The
Kjeldahl Method
for
Organic Nitrogen

The Kjeldahl Method for Organic Nitrogen

R. B. BRADSTREET

Petroleum Division, United States Testing Co., Inc.
Hoboken, New Jersey

1965

ACADEMIC PRESS   New York and London

547.04
B 72 K
53052
June 1966

ACADEMIC PRESS INC.
111 Fifth Avenue, New York, New York 10003

United Kingdom Edition published by
ACADEMIC PRESS INC. (LONDON) LTD.
Berkeley Square House, London W.1

LIBRARY OF CONGRESS CATALOG CARD NUMBER: 64-24653

PRINTED IN THE UNITED STATES OF AMERICA.

Preface

Since the inception of Kjeldahl's method for organic nitrogen, a large amount of data on this method has been published. Much of this material has been devoted either to the various phases of the method or to specific modifications for certain types of organic nitrogen compounds. Because this information is widely scattered among the various technical journals, it was felt that to bring together this material in one volume would be helpful both to those directly concerned with the method and to those seeking particular modifications.

This volume presents a broad and comprehensive survey of the method as applied to natural products and organic nitrogen compounds. Each of the several divisions of the method, e.g., salt addition, reduction, oxidation, catalysts, distillation, has been discussed in a separate section, and there is, of necessity, some overlapping of material. The bibliography in Part II has been classified according to the various headings, and here, too, there is some overlapping since some material is important enough—in the judgment of the author—to appear in more than one category. Although the effort has been made to present the material fairly, it is recognized that there will be sins of omission and commission. The author, therefore, will be grateful for all helpful criticism that will make the book of more benefit to the user.

The author wishes to express his thanks to those concerned with the typing of the manuscript, and collation of reference material.

July, 1965   R. B. BRADSTREET

Contents

CHAPTER 4
Distillation and Determination of Nitrogen

General Bibliography

CHAPTER I

Introduction to
the Kjeldahl Method

The quantitative determination of an element as widely distributed as nitrogen is of great importance, and the truth of this is borne out by the tremendous amount of literature published throughout the years. The analysis of nitrogen can be divided into two classes: inorganic and organic. The following chapters are concerned only with organic nitrogen compounds, and specifically their determination by the Kjeldahl method.

The historical background and the work leading to the evolution of the method to its present status are interesting, and give some conception of the ingenuity and resourcefulness of those investigators who contributed to the advancement of the method.

Johann Kjeldahl, son of a physician, was born August 16, 1849 at Jaegerpris, Zealand, Denmark, and died July 8, 1900 at Trivilde, Zealand. He received his education at the Gymnasium at Roskilde, graduating in 1867. From there he went to Copenhagen, specializing in chemistry and physics at the University and Polytechnische Hochschule. In 1876, after a short stay in the brewing industry, Kjeldahl became associated with the Carlsberg Laboratory — a philanthropic organization founded by J. C. Jacobson, a brewer, and the father of Kjeldahl's former employer. Here the work on problems relating to the brewing industry was continued.

The problem of protein changes in grain led directly to a search for a method that would overcome the inadequacies of those existing at the time. It was characteristic of Kjeldahl that he gave his entire time to the solution of this problem. When each detail and step of the method had been thoroughly tested, it appeared in *Zeitschrift für analytische Chemie* (1). The method was immediately successful. It was simple, it was more reliable, and also capable of improvement.

Kjeldahl, however, was aware of the limitations of his method, and that it was not applicable to all forms of nitrogen, and with many compounds he found that the nitrogen was only partially recovered. However, the method was well adapted for tracing the course of fermentation in grains.

Kjeldahl first tried Wanklyn's method, a distillation with alkaline permanganate, which gave low results. Better results were obtained with permanganate and dilute sulfuric acid, first boiling, then making alkaline with fixed alkali, distilling into standard acid, and titrating the excess. His final method was to heat the substance in concentrated sulfuric acid, close to the boiling point of the acid and then oxidize with powdered permanganate. He recommended addition of some fuming sulfuric acid and phosphoric anhydride to the sulfuric acid containing the sample, and heating for 2 hours. After the addition of the permanganate, the solution was subsequently diluted, transferred to a distilling flask, made alkaline, zinc added, and distilled into standard acid. Potassium iodide and iodate were added to the distillate, and the liberated iodine titrated with standard thiosulfate.

Heffner, Hollrung, and Morgen (2) compared Kjeldahl's method with that of Will-Varrentrapp on numerous organic compounds. In 94% of the compounds checked, Kjeldahl's method gave higher results. Petri and Th. Lehman (3) also checked the method using Ammonium sulfate, urea, uric acid, and hippuric acid.

Dafert (4, 5) explained the Kjeldahl reaction as the removal of the elements of water from the organic compounds. Heating of the carbonized mass reduced the sulfuric acid, and the resulting sulfur dioxide further reduced the nitrogenous compounds, resistant compounds being finally decomposed by potassium permanganate. Dafert divided nitrogenous compounds into two classes: (1) those compounds which need no previous treatment, such as amines, ammonium compounds, pyridine and quinoline derivatives, alkaloids, proteins and allied bodies; (2) substances requiring previous treatment such as nitro, nitroso, azo, diazo, aminoazo, hydrazines, and all others in which a nitrogen atom is linked to an oxygen atom or atoms, or to a second nitrogen atom. Bosshard (6) also applied Kjeldahl's method successfully to allantoin, leucine, tyrosine, asparagine, aspartic, glutaminic, and aminovaleric acids.

Modifications and improvements quickly followed the publication of the method. Asboth (7), using sucrose in the digestion, succeeded in obtaining good results on such compounds as azobenzene, nitrobenzene, and picric acid. By replacing sucrose with benzoic acid, still better results were obtained. Stebbins (8), also using sucrose, was able to determine the nitrogen in such compounds as dinitrobenzene, *m*-nitroaniline, and *o*-nitrophenol. Jodlbauer (9) substituted phenol, which is more readily nitrated, for benzoic acid. Still later, Scoville (10) and Cope (11) used salicylic acid respectively, for inorganic nitrates, and organic nitro compounds.

In his original method, Kjeldahl finished his digestion by the addition of powdered potassium permanganate. This was to assure complete oxidation, and conversion of any nitrogen not previously converted to ammonium sulfate by the acid digestion. Potassium permanganate, however, has been the subject of considerable controversy. It was finally discarded as being unsatisfactory and unnecessary.

It was soon found that the speed of reaction with concentrated sulfuric acid was accelerated by the use of catalysts, the search for which led investigators through most of the Periodic System. Wilfarth (12) reported on the addition of oxides of iron, mercury, manganese, bismuth, zinc, lead, and copper to the digestion mixture. Mercury, and salts of mercury form complexes with ammonia, resulting in a low recovery on distillation. This, however, was overcome by the use of alkali sulfide (13), sodium thiosulfate (13, 14), monosodium phosphate, or potassium xanthate (15) prior to distillation. Wilfarth's discovery of the catalytic action of various metals was probably the most important contribution to the Kjeldahl method, and from thereon the use of catalysts became universal.

The use of platinic chloride was suggested by Ulsch (16) who reported it to be satisfactory except when large amounts were used. Andersen (17) however, found it unsatisfactory for urine, hydrolyzed casein, old albumin solutions, and milk treated with pepsin or trypsin. The tremendous amount of work published on single catalysts and catalyst combinations has resulted in many claims regarding their relative efficiencies. Selenium, first suggested by Lauro (18), has considerable merit as a catalyst, although it has been the subject of some controversy. It is not as fast as mercury, but does possess the advantage that no pretreatment of the digest is necessary before distillation. Davis and Wise (19) believe that it is not as adaptable to general laboratory conditions as mercury, and that its use in combination with other catalysts, particularly mercury, should be discouraged.

The accelerating and retarding action of various elements was studied by Ranedo (20), who showed that the elements in the third and fourth groups of the Periodic System exhibited considerable retarding action. Working on the determination of nitrogen in a gluten flour, Osborn and Wilkie (21) examined thirty-nine metals and found that only ten or twelve catalyzed the reaction, mercury being the most satisfactory.

Milbauer (22) studied the effect of catalysts on the oxidation of such substances as hydrogen, carbon monoxide, carbon disulfide, and sucrose with sulfuric acid, and found that catalyst activity varied with temperature and the material being oxidized. The effectiveness of various catalysts was evaluated using sucrose as a standard for oxidation (23, 24). The reported results indicated selenium to be the most effective single catalyst, and selenium dioxide-mercuric sulfate (1:1) and selenium dioxide-copper sulfate (3:1) the most effective mixed catalysts. In the presence of the various catalysts, the passage of gases such as air, oxygen, ozone, nitrogen, carbon dioxide, chlorine, sulfur dioxide, hydrogen, and hydrogen chloride accelerated the oxidation of sucrose in concentrated sulfuric acid (25). Under these conditions, the most effective combination was chlorine with selenium dioxide-tellurium oxide as catalyst.

One objection to Kjeldahl's method was the length of time necessary, and the obvious disadvantage in having to use a small sample in order not to prolong the digestion. To increase the severity of the reaction, and thereby shorten the digestion time, Gunning (26) in 1889 proposed the addition of potassium sulfate as a means of raising the boiling point of the digestion mixture. This modification ranks in importance with Wilfarth's discovery of the catalytic effect of metals. He explained the action of potassium sulfate as that of first forming the acid sulfate, which in turn acted upon nitrogenous matter during digestion as does sulfuric acid under pressure above its boiling point.

The position of Arnold with regard to the Kjeldahl method is somewhat unique. The method generally referred to as the Kjeldahl-Gunning-Arnold procedure, is actually misnamed, since it involves the use of a single catalyst, and should properly be called the Kjeldahl-Gunning-Wilfarth method. Arnold's work (27) dealt with the use of a mixed catalyst of mercuric oxide and copper sulfate, which he considered more effective than either one alone. In collaboration with Wedemeyer (28), many pure organic compounds were analyzed using the mixed catalyst with sucrose and benzoic acid, first reducing, by Förster's (29) modification, with thiosulfate.

Potassium sulfate is apparently the most satisfactory boiling point raiser. A comparison of the sulfates of lithium, sodium, and potassium (30) has shown the latter to be the most effective. On the other hand,

Latshaw (31) reported that when an equivalent amount of sodium sulfate was used, no variation in results was noticed. Other compounds such as sodium pyrophosphate, potassium phosphate, and phosphoric acid have been used with varying degrees of success.

Regardless of the fact that sulfuric acid itself is a strong oxidizing agent, it is sometimes necessary to accelerate oxidation by other means. Kjeldahl used potassium permanganate, but as previously stated, the uncertainties attached to its use caused it to be discarded. Hydrogen peroxide is now used to a large extent as an oxidizing agent. The reaction is more or less violent and needs to be handled carefully. Digestion times are generally reduced considerably. Perchloric acid, also, has found some favor, but the possible hazards connected with its use offset the advantages.

The recovery of ammonia has been approached from various angles. Kjeldahl, in his original method, after adding alkali, distilled the ammonia into a known volume of standard acid, added potassium iodide and iodate, and titrated the liberated iodine with standard sodium thiosulfate. This more or less cumbersome method (as applied to macro digestions) has been almost entirely superseded by back titration of a known volume of standard acid, or direct titration by the use of boric acid as proposed by Winkler (32).

The value of Kjeldahl's work becomes apparent when prior methods are considered, and it may be of interest to review briefly the predecessors of the method.

Dumas (33) published his method for total nitrogen in 1831. With improved equipment, materials, and technique, it can be regarded at the present time as the sine qua non of total nitrogen procedure. However, for some years prior to the publication of Kjeldahl's method, the Dumas method was little used. Ten years later, in 1841, Will and Varrentrapp (34) published a procedure in which the sample was heated to redness with soda-lime. The ammonia was absorbed in hydrochloric acid and finally weighed as ammonium chloroplatinate. Peligot modified this latter step by absorbing the ammonia in a known volume of standard acid and titrating the excess. This method, however, was limited to compounds whose nitrogen could be directly converted into ammonia. At that time it filled a great need, and, within its limitations performed satisfactorily.

In the search for a quicker, simpler, method, and one requiring less specialized technique, Wanklyn (35) distilled samples with alkaline permanganate. This procedure, although inaccurate by reason of incomplete decomposition, for a while was widely used. Later, Grete

(1878) and Dreyfus (1883) gave their samples a preliminary treatment with concentrated sulfuric acid, and subsequently treated the charred residue according to the Will-Varrentrapp method.

In its present state, the Kjeldahl method represents a tremendous amount of investigation by many workers. Some indication of this progress is given in various reviews (36–41). There has been, however, comparatively little published work on the kinetics of the Kjeldahl digestion. Bredig and Brown (42) determined that the conversion and oxidation of aniline was a first-order reaction, and further work by Schwab and Agallidis (43) confirmed this.

The fact that losses of nitrogen occurred during the digestion of relatively simple compounds led both Self (44) and Carpiaux (45) to the observation that a definite amount of acid must be present at the end of the digestion. Self stated that an excess of at least 10 gm of acid is necessary, and also reported the approximate amounts of sulfuric acid necessary to decompose several types of organic materials, e. g., carbohydrates require 7.3 gm of acid, proteins 9 gm, and fats 17.8 gm. This has been more systematically approached by both Middleton and Stuckey (46), and Bradstreet (47).

Many modifications of Kjeldahl's method are in use today, and it would be unsound to designate a general method. However, in order to secure comparative results between various laboratories, industry or an association representing industry may outline definite specifications by which the method is to be used. As an example, the Association of Official Agricultural Chemists lists two official methods for the determination of nitrogen by the Kjeldahl method, one for the uncomplicated forms of nitrogen, and the other to include nitrates and nitro compounds. Under such conditions as these, even if the results obtained are not accurate, the precision of the method under specified conditions allows a comparison between different laboratories.

Broadly speaking, the Kjeldahl method involves an acid digestion and distillation. Most important is the digestion which may include a pretreatment — i.e., reduction of the sample by various means — salt addition for elevated temperatures, oxidation of organic matter by either oxidizing agents or catalysts, and after boil, or the boil period following the clearing of a digestion mixture. The recovery of ammonia is accomplished by addition of excess caustic and subsequent aeration, direct distillation, or steam distillation, and the amount present determined by titration, gravimetrically, Nesslerization or other colorimetric procedures, by pH measurement, or neutralization of the digest and direct estimation of ammonia without distillation.

The following chapters are concerned with specific phases of the Kjeldahl method, and each one will be discussed in detail.

REFERENCES

1. J. Kjeldahl, *Medd. Carlsberg Lab.* **2**, 1 (1883); *Z. anal. Chem.* **22**, 366 (1883).
2. Heffner, Hollrung, and Morgen, *Chem. Z.* **8**, 432 (1884).
3. Petri & Th. Lehman, *Z. physiol. Chem.* **8**, 200 (1887).
4. F. W. Dafert, *Z. anal. Chem.* **24**, 454 (1885).
5. F. W. Dafert, *Landwirtsch. Vers.-Sta.* **34**, 314 (1887).
6. Bosshard, *Z. anal. Chem.* **24**, 199 (1885).
7. A. Von Asboth, *Chem. Zentr.* **17**, 161 (1886).
8. Stebbins, *J. Am. Chem. Soc.* **7**, 108 (1885).
9. M. Jodlbauer, *Chem. Zentr.* **57**, 433 (1886).
10. M. A. Scovill, *Assoc. Offic. Agr. Chem.* pp. 51–54 (1887); *Div. Chem., U.S. Dept. Agr., Bull.* **16.**
11. W. C. Cope, *J. Ind. Eng. Chem.* **8**, 592–593 (1916).
12. H. Wilfarth, *Chem. Zentr.* **56**, 17, 113 (1885).
13. C. F. Davis and M. Wise, *Cereal Chem.* **8**, 349 (1931); cf. *Cereal Chem.* **10**, 488–492 (1933).
14. M. E. Pozzi-Escot, *Compt. rend.* **149**, 1380 (1910).
15. C. Neuberg, *Biochem. Z.* **24**, 423, (1910); *Chem. Abstr.* **4**, 1766 (1910).
16. K. Ulsch, *Z. ges. Brauw.* **9**, 81 (1886).
17. A. C. Andersen, *Skand. Arch. Physiol.* **25**, 96–104 (1911).
18. M. F. Lauro, *Ind. Eng. Chem. Anal. Ed.* **3**, 401–402 (1931).
19. C. F. Davis and M. Wise, *Cereal Chem.* **10**, 489–492 (1933).
20. J. Ranedo, *Anales soc. espan. fis. quim.* **31**, 195–200 (1933).
21. R. A. Osborn and J. B. Wilkie, *Assoc. Offic. Agr. Chem.* **18**, 604–609 (1935).
22. J. Milbauer, *Bull. soc. chim. France* **3**, 218–221 (1936).
23. J. Milbauer, *Chem. obzor* **11**, 183–185 (in English, p. 185) (1936).
24. J. Milbauer, *Chem. obzor* **11**, 208–211 (in English, p. 211) (1936).
25. J. Milbauer, *Chem. obzor* **12**, 17–19 (1937).
26. J. W. Gunning, *Z. anal. Chem.* **28**, 188 (1889).
27. C. Arnold, *Z. anal. Chem.* **25**, 581 (1886); **25**, 454 (1886); **26**, 249 (1887).
28. C. Arnold and K. Wedemeyer, *Z. anal. Chem.* **31**, 525 (1892).
29. O. Förster, *Z. Anal. Chem.* **28**, 422 (1889).
30. B. M. Margosches and E. Vogel, *Ber.* **55B**, 1380–1389 (1922).
31. W. L. Latshaw, *Ind. Eng. Chem.* **8**, 585 (1916).
32. L. W. Winkler, *Z. angew. Chem.* **26**, 231 (1913).
33. Dumas, *Ann. chim. phys. (Paris)* [2], **47**, 198 (1931).
34. H. Will and F. Varrentrap, *Ann.* **39**, 257 (1841).
35. J. A. Wanklyn and A. Gamage, *J. Chem. Soc.* **2**, 6, 25 (1868).
36. Schuette and Oppen, Wisconsin Academy of Science.
37. R. B. Bradstreet, *Chem. Rev.* **27**, No. 2, 331–350 (1940).
38. R. B. Bradstreet, *Anal. Chem.* **26**, 235 (1954).
39. P. L. Kirk, *Anal. Chem.* **22**, 354–358 (1950).
40. A. Friedrich, *Mikrochemie* **13**, 91–114 (1933).
41. H. B. Vickery, *J. Assoc. Offic. Agr. Chem* **29** 358–370 (1946).
42. G. Bredig and J. W. Brown, *Z. physik. Chem.* **46**, 502 (1903).
43. G. M. Schwab and E. Schwab-Agallidis, *J. Am. Chem. Soc.* **73**, 803–809 (1951).

44. P. A. W. Self, *Pharm. J.* **88**, 384–385 (1912).
45. E. Carpiaux, *Bull. soc. chim. Belges* **27** 13–14 (1912).
46. G. Middleton and R. E. Stuckey, *J. Pharm. and Pharmacol* **3**, 829–841 (1951).
47. R. B. Bradstreet, *Anal. Chem.* **29**. 944 (1957).

CHAPTER II

The Kjeldahl Digestion

Acid Requirements

The use of sulfuric acid as a digestion medium was not original with Kjeldahl, since it had been used in the preliminary treatment of organic material prior to completing the determination of nitrogen by the now obsolete Will-Varrentrapp method. While sulfuric acid alone may be used for the digestion of organic material, nevertheless it possesses certain disadvantages. The severity of the reaction is governed by the temperature which, in this case, is the boiling point of the acid. This also makes necessary the use of comparatively small samples, and a longer digestion time. Since time is an important factor in any laboratory, the use of sulfuric acid alone is seldom practical for macro digestions.

The decomposition of nitrogenous organic matter to carbon dioxide, water, and ammonia, requires varying amounts of sulfuric acid, depending upon the composition of the sample. Additional amounts of acid are necessary for the conversion of potassium sulfate to the acid sulfate, decomposition of sodium thiosulfate to the acid sulfate, conversion of salicylic acid to carbon dioxide and water, and loss by volatilization, which, in turn, is dependent upon the rate of heating, temperature, and digestion time. The total acid requirement will, obviously, vary according to whatever modification of the method is used. There are, however, certain basic requirements which will be considered, step by step. Potassium sulfate, added to concentrated sulfuric acid, is converted on heating, to the acid sulfate

$$K_2SO_4 + H_2SO_4 \rightarrow 2KHSO_4$$

If 10 gm of sulfate are used in the digestion, the conversion to acid sulfate will require

$$\frac{H_2SO_4}{K_2SO_4} \text{ or } \frac{98}{174.2} \times 10 = 5.6 \text{ gm } H_2SO_4$$

In cases where sodium thiosulfate and salicylic acid are used, as in the reduction of nitro groups, additional acid is needed. When 5 gm of sodium thiosulfate pentahydrate are used,

$$Na_2S_2O_3 + 2H_2SO_4 \rightarrow 2NaHSO_4 + SO_2 + S + H_2O$$

and the conversion requires

$$\frac{2H_2SO_4}{Na_2S_2O_3 \cdot 5H_2O} \text{ or } \frac{196}{248.2} \times 5 = 3.87 \text{ gm } H_2SO_4$$

There is also a secondary reaction taking place in the hot concentrated acid, converting the sulfur liberated from the thiosulfate to sulfur dioxide

$$S + 2H_2SO_4 \rightarrow 3SO_2 + 2H_2O$$

The sulfur liberated from the thiosulfate is

$$\frac{S}{Na_2S_2O_3 \cdot 5H_2O} \text{ or } \frac{32}{248.2} \times 5 = 0.645 \text{ gm } S$$

and the acid necessary for conversion to sulfur dioxide

$$\frac{2H_2SO_4}{S} \text{ or } \frac{196}{32} \times 0.645 = 3.99 \text{ gm } H_2SO_4$$

Salicylic acid is eventually decomposed into carbon dioxide and water

$$C_6H_4(OH)COOH + 14H_2SO_4 \rightarrow 7CO_2 + 17H_2O + 14SO_2$$

and requires

$$\frac{14H_2SO_4}{C_6H_4(OH)COOH} \text{ or } \frac{14 \times 98}{138} \times 1 = 10 \text{ gm } H_2SO_4/gm$$

The amount of acid lost by boiling during the digestion and boil period, irrespective of acid used for the sample and accelerators (e.g., dextrose, sucrose, salicylic acid), is dependent upon the rate of boiling, salt content, and total digestion time. The values shown in Table I were obtained from a series of determinations using 30 ml of concentrated sulfuric acid and varying quantities of potassium sulfate.

TABLE I
ACID LOSS ON BOILING

H_2SO_4 (ml)	K_2SO_4 (gm)	Boiling time (min)	Total acid lost (gm H_2SO_4)	Loss (gm/min)
30	10	90	3.18	0.0355
30	15	90	3.22	0.0358
30	20	90	3.49	0.0372
30	25	90	4.02	0.0448

The mixtures were boiled vigorously in 500 ml Kjeldahl flasks for ninety minutes and the loss of acid determined.

As stated above, the total loss of acid is in part dependent upon the digestion time, and increases with time. The rate of loss, however, is greater the shorter the digestion period, due to loss of water in the early stage of boiling and concentration of the sulfuric acid. The data in Table II show the losses on boiling 30 ml of concentrated acid for various times.

TABLE II

PROGRESSIVE LOSS OF ACID ON BOILING

H_2SO_4 (ml)	Boiling time (min)	Total loss (gm H_2SO_4)	Average loss (gm/min)
30	15	1.40	0.0933
30	30	1.89	0.0630
30	45	2.14	0.0476
30	60	2.53	0.0422
30	75	2.97	0.0396
30	90	4.10	0.0355

The loss of acid using various initial salt-acid ratios for digestion times up to 90 minutes is shown graphically in Fig. 1. When the initial concentration is 1.3 gm K_2SO_4/ml H_2SO_4, the digestion should not exceed 15 minutes at full boil, and for a concentration of 1.2 gm/ml the limiting time for digestion is 60 minutes. This is exclusive of acid necessary to decompose the sample. Digestion at full heat beyond these limits can cause loss of nitrogen.

At this point, using 10 gm of potassium sulfate exclusive of sample, there have been 21.1 gm of H_2SO_4 used, or, on a basis of 95.5 % acid strength and specific gravity of 1.84, — 11.98 ml, — representing conversion to acid sulfates, oxidation of sulfur and salicylic acid, and loss on 90 minutes boiling. This represents the minimum requirements of a digestion. For the usual procedure where 30–35 ml of acid are used, the excess of acid present (18–23 ml) is generally sufficient for the sample, and to prevent loss of nitrogen.

It has been pointed out by Self (1) and Carpiaux (2) that loss of nitrogen occurs when the final digest is solid, and Self further recommended that at least 15 gm of acid be present at the end of the digestion. Since the success of a Kjeldahl digestion depends in great part on the temperature, the excess of acid present at the end of a digestion should represent the minimum quantity from which no nitrogen is lost and the maximum temperature obtained.

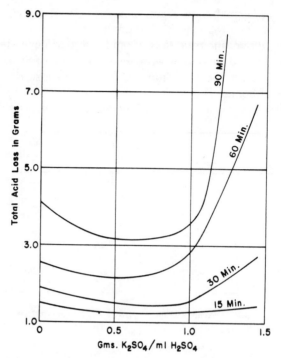

FIG. 1. Total acid loss for various digestion mixtures.

The determination of the minimum acid requirements of two modifications has been carried out by Bradstreet (3). In this study, a mixture of (1) 10 gm of potassium sulfate and sulfuric acid, and (2) 10 gm of potassium sulfate, 5 gm of sodium thiosulfate, and sulfuric acid were used. An equivalent amount of sodium sulfate (2.86 gm) was substituted for the thiosulfate, which would be representative of the condition existing after the thiosulfate had been oxidized to sodium sulfate. The amounts of acid necessary for the conversion to acid sulfate are 5.6 gm for (1) and 7.6 gm for (2). Each determination was given a 60 minute digestion representing the boil period after the clearing of a digestion when presumably all organic matter has been destroyed and only ammonium sulfate is present. The loss of acid during this boil period was prorated on the basis of a loss of 3.2 gm over a 90 minute period, or 2.1 gm. The basic acid requirements, therefore, are 7.8 gm (4.4 ml) and 9.7 gm (5.5 ml), respectively, for each modification. In each series the volume of sulfuric acid was varied from 5.00 to 12.50 ml, and 0.1 gm of ammonium sulfate added to each determination. After 60 minutes of boiling, the digests were cooled, diluted, and distilled in the usual manner. These results are shown in Table III, and indicate that the critical point lies between 7.50 and 10.00 ml. It is also apparent that as the digest approaches the composition of the acid sulfates, loss of nitrogen will occur. The physical appearance of the digest also gives an indication—a loss of nitrogen can be expected when the cooled digest is solid, or nearly so. From these results it will be seen that unless 10 ml of acid are present at the start of the boil period (i. e., after clearing of the digest), losses can be expected. This volume of acid (10 ml) represents the total acid present, including that necessary for the conversion of the sulfate to acid sulfate. The "free acid," therefore, is less than 10 ml by the amount used for conversion to acid sulfate. Under the usual conditions of the Kjeldahl digestion there will be sufficient acid present to prevent loss of nitrogen unless an excessive amount of sample is used, or a greatly extended boiling period is necessary. It can be recognized from the data in Table III that the ratio of acid to salt is important. By using the arbitrary loss factor of 0.0355 gm of acid per minute, the acid (volume) to salt (weight) ratio, or acid index, existing at the end of the boil period may be calculated. As an example, the loss of acid in the first determination, method *(1)* is

$$0.0355 \times 60 = 2.13 \text{ gm } H_2SO_4$$

$$\frac{2.13}{1.84} \times 0.955 = 1.22 \text{ ml conc. } H_2SO_4$$

At the start of the boil period the acid:salt ratio, or acid index is

$$\frac{5}{10} = 0.50$$

after 60 minutes of boil, the total acid present will be

$$5 - 1.22 = 3.78 \text{ ml}$$

and the acid index is

$$\frac{3.78}{10} = 0.38$$

The data appearing in Table IV were calculated in this manner. Examination shows that the critical point beyond which nitrogen will be lost is represented by an acid index of 0.88 for *(1)* and 0.68 for *(2)*. For optimum conditions, the acid index at the end of a digestion should not be lower than these limiting factors.

TABLE III

RECOVERY OF $(NH_4)_2SO_4$ FROM H_2SO_4-K_2SO_4 DIGESTION MIXTURES

H_2SO_4 present at start of boil period (ml)	Digestion mixture No. 1				Digestion mixture No. 2			
	State of digest when cold	$(NH_4)_2SO_4$ added (gm)	$(NH_4)_2SO_4$ recovered (gm)	% Recovered	State of digest when cold	$(NH_4)_2SO_4$ added (gm)	$(NH_4)_2SO_4$ recovered (gm)	% Recovered
5.00	Solid	0.1006	0.0962	95.67	Solid	0.1000	0.0965	95.50
	Solid	0.1004	0.0964	96.02	Solid	0.1005	0.0967	96.17
7.50	Solid	0.1006	0.0976	97.04	Solid	0.1007	0.0982	97.53
	Solid	0.1000	0.0970	97.00	Solid	0.1002	0.0975	97.32
10.00	Pasty	0.1002	0.1000	99.80	Fluid	0.1008	0.1008	100.00
	Pasty	0.1002	0.1001	99.90	Fluid	0.1003	0.1004	100.10
12.50	Liquid	0.1005	0.1006	100.10	Fluid	0.1001	0.1001	100.00
	Liquid	0.1000	0.1000	100.00	Fluid	0.1003	0.1003	100.00

TABLE IV
ACID INDEX

Ml H_2SO_4 before digestion	Acid index	Ml H_2SO_4 after 60 min digestion	Acid index
H₂SO₄-K₂SO₄ colspan			
5.00	0.50	3.78	0.38
7.50	0.75	6.28	0.63
10.00	1.00	8.78	0.88
12.50	1.25	11.28	1.13
H_2SO_4-K_2SO_4-$Na_2S_2O_3$-$5H_2O$			
5.00	0.39	4.78	0.37
7.50	0.58	6.28	0.49
10.00	0.78	8.78	0.68
12.50	0.97	11.28	0.88

Decomposition of Organic Material

In addition to the acid needed to form the acid sulfates, for decomposition of sodium thiosulfate and salicylic acid (if used), and to compensate loss on boiling, a definite amount is necessary for decomposition of the sample. The amount of acid required is dependent upon not only the size of the sample, but also upon the structure and molecular weight. With small samples, in the order of 0.1–0.2 gm, the amount of acid required may not be critical, but when it is necessary to decompose relatively large amounts (e. g., grains, petroleum), the volume of acid used may change the acid:salt ratio so that the final acid index falls below the critical point, and nitrogen is lost. For purposes of calculations, it will be assumed that complete decomposition takes place, and that all nitrogen will be converted to ammonia. (Strictly speaking, using the present Kjeldahl method and its modifications, this is not always true since some types of nitrogen linkages are extremely difficult, if not impossible, to reduce to ammonia. Some of these will be discussed later.) On the basis, therefore, that carbon is converted to carbon dioxide, hydrogen and oxygen to water, nitrogen to ammonia, the amount of acid necessary may be readily calculated. It must also be remembered that the reaction of boiling, concentrated sulfuric acid and organic matter is at best not a simple one, but inasmuch as the end products of carbon dioxide, water, ammonia, etc., are readily determined, and the compound identified by such means, the assumption of a formal reaction is justifiable.

The following reactions are given as examples of the amounts of sulfuric acid necessary to decompose completely various types of organic compounds. If, under the influence of temperature, sulfuric acid acts as a mild oxidizing agent, the following reaction may be expected to occur when oxidizable material is present:

$$H_2SO_4 \rightarrow H_2O + SO_2 + O$$

Sulfuric acid is a powerful dehydrating agent, and in the case of oxygenated compounds and at some critical temperature, will remove the elements of water, resulting in free carbon. Influence of higher temperature promotes oxidation of the free carbon and further decomposition of the sample. The reactions listed below are representative of saturated aliphatic primary amines.

(1) $CH_3NH_2 + 4H_2SO_4 \rightarrow CO_2 + 3SO_2 + 4H_2O + NH_4HSO_4$

(2) $C_2H_5NH_2 + 7H_2SO_4 \rightarrow 2CO_2 + 6SO_2 + 8H_2O + NH_4HSO_4$

(3) $C_5H_{11}NH_2 + 16H_2SO_4 \rightarrow 5CO_2 + 15SO_2 + 20H_2O + NH_4HSO_4$

Since secondary and tertiary saturated aliphatic amines have the same empirical formulas as the corresponding primary amine, the calculated amount of acid per mole will be the same.

The amount of sulfuric acid used increases by the ratio of 3 moles of acid to each CH_2 increase in molecular weight. In a homologous series, therefore, a general formula may be derived for saturated aliphatic amines.

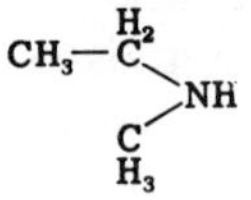

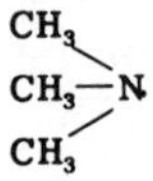

$$C_nH_{n+1}NH_2 + mH_2SO_4 \rightarrow nCO_2 + (m-1)SO_2 + 4nH_2O + NH_4HSO_4$$

where n = number of carbon atoms, and m = sum of carbon and hydrogen atoms in the alkyl group (or groups).

A similar procedure may be followed in determining the amount of acid necessary for homologous series such as the aliphatic amides, amino acids of the type $NH_2(CH_2)_xCOOH$ fatty acids, hydrocarbons, etc. A typical reaction and general formula are given below for several classes of compounds.

Amides:

$C_{17}H_{35}CONH_2$ + 53 H_2SO_4 → 18 CO_2 + 52 SO_2 + 69 H_2O + NH_4HSO_4

$C_nH_{2n-1}CONH_2$ + $(m+1)$ H_2SO_4 → $(n+1)$ CO_2 + $(m-1)$ SO_2 + $(4n+1)$ H_2O + NH_4HSO_4

Nitriles:

C_2H_5CN + 8 H_2SO_4 → 3 CO_2 + 7 SO_2 + 8 H_2O + NH_4HSO_4

$C_nH_{2n+1}CN$ + $(m+1)$ H_2SO_4 → $(n+1)$ CO_2 + m SO_2 + $4n H_2O$ + NH_4HSO_4

Nitroparaffins:

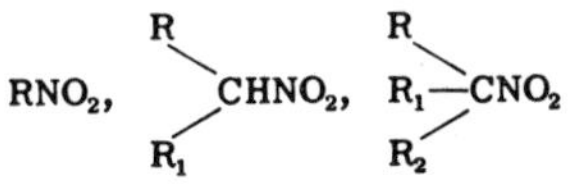

$$RNO_2, \quad \overset{R}{\underset{R_1}{>}}CHNO_2, \quad R_1-\overset{R}{\underset{R_2}{}}CNO_2$$

where R, R_1, R_2 are alkyl groups

$C_3H_7NO_2$ + 7 H_2SO_4 ---→ 3 CO_2 + 6 SO_2 + 8 H_2O + NH_4HSO_4

$C_nH_{2n+1}NO_2$ + $(m-3)$ H_2SO_4 ---→ nCO_2 + $(m-4)$ SO_2 + $(4n-4)$ H_2O + NH_4HSO_4

Amino Acids:

$NH_2(CH_2)_x COOH$

$NH_2CH_2CH_2CH_2COOH$ + 10 H_2SO_4 ---→ 4 CO_2 + 9 SO_2 + 12 H_2O + NH_4HSO_4

$NH_2(CH_2)_x COOH$ + $(m+1)$ H_2SO_4 ---→ $(n+1)$ CO_2 + m SO_2 + $4n$ H_2O + NH_4HSO_4

Fatty Acids:

$C_{11}H_{23}COOH$ 34 H_2SO_4 ---→ 12 CO_2 + 34 SO_2 + 46 H_2O

$C_nH_{2n+1}COOH$ + m H_2SO_4 ---→ $(n+1)$ CO_2 + m SO_2 + $(4n+2)$ H_2O

Paraffins:

C_nH_{2n+2}

$CH_3CH_2CH_2CH_2CH_3$ + 16 H_2SO_4 ---→ 5 CO_2 + 16 SO_2 + 22 H_2O

C_nH_{2n+2} + $(m-1)$ H_2SO_4 ---→ n CO_2 - $(m-1)$ SO_2 + $(4n+2)$ H_2O

In all cases, n = number of carbon atoms in the alkyl group, and m = sum of carbon and hydrogen in the alkyl group. The amount of acid per gram of sample, for various types of organic material is shown graphically in Figs. 2 and 3, and some calculated values are given in

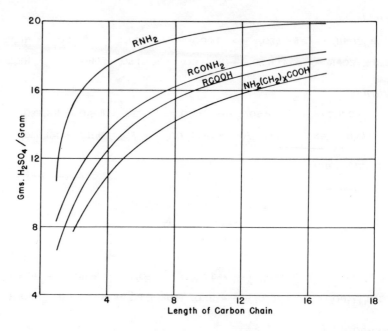

FIG. 2. Total acid necessary for decomposition of some organic compounds.

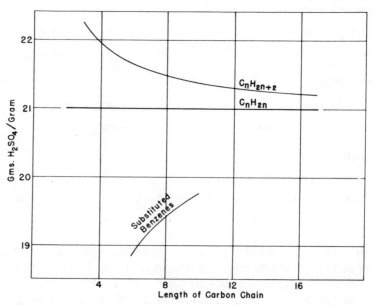

FIG. 3. Total acid necessary for decomposition of some hydrocarbons.

Table V. It will be noted that the curves for nitriles and amino acids are identical. This is an example of compounds having the same empirical formula.

The determination of the amount of acid used for the decomposition of a sample is a relatively simple matter, and may be carried out in the following manner (3).

A blank determination is first run using a mixture of 10 gm K_2SO_4 and 30 ml of concentrated H_2SO_4 (carefully measured by means of a burette). This is boiled for 90 minutes (the approximate time of digestion and boil period), cooled, diluted with distilled water, and transferred to a 250 ml volumetric flask. An aliquot is taken and titrated with standard alkali. The amount of acid lost during the 90 minute boiling period can now be calculated, basing the calculation on an acid of 1.84 specific gravity and 95.5% H_2SO_4.

The total weight of acid at the start of the boil is:

$$(1) \quad 30 \times 1.84 \times 0.955 = 52.7 \text{ gm } H_2SO_4$$

and after 90 minutes of boiling:

$$(2) \quad 0.049 \times \text{normality} \times \text{ml of alkali} = \text{gm } H_2SO_4 \text{ lost}$$

As an example, the average of several blank determinations was 3.2 gm of acid lost during the 90 minute boiling period. Prorating this

TABLE V

CALCULATED ACID REQUIREMENTS

No. of carbon atoms	RNH_2, R_2NH_1 and R_3N	RNO_2 $NH_2(CH_2)_xCOOH$	$RCONH_2$	RCN	$RCOOH$	C_nH_{2n+2}
1	10.65		8.30	11.95	6.53	24.50
2	15.24	5.23	10.74	14.25	9.22	22.87
3	16.61	7.70	12.40	15.62	11.09	22.27
4	17.45	9.51	13.58	16.53	12.45	21.96
5	18.02	10.89	14.49	17.18	13.45	
6	18.44	11.97	15.19	17.66	14.30	21.65
7	18.75	12.84	15.76	18.03	14.94	
8	19.00	13.73	16.23	18.33	15.50	21.49
9	19.19		16.62	18.58	15.95	
10	19.35	14.83	16.95	18.78	16.33	21.39
12	19.60	15.65	17.49	19.09	16.94	21.33
14	19.78	16.27	17.89	19.34	17.41	21.28
16	19.93	16.72	18.22	19.52	17.78	21.25
18		17.16	19.67			

Header spanning: Gm H_2SO_4/gm for compound type[a]:

[a] R=alkyl groups.

value gives an average loss of 0.0355 gm of acid per minute. While this is admittedly not an exact value, due to fluctuations in heating, external cooling of the flask, rate of boil, etc., nevertheless it is sufficiently accurate for purposes of calculation.

Samples of organic materials (1.0000 gm each) are digested in the above mixture, noting the time necessary for clearing of the digest. Each sample is then given a one hour boil. At the end of this period, the acid left is determined in the same manner as for the blank.

The total acid used, therefore, is:

(3)   Equation (1) − Equation (2) = total acid used

and the amount of acid used for the sample is:

(4)   Total acid used − (0.036 × time in minutes)

The average results of determinations of a number of natural products and various organic compounds are given in Table VI. There is, of course, some discrepancy between the calculated values and the actual values obtained. This is due mainly to the physical differences in a digestion. The temperature at which decomposition takes place will vary, depending upon such factors as the type of nitrogen linkage — whether amine, amide, nitrile, nitro, azo, nuclear (as pyridine), heterocyclic — and whether the compound is in the aliphatic or aromatic series. The position of the nitrogen-containing group or groups with regard to similar or other groupings has a bearing, as well, on the decomposition temperature. It may be said, in general, that since concentrated sulfuric acid is such a powerful dehydrating agent, oxygenated compounds will have a tendency to decompose easily, and at fairly low temperatures. The decomposition point, therefore, becomes important in those cases in which reduction of nitrogen in concentrated sulfuric acid by means of thiosulfate, salicylic acid and the like, precedes digestion, since if decomposition takes place before reduction,* nitrogen is lost. This fact is a partial explanation for some compounds being classified as refractory.

The basic requirements, therefore, for a Kjeldahl digestion may be summarized as follows:

1. Acid necessary to convert sulfates to acid sulfates.
2. Acid lost by boiling.
3. Acid used for oxidation of organic accelerators such as sucrose, benzoic acid, salicylic acid.

* In some cases, e.g., chlorinated aromatic compounds containing nitrogen, loss can can also occur through volatilization or sublimation.

TABLE VI
ACID REQUIREMENTS FOR THE DIGESTION OF VARIOUS SUBSTANCES

Sample	Total gm H_2SO_4 used	Digestion time (min)	Net gm H_2SO_4/ gm sample	Gm H_2SO_4 calc.
H_2SO_4	3.20[a]	90	—	—
Salicylic acid	13.11	75	10.04	10.0
Benzoic acid	15.03	75	12.37	12.05
Sucrose	11.73	95	8.36	6.88
Anthranilic acid	19.57	80	13.92	10.73
Aminosalicylic acid	12.87	75	10.22	8.92
Acetanilide	18.08	80	15.24	13.79
Oleic acid	23.42	100	19.87	17.72
Stearic acid	22.23	95	18.86	17.94
Crepe rubber	22.82	100	19.27	—
Buna rubber	19.24	95	15.87	—
Light lube oil	15.11	100	11.56	—
Heavy lube oil	15.65	105	11.92	—
Leather (chrome tan)	13.75	95	10.38	—
Wool (flannel)	11.49	95	8.12	—
Hemoglobin	12.21	100	8.66	—
Egg albumin	12.09	95	8.72	—
Blood albumin	11.73	95	8.36	—
Gelatin	19.94	90	16.74	—
Casein	13.04	95	9.67	—
Corn meal	9.82	100	6.27	—
Dextrin	10.66	95	7.29	—

[a] Loss over 90 minute boil period. All results calculated on a prorated loss.

4. Acid used for conversion of reducing agents such as sodium thiosulfate to sulfate (and oxidation of free sulfur to sulfur dioxide).
5. Acid necessary for oxidation of the sample.
6. A specific amount of acid in excess of the above requirements to ensure no loss of nitrogen through volatilization.

The amount of acid in item 6 should be enough to give an acid index representative of the highest possible temperature without incurring a loss of nitrogen. While there are other factors to be considered in the Kjeldahl digestion, these remain fundamental and must be observed.

Middleton and Stuckey (4) calculate the amount of sulfuric acid necessary for any given compound by a slightly different procedure. From the molecular formula, nitrogen as NH_3, carbon as CO_2, and sulfur (if present) as SO_2 corresponding to the number of nitrogen and oxygen atoms present, are deducted. A residual formula containing only carbon and hydrogen remains. The carbon-hydrogen ratio is reduced to its lowest terms (to the nearest one half or whole number), and the amount of sulfuric acid necessary to oxidize one gram of this ratio to carbon dioxide and water is taken as the factor for the calculation of acid consumed by the sample. For example, if the residual formula after subtraction of ammonia and carbon dioxide were C_9H_5, the carbon:hydrogen ratio would be represented by C_2H. This is an acceptable approximation since the amount of acid for a digestion is seldom measured with any greater precision than that obtained with a graduate. Once the factors have been obtained, calculation of acid for one gram of sample is as follows:

$$\frac{\text{Residual formula weight}}{\text{Molecular weight}} \times \text{Factor} = \text{ml } H_2SO_4/\text{gram}$$

The values of some factors taken from Middleton and Stuckey's article appear in Table VII.

TABLE VII
ACID REQUIREMENTS ACCORDING TO MIDDLETON AND STUCKEY

Lowest C/H ratio	Ml H_2SO_4 (sp.gr. 1.84)/ gm C/H ratio
C	8.9
CH	10.2
CH$_2$	11.4
C$_{1.5}$H	9.9
C$_2$H	9.6
C$_3$H	9.3
C$_4$H	9.1

In cases where sulfur is present as sulfide or in the ring, as for example, thiazole, the assumption is made that it is eliminated unoxidized. Sulfur, free or combined, is oxidized by boiling sulfuric acid, one gram of sulfur requiring 3.5 ml of concentrated acid. A real difference can, therefore, exist if the total sulfur content is not assumed to be oxidized.

Salt Addition

POTASSIUM SULFATE

Since all compounds do not decompose at the same temperature, and since many of them are not decomposed (or only partially) at the boiling point of concentrated sulfuric acid, it is necessary to increase the severity of the reaction by the addition of various salts, but chiefly by the addition of potassium sulfate.

Use of potassium sulfate was first made by Gunning (5) who digested up to one gram of sample with 20 to 30 ml of a mixture of one part of potassium sulfate in two parts of concentrated sulfuric acid. Digestion was considered complete when the mixture became colorless. Later, Arnold and Wedemeyer (6) combined the Gunning and Arnold methods (7). Arnold had previously used sulfuric acid and a mixed catalyst of mercuric oxide and copper sulfate. In the combined method, the concentration of potassium sulfate was considerably higher, in the order of 0.8 gm/ml of acid. By this means, many compounds heretofore considered refractory could be analyzed.

The effect of progressive salt addition on temperature is shown in Fig. 4, and if these temperatures are plotted against the acid indices, the curves in Fig. 5 are obtained. By selection of the proper acid index, the conditions of digestion can be regulated to give maximum temperature. The curves in Fig. 4 were obtained by progressive addition of potassium sulfate to *(1)* 30 ml of sulfuric acid and *(2)* 30 ml of sulfuric acid plus 2.86 gm of sodium sulfate (equivalent to 5 gm of sodium thiosulfate pentahydrate used in the salicylic acid method). The temperature was measured by a thermometer in a well which extended to

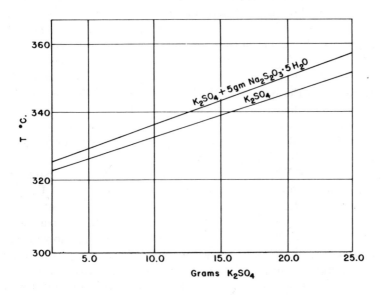

FIG. 4. Boiling points of H_2SO_4-K_2SO_4 digestion mixtures.

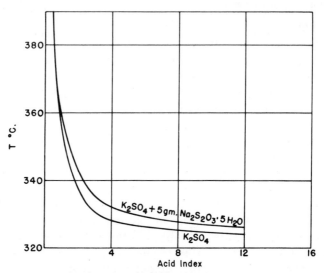

FIG. 5. Acid index of H_2SO_4-K_2SO_4 digestion mixtures.

within 1/4 inch of the bottom of a 500 ml flask. Measurement was made after the mixtures were boiling briskly.

Ogg and Willits (8) have measured by means of a thermocouple the temperature of boiling mixtures in both micro (30 ml) and macro (500 ml) flasks at six different points: — three liquid temperatures and at three points above the surface of the liquid. For concentrations of 0.375, 0.50, and 0.625 gm of potassium sulfate per milliliter of acid, the maximum temperatures (in 30 ml flasks) are 342°, 345°, and 353°C, respectively, at the bottom of the flasks, and 336°, 342°, and 349°C at the midpoint of digest. At a concentration of 0.625 gm/ml, the bottom temperature of a macro digest is 356° and 349°C at midpoint. Working with nicotinic acid, it was found that digestion time was approximately halved for each 10° rise in temperature.

McKenzie and Wallace (9) also measured the macro digestion temperatures at essentially the same points as Ogg and Willits. The average temperature taken at a point slightly above the bottom of the flask for a concentration of 0.66 gm/ml, 15 minutes after fuming, was 363°C. Their work with tryptophan as a refractory compound showed that a ratio of 1 gm/ml was necessary for complete recovery of nitrogen. The temperature during a 3 hour digestion varied from an initial of 384°C to a final of 418°C. This is close to the critical point at which loss of nitrogen can occur. Using an air condenser, the highest temperature after 3 hours digestion was 398°C, and after 6 hours, 400°C, with complete recovery of nitrogen.

From their work on the minimum temperature of digestion, Lake *et al.* (10) have shown that for a refractory compound such as pyridine, one hour digestion at 360°C is insufficient to recover all the nitrogen, and further, that a temperature of 370°C allows only a marginal safety factor. Experiments on the recovery of nitrogen from ammonium oxalate also showed that when the temperature rose much above 400°C, nitrogen was lost.

As part of an investigation on the effect of added salt and catalyst to the Kjeldahl digestion, Baker (11) measured the boiling points of various salt concentrations under conditions of vigorous boiling such that acid vapors just distilled from the mouth of a 30 ml flask, and with the bulb of the thermometer well immersed in the liquid.

Dahl and Oehler (12), in the course of their investigation of the critical factors involved in the determination of nitrogen in leather, measured the temperature of salt concentrations ranging from 0 to 1.4

TABLE VIII
BOILING POINTS OF K_2SO_4-H_2SO_4 Mixtures

Gm K_2SO_4/ ml H_2SO_4	Boiling point (°C)							
	1	2	3[a]	4[a]	5	6	7	8
0	345	—	328	—	—	310	329	320
0.25	354	332	337	—	—	329	—	327[b]
0.33	—	—	—	351	349	333	—	—
0.50	366	342	356	358	—	343	344	334[c]
0.625	—	—	370	—	363	346	—	—
0.75	385	354	382	369	—	—	—	350[d]
1.0	—	—	—	380	383	376	365	359
1.1	—	—	—	386	—	388	—	—
1.2	—	—	—	—	—	396	—	365
1.3	—	—	—	—	397	406	—	—
1.4	—	—	—	—	—	—	—	370
1.5	—	—	—	—	—	—	388	—
2.0	—	—	—	—	450	—	410	—

1. Snider and Coleman (152).
2. Ogg and Willets (8).
3. Middleton and Stuckey (4).
4. Lake *et al.* (10).
5. McKenzie and Wallace (9).
6. Bradstreet, unpublished data.
7. Baker (11).
8. Dahl and Oehler (12).

[a] Values interpolated from curve.
[b] 0.2 gm/ml.
[c] 0.4 gm/ml.
[d] 0.8 gm/ml.

gm/ml using both potassium and sodium sulfates. Temperatures were taken after 30 minutes of boiling, and keeping the condensation of acid within the limit of the neck of the flask. The temperature spread for potassium sulfate is 50°C and for sodium sulfate 41°C.

A summary of boiling points of salt concentrations reported by various workers is given in Table VIII.

Sodium Sulfate

From time to time, throughout the history of the Kjeldahl method, the use of salts other than potassium sulfate has been recommended. These attempts to replace potassium sulfate have generally been unsuccessful, except in the specific cases to which the particular salts were adapted. There is no question as to the use of various sulfates and phosphates. They can be, and are, used satisfactorily in many instances. Their limiting factor, however, is their solubility in sulfuric acid. This is probably the reason why potassium sulfate is more suitable than any other salt. Maintaining a high digestion temperature is necessary in many cases, particularly in the case of compounds containing a pyridine nucleus. The maximum digestion temperature is reached when a saturated solution of the salt in concentrated sulfuric acid is obtained (comparable to a cooled digest which is fluid). Exceeding this limit will result in loss of nitrogen, since the final digest will be solid, or nearly solid, when cooled. This has been pointed out in the case of potassium sulfate (Table III), and it will be shown, subsequently, that this condition exists for other salts, and to a much greater degree than for potassium sulfate. From the limiting amounts of acid and salt, the calculated acid indices will show the temperature range in which the digestion will take place.

Sodium sulfate has been used by many workers and has, in most cases, given satisfactory results. Also, in these cases direct substitution of potassium sulfate by sodium sulfate has not altered the final results. However, where a relatively high digestion temperature is necessary, it is unsatisfactory because solid digests are obtained unless a relatively large excess of sulfuric acid is present. This is, in effect, another way of saying that the solubility of sodium sulfate in sulfuric acid is low. This effectively eliminates the use of this sulfate in the determination of nitrogen in refractory compounds.

The progressive addition of sodium sulfate to 35 ml of concentrated sulfuric acid, and the consequent temperatures are shown in Fig. 6. If

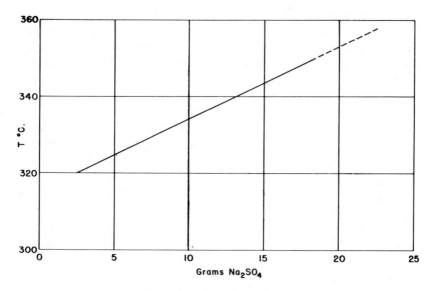

FIG. 6. Boiling points of H_2SO_4-Na_2SO_4 digestion mixtures.

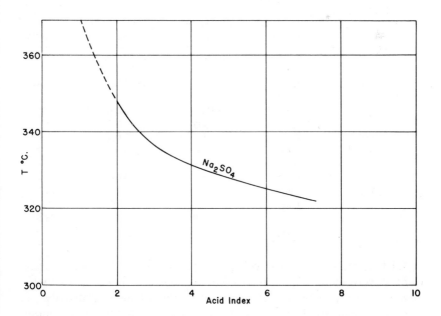

FIG. 7. Acid index of H_2SO_4-Na_2SO_4 digestion mixtures.

the acid indices are now calculated and plotted against temperature, the curve in Fig. 7 is obtained. The recovery of ammonium sulfate from simulated digests was carried out (3) in the same manner as for potassium sulfate (q.v.). In these experiments, 12.8 gm of sodium sulfate, equivalent gram for gram of potassium sulfate plus the equivalent amount of sodium sulfate (2.86 gm) in place of 5 gm of sodium thiosulfate pentahydrate. These results are shown in Table IX, and indicate that the same condition exists as with potassium sulfate — when the cooled digest is solid, there will be a loss of nitrogen. If the acid indices are calculated both before the boil period and after it, the maximum temperature range during which no nitrogen will be lost, is obtained. It must also be remembered that this range is based on a one hour boil period, presumably after the clearing of a digestion. Nitrogen will be lost on continued boiling, and if a longer boil period is anticipated, the acid:salt ratio should be adjusted so that the acid index of the final digest does not fall below that representing the maximum temperature beyond which nitrogen will be lost.

TABLE IX

RECOVERY OF $(NH_4)_2SO_4$ FROM H_2SO_4-Na_2SO_4 DIGESTION MIXTURE

Ml H_2SO_4 present at start of boil period	State of digest when cold	Gm$(NH_4)_2SO_4$ added	Gm $(NH_4)_2SO_4$ recovered	% Recovery
5.00	Solid	0.1083	0	0
	Solid	0.1001	0	0
7.30	Solid	0.1029	0	0
	Solid	0.1014	0	0
10.00	Solid	0.1001	0.0975	97.45
	Solid	0.1005	0.0977	97.21
12.50	Solid	0.1006	0.0987	98.12
	Solid	0.1000	0.0979	79.90
15.00	Solid	0.1011	0.0979	96.78
	Solid	0.1007	0.0972	97.01
17.50	Pasty	0.1036	0.1018	98.28
	Pasty	0.1028	0.1003	98.37
20.00	Fluid	0.1020	0.1009	99.87
	Fluid	0.1004	0.1003	99.92

Earlier, many attempts to replace potassium sulfate with sodium sulfate were made. If the material being analyzed had a relatively low decomposition point, the change to sodium sulfate was usually successful. Latshaw (13) found no difference when an equivalent amount of sodium sulfate was used. On the other hand, Brill and Agcaoili (14) analyzing samples of pyridine, found that while neither sulfate was satisfactory, sodium sulfate gave much lower results. The evidence of Dowell and Friedemann (15) supports that of Latshaw. They used sodium sulfate and sodium sulfate decahydrate and found no difference in digestion time. Furthermore, no appreciable difference was found between the use of 5 and 10 gm of potassium sulfate with 30 ml of sulfuric acid. The materials examined were oat feed, cottonseed meal, dried blood, and mill run bran. It would seem that this is an example of materials having a low decomposition temperature and without formation of intermediate compounds having a high decomposition point. Phelps and Daudt (16) reported varying results with sodium sulfate, unless conditions were rigidly controlled. From their data on refractory compounds, they concluded that the differences in the the behavior of the two sulfates were due to differences in the tendencies of the acid sulfates to retain water. In their investigation of the effect of either potassium or sodium sulfate in sulfuric acid, they used lead return condensers to prevent loss of acid. It was found that under these conditions, the hydrolysis of 0.4 gm of pyridine zinc chloride with 0.7 gm of mercuric oxide, 15 ml of sulfuric acid, and 10 gm of potassium sulfate was incomplete in one hour, but complete in 1.5 hours, while with 15 gm of potassium sulfate it was complete within an hour. Larger amounts of acid took correspondingly longer times. Substituting 8.2 gm of sodium sulfate for 10 gm of potassium sulfate, and using 15–20 ml of sulfuric acid, required 2 hours for complete hydrolysis. In subsequent collaborative tests on protein materials by Daudt (17), it was stated that when 20 ml of sulfuric acid were used, 8.2 gm of sodium sulfate could be substituted for the usual 10 gm of potassium sulfate, but that a total digestion time of 2.5 hours was necessary unless it was known that the substance in question required less than this. Harrel and Lanning (18) also investigated the effect of sodium sulfate on digestion time in the determination of protein. They concluded that low protein results could be explained by failure to use a high salt concentration with a given heat source and time of digestion, and that when larger amounts of sodium sulfate are used, copper is a more desirable catalyst than mercury.

In spite of the obvious disadvantages of sodium sulfate, investigators have continued to recommend its use. Barker and Shuttleworth (19) studying minimum digestion times for leather samples, used a mixture of 10 gm of sodium sulfate, 5 gm of copper sulfate pentahydrate, and 1 gm of sodium selenate in sulfuric acid. Complete digestion was accomplished in 30 minutes. Pepkowitz et al. (20) in conjunction with perchloric acid, used 25 ml of sulfuric acid and 10 gm of sodium sulfate. These workers stated, however, that in the digestion of soils, the sulfate should be omitted since in combination with perchloric acid it has a tendency to oxidize materials present in the soils. For the nitrogen in foodstuffs, Alcock (21) recommends the use of 40 gm of sodium sulfate, 1.6 gm of copper sulfate per 100 ml of sulfuric acid, and a 6 hour digestion time. Examination of these data will reveal that the acid index is high, and that under such conditions, a high digestion temperature cannot be obtained. Also, in the case of many natural materials, a particularly high temperature is not necessary, and either sulfate may be used with equal success. Paul and Berry (22) compared both sulfates, but found no difference. Margosches (23, 24), working with organic nitro compounds, made comparisons of potassium sulfate with sodium sulfate, lithium sulfate, and borax, and found that although in some cases the theoretical amount of nitrogen was not obtained, potassium sulfate was superior. Other workers (25–28) have used sodium sulfate, mainly in conjunction with oxidizing agents, and various catalysts, and have reported satisfactorily on its use. It must be pointed out, however, that wherever a high digestion temperature is necessary, or desirable, sodium sulfate should not be used.

PHOSPHATES, PHOSPHORIC ANHYDRIDE, AND PHOSPHORIC ACID

The use of phosphoric acid and phosphorus pentoxide goes back to Kjeldahl's original method. Kjeldahl, himself, recommended the addition of phosphoric anhydride and fuming sulfuric acid to the digestion mixture. Heffner, Hollrung, and Morgen (29) in their comparison of Kjeldahl's method with that of Will and Varrentrap also used this combination successfully. Kulisch (30) used a mixture of concentrated sulfuric acid and fuming sulfuric acid containing 100 gm of phosphoric anhydride per liter. Asboth (31), however, found equally good results whether or not phosphoric anhydride was present. A mixture which has been claimed to give a quick digestion of casein (32) is the following: 5 gm of potassium sulfate, 5 ml of sulfuric acid, and 15 ml phosphoric acid (85%). After decoloration, it is necessary to continue heating for 15 or 20 minutes. By using this method (33), good results have been obtained with such compounds as dimethylamine, aniline, phenacetin, uric acid, caffeine, piperazine, morphine, brucine, betaine, and atropine. Folin and Wright (34) in describing a method for nitrogen in urine, use a 5 ml sample and add to it 5 ml of a mixture of 50 ml of 5% copper sulfate (in water), 300 ml of 85% phosphoric acid, and 100 ml of concentrated sulfuric acid. Two milliliters of 10% ferric chloride are then added and the mixture boiled vigorously until the flask is filled with white fumes. The mouth of the flask is covered and boiling continued for 2 minutes. Gentle boiling is continued for 2 minutes longer. Acid digestion of malt, beer, wort, etc., according to Lunden and Ellborg (35) is carried out, in conjunction with hydrogen peroxide, by using 1–2 grams of sample and 10 ml of a mixture of 3 volumes of sulfuric acid and 2 volumes of 85% phosphoric acid. Hydrogen peroxide (10–20 ml of 30%) is first added to the sample along with 0.5 gm of copper wire. After the vigorous reaction is over, 7 gm of potassium sulfate are added, and the mixture boiled strongly for 5 minutes. Gerritz and St. John (36) state that 10 gm of anhydrous potassium hydrogen phosphate (or 12 gm of the trihydrate) can be substituted for 10/16 of either sodium or potassium sulfate thereby shortening the digestion time to 25 minutes or less. Such material as dried blood, fish meal, and soy bean meal required less than 15 minutes. These authors found that low results were obtained when all the sulfate was replaced by the phosphate. For the micro digestion of milk or blood, Winkler (37) used a mixture of 300 ml of 85% phosphoric acid and 100 ml of concentrated sulfuric acid. To each 100 ml of this mixture was added 10 ml of 6% copper sulfate solution and 10 ml of water. The digestion was carried out in a 50 ml test tube, 2 ml of the sample and 2 ml of the digestion mixture being used. Riehm (38) using essentially the method of Lunden and Ellborg (35) on beet products reported that this procedure eliminated foaming with a short digestion period. Stubblefield and DeTurk (39) in the determination of nitrogen in alfalfa, cereal products, vegetables, and milk, recommend a mixture of 10 gm of potassium hydrogen phosphate (12 gm of the hydrate), 6 gm of ferric sulfate, 25 ml of concentrated sulfuric acid and 0.6 gm of mercuric sulfate. Their results agreed with the official Kjeldahl-Gunning-Arnold method. The time of digestion, however, was reduced from 2.5 hours to 30 minutes. These authors state that the use of the phosphate prevents bumping. A comparison of sodium pyrophosphate and potassium sulfate (40) used in the analysis of gelatin showed the pyrophosphate to be less efficient. However, in this case, instead of an equivalent amount, 2 gm and 5 gm of pyrophosphate were compared with 10 gm of potassium sulfate.

It has been pointed out that the addition of various salts raises the boiling point of the digestion mixture. This is no less true of the phosphates, but, as in the case of other salts, the effective digestion temperature is limited by the solubility of the phosphate used, and the appearance of a solid digest is a reasonably good indication that a loss of nitrogen has occurred. Again, it must be repeated, that if it is necessary to increase the acid index either by reducing the amount of salt used, or by increasing the amount of acid, in order to obtain a fluid digest, or one in which no loss of nitrogen occurs, one of the primary functions of an acid-salt mixture is defeated, i.e., a high digestion temperature.

The addition of phosphates, while successful in many cases, requires a higher acid index than potassium sulfate. Their use, therefore, is limited. As an example, two series of determinations using mixtures of potassium sulfate and potassium hydrogen phosphate were made according to the procedure outlined for potassium sulfate. The results are shown in Table X. It will be seen that before 100% recovery can

TABLE X
RECOVERY OF $(NH_4)_2SO_4$ FROM H_2SO_4-K_2HPO_4 DIGESTION MIXTURES

Ml H_2SO_4 present at start of boil period	Staet of digest when cool	Gm $(NH_4)_2SO_4$ added	Gm $(NH_4)_2SO_4$ recovered	% Recovery
7.50	Solid	0.1004	0	0
10.00	Solid	0.1003	0.08939	89.12
12.50	Solid	0.1045	0.1032	98.76
15.00	Fluid	0.1006	0.0991	98.51
17.50	Fluid	0.1040	0.1022	98.31
20.00	Fluid	0.1022	0.1023	100.09

be attained, the amount of acid present at the start of the boil period must be at least 20 ml. The acid index, therefore, at the start of the boil period is 2, and if the arbitrary loss factor of 0.0355 gm of sulfuric acid per minute of boil is applied, the acid index at the end of the digestion is 1.88. Since the addition of phosphates to sulfuric acid, before the appearance of a solid or very viscous digest, does not contribute materially to a rise in temperature above that produced by potassium sulfate, the consequent advantage is small.

The problem of obtaining a sufficiently high temperature during digestion in order to insure complete decomposition of highly refractive residues has prevented the Kjeldahl method from becoming a general one for all types of organic nitrogen linkages. The temperature of a digestion mixture can be raised considerably without increasing the salt content by the use of glacial phosphoric acid (85%). Phosphoric acid acts chiefly as a boiling point raiser and diluent of the sulfuric acid, and contributes little to the actual oxidation of carbonaceous matter. The rate of oxidation, therefore, is retarded somewhat, depending upon the amount of phosphoric acid present.

The limiting factor governing the maximum temperature of an acid-salt mixture is the solubility of the salt in sulfuric acid. There is more latitude in the use of sulfuric-phosphoric acid mixtures, and a subsequent increase in working temperatures. On boiling these mixtures, sulfuric acid will distill in proportion to its concentration, and the temperature will rise slowly as sulfuric acid is lost, either by distillation or through reduction by the organic matter present. Since phosphoric acid (85%) under the influence of heat is converted to metaphosphoric acid, continued heating will eventually result in solid digests. The changes on heating glacial phosphoric acid may be represented thus:

$$85\% \ H_3PO_4 \xrightarrow{\text{150°C}} H_3PO_4 \text{ (anhydrous)}$$

$$2 \ H_3PO_4 \xrightarrow[\text{213°C}]{-H_2O} H_4P_2O_7$$

$$2 \ H_4P_2O_7 \xrightarrow[\text{-300°C}]{-2 \ H_2O} 4 \ HPO_3$$

The addition of water to the cooled digest converts the metaphosphoric acid to the orthophosphoric acid.

$$HPO_3 + H_2O \longrightarrow H_3PO_4$$

There is actually little advantage in the use of sulfuric-phosphoric acid mixtures when compared with sulfuric acid and potassium sulfate. Assuming that a reasonable working range of mixed acids does not exceed 40% of phosphoric acid, the differences in temperature between these mixtures and mixtures of sulfuric acid-potassium sulfate become negligible, while actual clearing time of the digest tends to increase with increasing percentage of phosphoric acid. However, if potassium sulfate is added to sulfuric acid-phosphoric acid, the temperature change becomes significant. This is apparent from the curves shown in Fig. 8. These temperatures were determined by boiling in a Kjeldahl flask (1) 35 ml mixtures of sulfuric acid-phosphoric acid, (2) 35 ml of mixed acids and 10 gm of potassium sulfate, and (3) 35 ml of mixed acids, 10 gm of potassium sulfate, and 2.86 gm of sodium sulfate (equivalent to 5 gm of sodium thiosulfate pentahydrate). In Fig. 9, the temperatures produced by progressive addition of potassium sulfate to 35 ml of specific combinations of mixed acids are shown. The acid

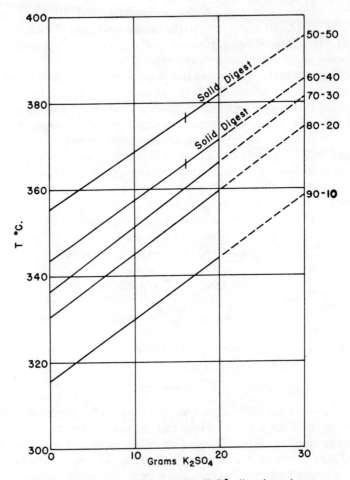

FIG. 8. Boiling points of H_2SO_4-H_3PO_4-K_2SO_4 digestion mixtures.

indices of 80%–20% and 70%–30% mixtures based on the total volume of acid are shown in Fig. 10.

Although it can be somewhat a matter of preference in selecting a combination of mixed acids, mixtures of 70%–30%, and 80%–20% sulfuric acid-phosphoric acid with potassium sulfate have been arbitrarily selected for reasons of high temperatures, liquid digests, and only slight differences in oxidation time of sample as compared with sulfuric acid-potassium sulfate mixtures. If 16 gm of potassium sulfate are used with 35 ml of mixed acids, the initial boiling temperatures are approximately 360°C for 70%–30% acid and 354°C for 80%–20% acid. These temperatures will increase somewhat as the digestion proceeds.

An average loss of acid from the above-mentioned mixtures was determined in the following manner:

Sixteen grams of potassium sulfate were added to 35 ml of a mixture containing *(1)* 20% phosphoric acid and *(2)* 30% phosphoric acid. Burettes were used to measure the exact volumes of acids. The samples were brought to a boil and boiled steadily for 90 minutes. The digests were then cooled, and diluted with distilled water to 250 ml. Total acidity (as H_2SO_4) and total phosphorus were determined, and sulfuric acid calculated by difference.

The results of two runs on each mixture are shown in Table XI. From these data, the loss of sulfuric acid appears to be fairly constant, although the total amount of acid lost varies with the acid ratio. For the 80%–20% acid mixture, an average constant loss of 0.081 ml/minute is obtained, and for the 70%–30% mixture, 0.101 ml/minute. As has been pointed out before, this rate of loss must be considered as an arbitrary factor, and will be influenced by the variables of the determination. It does, however, place the magnitude of loss, and therefore allows a basis for calculations.

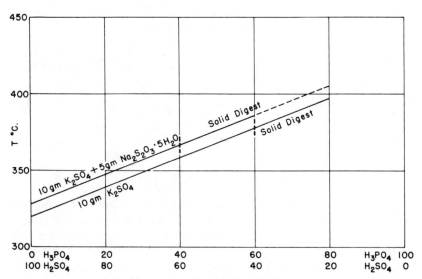

FIG. 9. Boiling points of H_2SO_4-H_3PO_4 digestion mixtures.

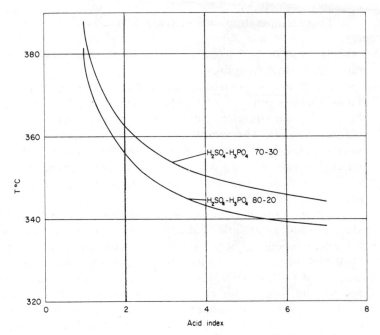

Fig. 10. Acid index of 70-30 and 80-20 H_2SO_4-H_3PO_4 digestion mixtures.

TABLE XI
ACID LOSS FROM H_2SO_4-H_3PO_4-K_2SO_4 MIXTURES

Start of digestion			After 90 minute digestion			Ml Acid loss	
Acid ratio	Acid index	T°C	Acid ratio	Acid index	T°C	H_2SO_4	H_3PO_4
80–20	2.19	354	76–24	1.75	360	7.16	0.26
80–20	2.19	356	76–24	1.76	363	7.00	0.30
70–30	2.19	362	67–33	1.63	367	7.18	1.80
70–30	2.19	3.60	67–33	1.61	368	7.42	1.75

Miscellaneous Salts

Other salts have, at times, been used as substitutes for potassium (or sodium) sulfate with little or no success. The rise in boiling point of an acid-salt mixture is dependent, for the most part, upon the solubility of the salt in concentrated sulfuric acid. When this solubility is exceeded, bumping and sometimes foaming generally occurs during digestion. The effective temperatures produced by substituting

TABLE XII
BOILING POINTS OF ACID-SALT MIXTURES

Mixture	T°C
Sulfuric acid	310
35 ml Sulfuric acid + 10 gm potassium sulfate	329
35 ml Sulfuric acid + 15 gm magnesium sulfate	318
35 ml Sulfuric acid + 7 gm manganese sulfate	318
35 ml Sulfuric acid * 7.5 gm lithium sulfate	343
35 ml Sulfuric acid + 17 gm zinc sulfate	322
35 ml Sulfuric acid + 22 gm sodium borate	351
35 ml Sulfuric acid + 16.5 gm ferrous sulfate	338

equimolar amounts of various salts for 10 gm of potassium sulfate are shown in Table XII.

Of the salts listed in the table, other than potassium sulfate, it is possible to use lithium sulfate and borax, although there is no particular advantage to either. Margosches and Vogel (23) made a comparison of potassium, sodium, and lithium sulfates while working with mononitrophenols, mononitrobenzoic and mononitrocinnamic acids. The reported results were low with both sodium and lithium sulfates. However, this can possibly be attributed in part to the lower digestion temperatures obtainable with either sulfate.

The recovery of ammonium sulfate from simulated digests is shown in Table XIII. Varying amounts of sulfuric acid were added to 10 gm of lithium sulfate, along with 0.1 gm of ammonium sulfate, and the mixtures boiled for one hour. In all cases with the exception of the digest containing 20 ml of acid, the residues are solid, although no ammonia is lost. This can perhaps be explained on the basis that the final digestion temperatures do not approach the decomposition point of ammonium sulfate. The initial concentrations at the start of the

TABLE XIII
RECOVERY OF $(NH_4)_2SO_4$ FROM H_2SO_4-Li_2SO_4 DIGESTION MIXTURES

Ml H_2SO_4 at start of boil period	State of digest when cold	Gm $(NH_4)_2SO_4$ added	Gm $(NH_4)_2SO_4$ recovered	% Recovery
7.5	Solid	0.1000	0.1002	100.20
10.0	Solid	0.1001	0.1000	99.90
12.5	Solid	0.1002	0.1002	100.00
15.0	Solid	0.1000	0.1002	100.20
17.5	Solid	0.1003	0.1002	99.90
20.0	Thick, pasty	0.1000	0.1001	100.10

digestions vary from 1.33 to 0.5 gm/ml, and it is obvious from the temperatures shown in Table XIV that even deducting the amount of acid lost on boiling (±1 ml), the final temperatures are well below the critical point at which ammonia may be lost.

TABLE XIV

BOILING POINTS OF H_2SO_4-Li_2SO_4 MIXTURES

Gm $Li_2SO_4/$ ml H_2SO_4	T°C
0.2	342
0.3	348
0.4	353
0.6	360
0.8	366
1.0	373
1.2	379
1.4	387

Substitution of part of the potassium sulfate (40%) by borax is also possible, and the recovery of ammonium sulfate is shown in Table XV. Here again it is necessary for a large excess of acid to be present before complete recovery is possible.

TABLE XV

RECOVERY OF $(NH_4)_2SO_4$ FROM H_2SO_4-K_2SO_4-$Na_2B_4O_7$ DIGESTION MIXTURES

Ml H_2SO_4 present at start of boil period	State of digest when cool	Gm $(NH_4)_2SO_4$ added	Gm $(NH_4)_2SO_4$ recovered	% Recovery
7.50	Solid	0.1028	0	0
10.00	Solid	0.1005	0.07793	77.54
12.50	Solid	0.1016	0.09609	95.46
15.00	Thick, glassy	0.1035	0.1002	98.60
17.50	Viscous	0.1000	0.09732	97.32
20.00	Viscous	0.1067	0.1067	100.00

Potassium bisulfate has been used occasionally in place of the sulfate, but there appears to be no particular advantage attached to it, other than the convenience of adding less acid than is customary when the normal salt is used. Goswami and Ray (41) in their evaluation of selenium and yellow mercuric oxide as catalysts for the digestion of proteins used 10 ml of concentrated sulfuric acid, 5 gm of potassium bisulfate, 0.5 gm copper sulfate, 0.05 gm selenium, and 0.1 gm yellow mercuric oxide. Dumazert and Marcelet (42) used a catalyst mixture of 24 parts of bisulfate and one part of mercuric selenite. For digestion, 20 mg were used for each milliliter of acid. After reduction of the nitro group, Soler (43) digested the sample (0.3–0.8 gm) with 10 gm of potassium bisulfate and 10–20 ml of sulfuric acid for one hour.

Oxidizing Agents

POTASSIUM PERMANGANATE

The oxidation of organic matter in boiling sulfuric acid is normally a slow process. It can be accelerated by the addition of salts such as potassium, or sodium, sulfate, by catalysts, or by the addition of an oxidizing agent. In his original method Kjeldahl (44) first heated the sample in concentrated sulfuric acid, close to the boiling point, and added powdered potassium permanganate to complete oxidation of the carbonized material. The use of permanganate has been the subject of much controversy. The variations in the amounts of recoverable nitrogen finally led to its discontinuance. In the early days of Kjeldahl's method, it represented an important advance, and at least, historically, is deserving of mention.

Gibboney (45), in making a comparison of the Gunning modification using permanganate and the alkaline permanganate method, found that variable results were obtained but were generally higher than those by the use of the alkaline permanganate and within the limits of acceptability. Siegfried and Weidenhaupt (46) state that if permanganate is added in small amounts to the digestion mixture and then boiled, there is no danger of loss of ammonia. Oxidation is complete if there is no decoloration after boiling for 3 minutes. In the determination of nitrogen in coal, Fieldner and Taylor (47) observed no loss of nitrogen on addition of permanganate, but found it necessary to prolong the digestion for 2 hours after the digest became colorless. It has also been noted by Frear, Thomas, and Edmiston (48), that the time at which the permanganate is added has an apparent effect on the amount of nitrogen recovered. If it is added immediately after removal of the heating source, a loss is observed. However, if the temperature is allowed to drop approximately 100°C, no loss of nitrogen occurs. Satisfactory results were obtained by Ashton (28) in the analysis of soils when 5 gm of permanganate were added after clearing of the digestion. This same procedure when applied to grass, gave low results. Beet (49) points out that if the permanganate is added before the digestion is complete, low results will be obtained.

In the analysis of feed stuffs and feces, Cochrane **(50, 51)** found that addition of permanganate gave higher results. However, in this case, a comparison was being made using the Kjeldahl method per se, with and without permanganate. Collaborative tests reported by Phelps **(52)** on the use of permanganate in the modified method for nitrates showed variable results. On the basis of these analyses, it was recommended that the use of permanganate be discontinued. Salkowski **(53)** also reported that permanganate should not be used, particularly if halogenated compounds were present. Other workers **(15, 54)** reporting on the variation in results, turned to the use of alkali sulfates and catalysts. Recently, however, Beet **(55)** has used permanganate in a semi-micro method for nitrogen in coal. Samples containing 0.2–1.0 mg of nitrogen are first digested for 5 minutes in 8×1 inch test tubes, and after cooling somewhat, are oxidized with permanganate added in small amounts until a sage green color is produced. Digestion is continued for one minute. The distillation period is 6 minutes, and the ammonia is collected in 2 ml of 0.75% boric acid.

Hydrogen Peroxide

Hydrogen peroxide is an energetic oxidizing agent, and its addition to concentrated sulfuric acid containing organic matter gives rise to a more or less violent reaction. It has been used successfully in both the macro and micro Kjeldahl methods, and its use eliminates the uncertainties attached to potassium permanganate.

The chief difficulties encountered in the Kjeldahl digestion, even with official methods, and particularly with natural products, are *(1)* length of digestion time and *(2)* excessive foaming. Kleeman **(54)** recommended the use of 30% hydrogen peroxide as a means of avoiding these troubles. A sample of one gram of air dried, or 5 gm of fresh plant or animal material and 25 ml of peroxide are mixed, and 40 ml of concentrated acid are added slowly with shaking. It is stated that approximately 80% of the nitrogen is converted quickly to ammonia. After addition of 15 gm of potassium sulfate, 10–15 minutes boiling is sufficient for complete conversion. However, the recommended time is 45 minutes. In the case of fat-rich milk, 60 minutes have been allowed. Experiments carried out with ammonium sulfate showed that in spite of the violent oxidizing conditions, and continued boiling for 3 hours, no nitrogen was lost. Huess **(56, 57)** followed Kleeman's procedure closely, but stated that in the analysis of barley, the amounts of reagents may be reduced, viz., on a sample of 1.75 gm, 15 ml of 30% peroxide, 20 ml of sulfuric acid, and 7–8 gm of potassium sulfate were satisfactory. The time for complete digestion was reduced from 80 to 45 minutes. Skutil (58) used Kleeman's method, but cooled the flask during addition of the concentrated acid. Riehm (38) also followed Kleeman's procedure although the proportion of materials was different. Copper, 0.5 gm, and mercuric sulfate, 0.8 gm, were used as a combination catalyst, and 10–20 ml of hydrogen peroxide added to the flask containing the sample. A mixture of 3 volumes of concentrated sulfuric acid and 2 volumes of glacial phosphoric acid, 20 ml, was added slowly. After the violent reaction ceased, the mixture was heated gently until SO_2 was given off. The mouth of the flask was then covered with a watch glass, and heating continued until the mixture cleared (between 6–10 minutes). At this point, 14 gm of potassium sulfate were added, and heating continued for 6 minutes. Riehm used this method on beet products, claiming a short digestion time, and elimination of foaming when analyzing beet juices. Lunden and Ellborg (35) claimed that digestion of beer, malt, and wort could be completed in 8–12 minutes using copper as a catalyst, and half the quantities of mixed acid and sulfate as were used by Riehm. In a study of various digestion methods, Rautenberg and Benischke (59) found that variable results were obtained on casein and carbazole on short digestion, but comparable results using a 2 hour boil period.

Various other workers, however, have used hydrogen peroxide for quick oxidation after carbonization of the organic matter present. Koch and McMeekin (60), in developing a micro method for nitrogen, claim complete recovery of nitrogen as ammonia by successive addition of peroxide (1–5 drops of 30% to the carbonized digest), heating until fumes appear, and again reheating after each addition. Moore (61), also, adds peroxide after first heating for 5 minutes over a low flame. Additional acid, copper sulfate as catalyst, and potassium sulfate are added, and the mixture heated until fumes are given off. Peroxide is added until the solution remains blue, and the digest is then heated for an hour with a high flame. Portner (62), also using a micro method on protein solutions in 50% glycerine first added bromine after charring, and reheated the digest. Bromine was again added with several drops of hydrogen peroxide. Finally after 4 or 5 additions, peroxide alone can be added. Careful heating is necessary after addition of bromine to avoid spontaneous carbonization. Saccardi (63), working with flour, leather, and cheese, first heated the samples with 5% oleum for 20 minutes. After charring, peroxide, in the amount of 10% of the acid, is added to the cold digest. After 5 minutes of heating, this is repeated. According to the author, very resistant compounds require an additional treatment. On samples of tobacco, linseed cake, leather, and wool, Cartiaux (64) treated 0.7–3.0 gm of sample with 5 ml of concentrated sulfuric acid and allowed the mixture to stand for 15 minutes at room temperature before heating for several minutes. After cooling, 10–20 ml of peroxide are added in small portions, avoiding a large evolution of gas. After heating to expel the gas, the digest is boiled for 5 minutes and the process repeated until a clear solution results. Various modifications involving methodic changes (65–72) have apparently been used successfully. The fact remains, however, that the use of a powerful oxidizing agent does not tend to broaden the scope of the Kjeldahl method. It is quite possible that at the time of carbonization the nitrogen is not completely reduced. Addition of an oxidizing agent at this point may keep the nitrogen from being reduced, if it is already present in a higher valence state, or oxidize it if it is present as ammonia or a reduced form. It is better to depend on the higher temperatures obtained by salt addition than on the addition of an accelerator to promote oxidation of organic matter.

Perchloric Acid

Perchloric acid is another oxidizing agent that has found favor for the rapid oxidation of carbonized material. In general, most workers advocate the use of perchloric acid after the material has been carbonized, although a few add it directly to the sample and sulfuric acid generally as a 35% solution. The same reasoning applies here for perchloric acid as for potassium permanganate and hydrogen peroxide. The addition of a powerful oxidizing agent, particularly in the presence of a catalyst, favors the oxidation of nitrogen even when added after carbonization. However, the reported results, for the most part, seem to indicate otherwise.

For digestion of the sample, Mears and Hussey (72) use 25 ml of sulfuric acid, 1 gm of copper sulfate, and 2 ml of concentrated perchloric acid. They report a clearing time of 3–7 minutes and recommend boiling the digest for at least 15 minutes after clearing. They also state that the accuracy of the determination is not affected by the use of perchloric acid. Parker and Terrell (73) determining the nitrogen in leather, heat the sample (0.8 gm) in a mixture of 15 ml of sulfuric acid, 1 gm of copper sulfate, and 6 ml of perchloric acid ($d = 1.12$) for 15 minutes, then increase the heat and boil for 45 minutes after clearing. Kitto (26) recommends using a digestion mixture composed of 70 ml of sulfuric acid, 6 ml of water, 20 ml of perchloric acid and 15 gm of sodium sulfate, with sodium selenate as a catalyst. A volume of 12.5

ml is used with 0.5 gm samples of flour, or 2 ml of milk. Pepkowitz, Prince, and Bear (20) treat the sample with 25 ml of sulfuric acid, 10 gm of sodium sulfate, using selenium oxychloride as a catalyst. After heating strongly for 10 minutes, the digest is cooled and 10 drops of 35% perchloric acid added, then heated over a low flame for 10–15 minutes, or until clearing. In the analysis of soils, the sulfate is omitted. The authors state that the materials contained in soils will oxidize ammonia in the presence of sodium sulfate-perchloric acid. A further modification (74) applied to the micro method for nitro compounds uses 1 ml of sulfuric acid containing 32 gm of salicylic acid per liter for 10–50 mg of sample. Nitro compounds are reduced with 3 drops of 30% sodium thiosulfate solution. The digest is heated moderately for one minute, and vigorously for 10–15 minutes. After cooling, 2 drops of perchloric acid, 35%, are added, and digestion continued below the boiling point until clear. For grain, starch, and potato, Koch (75) treats 0.1–0.2 gm samples in a beaker with 15 ml sulfuric acid. After an initial heating period, and when the foaming has subsided, perchloric acid is added dropwise until the digest clears. LeTourneur-Hugon and Chambionnot (76) using the Gunning modification digest the sample for 10 minutes and then add perchloric acid, dropwise, during boiling until clearing. They state that for flour and saffron the digestion can be made in 30 minutes. By the use of perchloric acid and selenium as a catalyst, Pacheco, Lopéz-Rubio, and Marquez (77) report comparable results on soils using this and the official Spanish method (Gunning-Hibbard). The time of digestion was shortened from 4 hours (official method) to 15 minutes. Both Wicks and Firminger (78), and Ribas-Marques and Capont (79) observe losses by the use of perchloric acid. The latter report poor results with such compounds as glycine, asparagine, aspartic acid, acetanilide, antipyrine, caffeine, cinchonine hydrochloride, ammonium oxalate, and ammonium sulfate.

POTASSIUM PERSULFATE

Potassium persulfate has been used by Scott and Meyers (80) as an oxidizing agent in the determination of nitrogen in urine, in both macro and micro Kjeldahl methods. In the procedure, 5 ml of urine are treated with 10 ml of concentrated sulfuric acid and 0.25 gm of copper sulfate, and boiled until the mixture is light brown or yellow. After cooling, 1.5–2.0 gm of potassium persulfate are added. Heat is applied until the reaction starts, the flask is then removed and the contents rotated until the reaction ceases and the digestion mixture colorless. This process is repeated, if necessary. The flask is again heated and boiling continued until the acid refluxes in the neck of the flask. At this point heat is removed, the flask cooled, and the nitrogen determined by distillation. The reaction of persulfate and sulfuric acid probably takes place as follows:

$$K_2S_2O_8 + H_2SO_4 \longrightarrow K_2SO_4 + 2 SO_3 + H_2O + O$$

The reaction takes place at a relatively high temperature, so that the entire amount of persulfate may be added at once, after the flask has cooled somewhat.

Huguet (81) first heated the sulfuric acid to vaporization and cautiously added a mixture of 10 ml of urine and 25 ml of 20% sodium persulfate, finally boiling the mixture until colorless. Nitrogen was determined by the hypobromite method. Steinitz (82) using a micromethod, first digested a sample containing 0.02–0.35 mg of nitrogen with 2 ml of sulfuric acid-phosphoric acid containing 0.1 gm of $Ti(OH)_4$ per 100 ml [difference from Rappaport's mixture (83) which contained 1 gm per 100 ml], until the sample carbonized. Potassium persulfate, 0.1 gm, is carefully added without allowing it to touch the side of the flask. The flask and contents are agitated for one minute, and the neck of the flask washed down with a few drops of water. If no yellow color of titanium peroxide appears, less than 0.3 mg of persulfate is present, and the digestion is continued until dense fumes form in the flask. Willard and Cake (84) used persulfate in the determination of nitrogen in flour, albumin, gelatine, and peptone. The sample, added to 15 ml of concentrated sulfuric acid is heated to charring and until evolution of sulfur dioxide ceases. The flask is cooled and ten times the sample weight of persulfate added. Gentle heat is applied and the flask swirled until the contents are colorless, generally in about a minute. After the digest has cleared, heating is resumed for 5 minutes to destroy any excess. It is stated that losses occur if too large an excess of persulfate is present.

For the macro digestion of urine, blood, and milk, Wong (85) uses relatively large amounts of potassium persulfate. A sample of 0.5 gm of dry protein or 5 ml of liquid is digested with 2 ml of 5% copper sulfate, 5 gm of potassium sulfate and 20 ml of acid and with gentle heat until frothing has stopped, and then strongly until the digest is amber colored. After cooling for 10 minutes, 3 ml of water are added and allowed to flow down the neck of the flask. Ten grams of persulfate (3 gm for urine samples) are now added carefully. After thorough mixing, the digest is heated until clear, and nitrogen estimated in the usual manner.

A gasometric micro method by Van Slyke (86) also uses persulfate as an oxidizing agent. Digestion is carried out in 200 × 25 mm test tubes with 1 ml of sulfuric acid-phosphoric acid mixture (3:1) and one gram of persulfate. Heating is continued until the mixture clears or until the appearance of white fumes. The amount of water present at the start of the digestion should not exceed 1 ml per milliliter of sulfuric acid.

The Boiling Period after Digestion

The expression "after boil" is used to designate the period of boiling after a digestion has cleared or become colorless. It is an arbitrary factor and is usually governed by the type of material under examination, the composition of the digest, and the temperature.

It frequently happens that the intermediate compounds formed during the early stages of digestion are more resistant to decomposition than the parent compound. Under a given set of digestion conditions it is possible that the maximum temperature obtainable is not sufficient to bring about complete decomposition on clearing. If the temperature is at or near the decomposition point of the intermediate, an extended period of boiling is necessary, since the thermal decomposition proceeds only slowly from left to right. In theory, the boiling period should be determined for each compound under specified digestion conditions. Since in practice this is not generally possible or practical, a factor of 2 or 3 times the clearing time is usually sufficient.

The progress of a digestion is easily followed by stopping the digestion at specified time intervals and determining the nitrogen in the usual manner. The recovery of nitrogen from several type compounds is shown in Fig. 11. The samples were digested using the salicylic acid-thiosulfate method, with 18 gm of potassium sulfate, 0.1 gm of selenium, and 35 ml of concentrated sulfuric acid. After reduction with 5 gm of sodium thiosulfate ($Na_2S_2O_3 \cdot 5H_2O$) the mixtures were brought to boiling. The average time of clearing was 30 minutes. Nitrogen was determined at 10, 20, 30 (time of clearing), 60, 90, 120, and 150 minute intervals. The amount of nitrogen converted to ammonia at the point of clearing is between 95 and 100%. For examples shown, an hour boil period after clearing is more than sufficient for complete recovery of nitrogen.

It might be reasonably expected, in theory, at least, that if a high enough temperature were maintained, digestion need not proceed

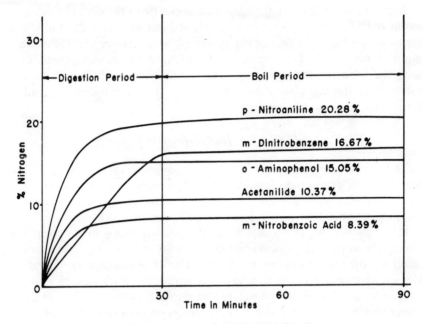

FIG. 11. Progress of the Kjeldahl digestion.

beyond the point of clearing. While this may be true in many cases, it is not generally so, since the maximum temperature of a digestion is necessarily limited by the amount of acid which must be present at the end of a digestion to prevent loss of nitrogen.

If a digestion is designed so that the final temperature is close to the critical point, and the temperature differential between the beginning and end of a digestion is small, it may be considered complete at the point of clearing. Under these conditions, clearing can take place in 20 minutes or less. Since with this high salt:acid ratio, both time and temperature are critical, and the digestion (at full heat) cannot be prolonged after clearing.

As an example of this type of procedure, some of the amino acids have been determined using 1.3 gm of potassium sulfate per milliliter of acid, and digesting with full heat until clearing. Average results of duplicate determinations are shown in Table XVI. Digestions were carried out in 500 ml flasks using 0.1–0.2 gm samples, 19.5 gm of potassium sulfate, 15 ml of acid, and 0.5 gm of mercury. Where possible, full heat was applied at once. However, many of the amino acids have a tendency to foam, so that low heat and frequent shaking are

TABLE XVI

RECOVERY OF NITROGEN FROM AMINO ACIDS WITHOUT THE BOIL PERIOD [a]

Compound	Gm $K_2SO_4/$ ml H_2SO_4	Digestion time (min)	%N Found	%N Calc.
Tryptophan	1.1	13	13.12	13.71
	1.2	17	13.49	
	1.3	15.5	13.84	
	1.3	16	13.73	
l-Lysine				
monohydrochloride	1.3	15	15.38	15.33
l-Cystine	1.3	10	11.56	11.66
Methionine	1.3	14	9.28	9.39
Phenylalanine	1.3	16	8.45	8.48
l-Histidine				
monohydrochloride[b]	1.3	16	20.01	20.04
dl-Valine	1.3	17	12.08	11.97
Arginine				
monohydrochloride	1.3	9	26.75	26.62
Glycine	1.3	15	18.96	18.68
Hydroxyproline	1.3	10.5	10.64	10.69
Leucine	1.0	21	10.71	10.69
	1.3	15	10.71	
Alanine	1.3	9	15.69	15.74
Glutamic acid	1.1	11	9.59	9.52
	1.3	9	9.56	
Aspartic acid	1.1	12	10.54	10.52
	1.3	10	10.50	
Tyrosine	1.3	12	7.69	7.73

[a] Catalyst: 0.5 gm Hg.
[b] With one mole of water.

necessary. As soon as the foaming is reduced to a minimum, full heat can be applied. Since the salt to acid ratio is close to the critical point, prolonged digestion at full boil beyond the point of clearing may cause loss of nitrogen. McKenzie and Wallace, and Perrin (see below) have both made use of high salt concentrations in order to reduce total digestion time.

Tryptophan (α-amino-β-3-indolepropionic acid), is difficultly decomposable and requires either a high temperature or long digestion. Furthermore, as shown in the table, total decomposition is not complete on clearing when the salt:acid ratio is less than 1.3:1. This is true also of lysine which can form, by ring closure a piperidine carboxylic acid. Conversely, other amino acids such as glutaric, aspartic, and leucine are easily digested with a salt:acid ratio of 1:1.

The method can be further extended to include other nitrogen linkages and natural products (Table XVII).

The recommended times of the boil period after clearing of a digestion have varied from 0 to 235 hours. Beet (87) states that the digestion of rice and wheat flour, oatmeal, and bran is complete when the digestion mixture has cleared. On the other hand, the digestion of certain coals required 235 hours boiling period to produce maximum recovery of nitrogen. Kitto's (26) experiments with wheat flour and milk showed the average length of the boil period to be 1.75 times the length of time for the digestion to clear. In determining the nitrogen in pyridine and nicotinic acid by the AOAC method using mixed catalysts, Shirley and Becker (88) found that 3–4 hours were required for practically complete recovery of nitrogen, and that usually the boil period after clearing could be estimated as 1.5 times the clearing time. In studying the effect of every variable in the digestion of cottonseed oil, Paul and Berry (22) found that the normal clearing time for a 2 gm sample was

TABLE XVII

RECOVERY OF NITROGEN FROM SOME NATURAL PRODUCTS AND ORGANIC COMPOUNDS
WITHOUT THE BOIL PERIOD[a]

Material	Gm K_2SO_4/ ml H_2SO_4	Digestion time (min)	%N	
			Found	Calc.
Leather, chrome tanned	1.3	15	12.37	12.68[b]
Leather, chrome tanned	1.3	16	11.93	11.85[b]
Flour	1.3	14	1.88	1.88[b]
Flour	1.3	14	1.60	1.62[b]
Flour	1.3	15	1.90	1.89[b]
Hide powder	1.3	21	13.47	13.42[b]
Corn meal	1.3	30	1.24	—
Oats	1.3	26	2.75	2.73[b]
Casein	1.3	23	13.34	13.36[b]
Egg albumin (soluble)	1.3	23	12.22	12.23[b]
Nicotinic acid	1.3	18	11.38	11.37[b]
Nicotinamide	1.3	18	23.05	22.94[b]
Imidazole	1.3	15	41.40	41.16
Betaine hydrochloride	1.3	15	9.16	9.13
Barbituric acid	1.2	11	21.65	21.78
p-Chloroaniline	1.2	11	10.91	10.98
o-Aminophenol	1.2	10	12.77	12.82
Anthranilic acid	1.2	10	10.23	10.21
Acetanilide	1.2	11	10.34	10.36
Urea	1.2	11	46.68	46.62

[a] Catalyst: 0.5 gm Hg.
[b] Nitrogen determined by Official Methods.

1–1.5 hours and that a boil period of 3 hours was necessary for complete recovery of nitrogen, using a digestion mixture of 5–10 gm of either sodium or potassium sulfate and 30 ml of sulfuric acid. The digestion period will obviously vary according to the proportions of the reagents and size of sample. Unless the digestion time is known for a given compound, Daudt (17) states that a minimum of 2 hours should be allowed. Andersen and Jensen (89), using a digestion mixture of 20 ml of sulfuric acid and 10 gm of potassium sulfate, also found that 2–4 hours were required for complete recovery and that in the case of refractory compounds, an even longer time was necessary. An exhaustive study of digestion conditions has been made by McKenzie and Wallace (9). These authors note that general procedure for the micro method is a ratio of 0.33 gm of potassium sulfate per milliliter of acid. Tryptophan was used as a typically resistant amino compound for the microdetermination of nitrogen. Varying amounts of potassium sulfate (0.5–3.0 gm), 1.5 ml of acid, catalyst and sample were digested. The most effective combination was a 1:1 ratio of salt and acid, giving a clearing time of 25 minutes. An additional 30 minutes boiling period with tryptophan gave a recovery of 99.1%. As a general procedure, and with such compounds as amino acids, nicotinic acid, and acetanilide, a 15 minute boiling period showed recoveries of 99.2–99.9%. A greatly shortened digestion procedure has been proposed by Perrin (90) in which 12 gm potassium sulfate, 15 ml of sulfuric acid, and 1.3–1.5 gm of mercuric oxide gave a total digestion time of 13–20 minutes. Sixty different protein samples determined by this method were compared with the official AOAC procedure. Agreement between the methods is within 0.3 percentage unit. For feeds and wheat products, complete digestion of 2 gm samples was accomplished in 25 minutes (36) with a mixture of 10 gm of dipotassium phosphate (or 10/16 of the amount of sodium or potassium sulfate), 25 ml of sulfuric acid, 0.7 gm mercuric sulfate, and 0.3 gm copper sulfate as catalysts. The digestion clears in 15–20 minutes. An additional 5 minute boil completes the digestion. Results indicate good agreement. Van der Bie (91) also reports a short period of boiling – 10 minutes – after clearing, in the determination of nitrogen in crude rubber, using a digestion mixture of 9.4 gm potassium sulfate, 30 ml of sulfuric acid, and catalyst. In the digestion of beets and sugar products (38), Riehm uses a digestion mixture of 20 ml of 60–40 sulfuric acid-phosphoric acid, boiling until clear (generally 6–10 minutes), adding 14 gm of potassium sulfate and continuing boiling for exactly 6 minutes. In contrast, Davies and Dowden (92) recommend that a one

hour boil after clearing is necessary for recovery of the betaine content in beet molasses and beet by-products. It may be pointed out,
however, that these workers did not use mixed acid for digestion. In
a study of the use of hydrogen peroxide to promote decomposition of
plant and animal substances, Kleeman (54) states that conversion
usually can be accomplished in 25–30 minutes after clearing, although
45–60 minutes is recommended. Using a semi-micro method for protein
hydrolyzates and proteins, Jonnard (93) reports that the digestion is
usually complete in 2–5 hours.

It is of interest to note that in the majority of cases where an extended boil period is recommended, the acid:salt ratio is high, giving
an acid index from 1.6 to 6.0. Under these conditions, even account-
ing for the acid used for decomposition of the sample and that lost
through boiling, it is understandable, in most cases, that a relatively
long boil period is necessary.

Every organic substance has its own decomposition point. Consequently, for greatest efficiency and minimum time of boil period, the
temperature of the digestion mixture should be above this point, but
below the point at which ammonium acid sulfate will be lost through
volatilization.

Reducing Agents

Originally, Kjeldahl's method was designed for the determination of
proteins. Digestion in sulfuric acid alone limited the method to those
compounds easily decomposed at the boiling point of sulfuric acid and
whose nitrogen was easily reduced to ammonia. The addition of either
sodium or potassium sulfate greatly increased the scope of the method.
There were, however, still many compounds classed as refractory since
their nitrogen could not be recovered quantitatively by this modification. It became necessary, therefore, to reduce these compounds prior
to actual digestion.

Reduction of nitrogen compounds may be effected in two general
ways: (1) as a pretreatment before actual digestion, and (2) addition
of compounds which are easily carbonizable to concentrated acid containing the sample. Where a large number of nitrogen determinations
are made daily, it is more convenient to add the reducing agent directly to the acid and sample. There are, however, numerous compounds which cannot be reduced by this procedure, and must,
therefore, be reduced by other means.

The following sections on reduction are more or less general, and other methods relating to specific materials may be found under Digestion Procedures.

REDUCTION BY PRETREATMENT

As early as 1887, Dafert (94) had broadly classified nitrogen compounds as belonging to a group not requiring pretreatment (amino, alkaloids, those containing the pyridine nucleus) and those in which the nitrogen was linked to oxygen or to another nitrogen and which required reduction before digestion. Flamand and Prager (95) using Dafert's procedure, reduced azo compounds with zinc and hydrochloric acid. A sample of 0.15–0.20 gm is dissolved in 10 ml of alcohol, 2–5 ml of concentrated hydrochloric acid, and 0.5–1.0 gm of zinc dust added. Reduction is complete when the solution becomes colorless. Ten milliliters of concentrated sulfuric acid and 0.5 gm of copper sulfate are added, and the mixture heated until fuming commences, at which point the flask and contents are cooled and 6 gm of potassium sulfate added. Digestion is continued until clearing, and the usual procedure for distillation followed. Close agreement with calculated values are reported. The method fails, however, with hydrazines.

Eckert (96) reduced nitro groups by mixing up to 0.5 gm of sample with 15–20 ml of 30–40% sulfuric acid and 0.4 gm of sulfur. Reduction takes place after one hour at steam bath temperature, and is followed by the usual Kjeldahl digestion. Reduction of azo compounds by powdered copper has been made by Kuznetsov (97). The sample is dissolved in concentrated sulfuric acid and a 50–100% excess of powdered copper (based on the sample weight) is carefully added. Instantaneous reduction is reported to take place and is evidenced by the clearing of the mixture. Digestion is completed in the usual manner. It is also stated by this author that azo compounds containing the anthraquinone ring cannot be analyzed. For the reduction of nitro compounds, Soler (43) used titanous chloride. The sample, 0.3–0.8 gm, is dissolved in 20 ml of acetone, 3–5 ml of 30% sulfuric acid, and 10–20 drops of a 10% titanous chloride solution added. The mixture turns violet and then decolorizes. Powdered zinc (1–2 gm) is then added with several drops of $PtCl_2$ solution to catalyze the reaction. If the violet, or violet-red color does not reappear, more zinc must be added. The flask and contents are gently heated to complete reduction. The acetone is carefully evaporated and the residue heated to fumes. Ten grams of potassium sulfate and 20 ml of concentrated sulfuric acid are now added. Digestion is continued for about an hour, then cooled, diluted, and distilled.

Rose and Ziliotto (98) determine the nitrogen in nitriles, both aliphatic and aromatic, by reduction with potassium iodide using the following procedure: 40–60 mg of sample is added to 30 ml of concentrated sulfuric acid and 1.5 gm of potassium iodide and heated on the steam bath for 45 minutes with occasional shaking. After this treatment 10 gm of potassium sulfate and 0.1 gm each of anhydrous copper sulfate and selenium are added and the mixture heated gently at first, and then boiled vigorously. After clearing, the mixture is boiled for one hour. Any free iodine remaining in the neck of the flask is removed by gently heating with a burner. The method is not suitable for all nitro compounds, or for hydrazines, pyridine, or inorganic nitrates. Substituents in azo compounds may also hinder complete recovery of nitrogen.

Reduction with sodium hydrosulfite ($Na_2S_2O_4$) has given satisfactory results in many cases. Simek (99), working with nitro and azo compounds, dissolved the sample (0.1–0.3 gm) in a minimum quantity of alcohol, in a 300 ml Kjeldahl flask. After addition of 20 ml of a freshly prepared saturated solution of sodium hydrosulfite, the mixture is allowed to stand on the steam bath for 30 minutes. In general, this is sufficient for complete reduction. The excess of hydrosulfite is destroyed by addition of 20 ml of concentrated sulfuric acid. The mixture is heated gently at first to drive off the water, and then digested until clear. In determining the nitrogen in 4,6-dinitrobenzene-2-diazo-1-oxide (diazodinitrophenol), Schaefer and Becker (100) modified Simek's method for reduction of the nitro groups, and also for total nitrogen, using the following procedure: 0.25 gm of sample is dissolved in 25 ml of alcohol in a 200 ml Kjeldahl flask, warming to effect solution. After addition of 25 ml of hot water, the solution is heated for a few minutes. At this point the mixture should be clear. Five grams of hydrosulfite in 25 ml of hot water are now added quickly and the solution warmed on the steam bath for several minutes with occasional shaking. The flask is now cooled in running water and the excess of hydrosulfite decomposed by addition of 5 ml of 50% H_2SO_4 followed by 20 ml of concentrated acid. The contents of the flask are heated over a low flame until the water and alcohol have evaporated. Heat is increased, and the mixture digested until straw colored, and heating continued for an additional 30 minutes. It is then diluted, transferred to a 500 ml Kjeldahl flask and distilled in the usual manner. Using this procedure, the standard deviation was −0.04.

In contrast to the relatively large amounts of hydrosulfite (see above), Csuros *et al.* **(101)** use 0.2–0.5 gm per 0.1–0.2 gm of sample. The compound is dissolved in either 25 ml of water, dilute caustic, dilute HCl or H_2SO_4, or, if it is insoluble in these solvents, 15–20 ml of acetone and 20 ml of water. After addition of hydrosulfite, it is allowed to stand on the steam bath for one hour. At the end of this period, 20 ml of concentrated sulfuric acid are added, and the water and solvent evaporated. The usual Kjeldahl procedure is followed, with selenium as a catalyst. The method is reported to give excellent results with azo compounds, and has been extended to include nitro and nitroso nitrogen **(102)**.

Sisley and David **(103)** determined the nitrogen in a large number of azo dyes and intermediates using hydrosulfite as the reducing agent followed by the usual Kjeldahl digestion with copper sulfate as the catalyst.

The reduction is carried out in the following manner: 0.5–1.0 gm of sample is weighed into a 250 ml Kjeldahl flask, 10 ml of alcohol and 5 ml of water added, and the mixture warmed. Sodium hydrosulfite, 2–4 gm, is added one gram at a time, heating to boiling and allowing the flask and contents to cool after each addition. Reduction is generally complete within 10–15 minutes. When the flask is cool, 10 ml of sulfuric acid are added, and most of the alcohol driven off by moderate heating. After cooling, 6–8 gm of potassium sulfate are added, depending on the quantity of hydrosulfite used, 12 ml of sulfuric acid, and 0.5 gm of copper sulfate. The mixture is heated first moderately, and then strongly until clearing. The digestion which generally takes 20–30 minutes is stopped at this point and nitrogen determined by distillation. The method is general in scope and applicable to mono- and polynitro compounds, azo, azoxy nitrogen, and many azo dyes.

An exploratory study by Woods, Scheirer, and Wagner **(104)** of such reducing agents as hypophosphorous acid, chromous chloride or sulfate, sodium and methanol, and electro reduction was made using nicotinic acid as a type compound. While the data are admittedly incomplete the results are close enough to induce further work. Aqueous hypophosphorous acid (50%) is added to the sample, and CO_2 passed into the flask, since phosphine is formed and may flash or explode. Results by this method averaged 94% recovery. Reduction with sodium and methanol yielded results which were reasonably acceptable, having a spread of 11.04–11.48% (11.38% theory). Electrolytic reduction was made on nicotinic acid in 80% H_2SO_4 using platinum electrodes and passing a current of 0.7 amperes and 4 volts through the solution. Reduction is followed by digestion.

Reduction of the nitrogen of osazones with zinc and hydrochloric acid was made by Dorfmüller (105) who reported that this reduction followed by the Kjeldahl digestion gave satisfactory results with the osazones of disaccharides, but was not adaptable as a general method for all osazones and hydrazones. Weizmann *et al.* (106) reduced nitro compounds by the following method: A sample, 0.1–0.2 gm, is treated in a 100 ml Kjeldahl flask with 5 ml of fuming sulfuric acid (containing 7% SO_3), and 2 gm of zinc dust. The zinc should be added slowly and without the development of too much heat. After the final addition, the mixture is allowed to stand for several hours or preferably overnight. The digestion following this reduction is extremely long. After addition of potassium sulfate, with copper sulfate as catalyst, the mixture is heated gently for 5 or 6 hours, then strongly for 6 to 20 hours until clearing, after which time the distillation is made in the usual manner. For the best results, at least four times the theoretical amount of zinc should be used.

A semi-micro method using zinc and hydrochloric acid has been proposed by Fish (107). The sample is weighed in a tin foil cup and dropped into the Kjeldahl flask. One milliliter of acetic acid is added and the mixture warmed to dissolve the sample. After solution and cooling, 200 mg of zinc powder and 1.5 ml of methanol are added. Concentrated hydrochloric acid, four drops, is added and the mixture warmed gently over a small flame. After 2–3 minutes, 4 drops of acid are again added, continuing to warm the solution. This procedure is repeated until 16 drops of acid have been added. The greater portion of the solvents is removed by gentle boiling, care being taken not to allow complete evaporation, since there is a possibility of nitrogen being lost. Digestion is carried out after addition of 3 ml of concentrated sulfuric acid, heating the solution to expel the water,—and subsequent addition of 1.5 gm of catalyst mixture (150 gm K_2SO_4, 10 gm HgO and 5 gm Se). When the digestion mixture clears, it is given an additional 45 minute boiling period. After cooling and diluting, it is distilled into boric acid. It is stated that the solvent apparently has an effect on the reductive treatment. Acetic acid, or methanol alone, gave low results with some carbazones and hydrazones. The method is applicable to azines, semicarbazines, oximes, and hydrazones.

For the reduction of nitro compounds, Dickinson (108) uses the following procedure: 0.35 gm of the nitro compound is weighed into a 500 ml Kjeldahl flask, and 5 ml of 88% formic acid and 2 ml of hydrochloric acid added. The mixture is warmed until the sample is in solution, 2 gm zinc dust added, and the flask swirled for 2 minutes. After standing on the steam bath for 5 minutes one gram of iron powder (reduced by hydrogen) is added and the flask swirled again for 2 minutes. Two milliliters of hydrochloric acid and 5 ml of alcohol are added and the mixture allowed to stand on the steam bath for 5 minutes. This process is repeated until nearly all the iron has dissolved, after which 25 ml of sulfuric acid are added slowly with swirling. The flask and contents are then heated over a Bunsen burner until ebullition ceases. Either potassium or sodium sulfate (12–14 gm) is added, the mixture digested for one hour, cooled, diluted, and distilled. If the compound is not soluble in formic acid, but melts under heat, vigorous swirling to keep the sample in contact with the metal usually gives theoretical results. In the event the sample neither melts nor goes into solution, 5 ml of acetic acid or 85% phosphoric acid may be substituted for formic acid, giving a recovery of about 98.5% of the nitro compound. Iron powder is used rather than additional zinc because it does not agglomerate in the acid and lose its effectiveness as zinc does. A further method of reduction, effective only on aromatic nitro compounds, uses aluminum as the metal. The sample (0.35 gm) is dissolved, on the steam bath, in 20 ml of concentrated sulfuric acid. The temperature of the solution is adjusted to 30°C and 0.4 gm of aluminum added. The flask and contents are shaken and allowed to stand for 10 minutes or until foaming starts. Reduction time is 30 minutes at 30°C. After this period, 12–14 gm of potassium sulfate are added, the mixture digested one hour and distilled. Recovery is stated to be 0.2% higher than theory.

Steyermark et al. (109) adapted Dickinson's method of reduction to micro procedure for azo, nitro, oxime, isoxazoles, hydrazine, and hydrazone groupings. A sample of 5–8 mg, 0.2 ml of formic acid (98–100%), and 0.1 ml of concentrated hydrochloric acid are warmed in a water bath until solution takes place. This is treated with 80 mg of nitrogen-free zinc, mixing for 2 minutes by swirling the contents of the flask, and heating for 5 minutes in a water bath, after which 40 mg of iron powder (by hydrogenation) are added. After mixing for 2 minutes, 0.1 ml of concentrated hydrochloric acid and 0.15 ml of methanol are added and the mixture heated on the water bath for 5 minutes. Increments of 0.1 ml of hydrochloric acid are added every 5 minutes until the iron has dissolved. One milliliter of concentrated sulfuric acid is added slowly and heating continued on the water bath until evolution of hydrogen chloride ceases. Potassium sulfate, 0.65 gm, mercuric oxide, 0.016 gm, and sulfuric acid, 0.5 ml, are added. The mixture is digested for 4 hours, regulating the boiling so that the acid refluxes half way up the neck of the flask. Distillation is carried out for 8 minutes with the delivery tube below the surface of the boric acid solution, and for 2 minutes above it.

The method is stated to be not reliable for heterocyclic rings containing two or more nitrogens linked together such as 1, 2-diazines, 1, 2, 3-triazoles, and pyrazolones.

Friedrich (110) reduces the nitrogen of azo, nitro, nitroso, and hydrazine compounds with hydriodic acid and red phosphorus. The sample is treated with 1 ml of hydriodic acid and a small amount of red phosphorus, and warmed gently for half an hour. The flask is washed with water until about half full, and 2 ml of concentrated sulfuric acid added. After the water, hydriodic acid, and iodine have been boiled off, 0.5–1.0 gm of potassium sulfate and 0.1 gm of mercuric acetate are added and the mixture digested until clear. The digestion takes approximately 30–60 minutes. An objection to the method, although not a serious one, is the time necessary to boil off the water and free the mixture of iodine. It is intended to cover a wide range of nitrogen linkages, and Friedrich reported good results with various hydrazines, hydrazones, a semicarbazone, and antipyrine. The method works best, however, with nitro, nitroso, and azo compounds.

A micromethod involving reduction of aromatic nitro and polynitro compounds with lithium aluminum hydride has been reported by Bezinga, Ovechkina, and Gal'pern (111). A 3–5 mg sample is weighed into a 30–40 ml Kjeldahl flask and treated with 1–3 ml of a suitable solvent and 40–50 mg of the hydride. It is digested on a water bath for 30 minutes at a temperature 10°C below the boiling point of the solvent. After cooling, the excess hydride is destroyed by adding cautiously 3 ml of water dropwise with continuous shaking. The nitro group is reduced to azo which is further reduced by addition of 0.1 gm of sodium bisulfite. The solution is digested on a water bath for 15 minutes, then evaporated nearly to dryness. The residue is then digested with 5 ml of sulfuric acid, 250 mg of a 1:3 mixture of potassium sulfate and copper sulfate, and 20 mg of mercuric oxide until clear and distilled in the usual manner.

Albert (112) reduces oximes, nitro, and nitroso compounds by the use of ethylenebis(mercaptoacetate). A weighed sample is treated with one milliliter of concentrated sulfuric acid and two drops of the reagent and heated slowly to 180°–190°C for 15 minutes. Reduction is complete within this period, and digestion is carried out in the usual manner after addition of 0.65 gm of potassium sulfate, 0.016 gm of mercuric oxide, and 0.2 ml of sulfuric acid.

Reduction of nitro compounds with alkaline stannite has been made by Lunt (113). The reagent is prepared by dissolving stannous chloride hexahydrate in the minimum quantity of concentrated hydrochloric acid. This is cooled, and 30% NaOH added carefully with continued shaking and cooling. Sodium chloride is first precipitated, then a pale yellow curdy precipitate is formed which dissolves on further addition of caustic. The solution, which should contain 1.5 times the stoichiometrical amount of stannous chloride hexahydrate necessary for reduction of $-NO_2$ to $-NH_2$, is added immediately to the sample dissolved in aqueous methanol containing a drop of caustic. Reduction is complete after warming the solution gently for several minutes, although occasionally heating to a boil may be necessary. Reduction is complete when the deep yellow color has been discharged. The solution is cooled and diluted with water before addition of sulfuric acid and catalyst. The preparation of the alkali stannate must be done with fairly cold solutions and addition of caustic made very slowly, other-wide a dark precipitate containing metallic tin may result. If this happens, it is recommended that fresh reagent be prepared.

Takeda and Senda (114) heated aromatic mononitro compounds with potassium hydroxide in ethanol prior to digestion. The results by this method agreed well with calculated values, but with polynitro compounds complete recovery is not possible.

Salicylic Acid and Related Compounds

The function of compounds such as salicylic acid is to supply a reducing effect during the Kjeldahl reaction. The breakdown of such compounds to free carbon, and subsequent reduction of sulfuric acid to sulfur dioxide supplies the reducing effect of the Kjeldahl reaction.

The first mention of the use of oxygenated, or hydroxy, compounds was made by Stebbins (115) who used 0.5 gm of sucrose in the determination of nitrogen in nitro compounds, using 2 gm of phosphoric anhydride and 20 ml of a digestion mixture of 4 volumes of concentrated sulfuric acid and one volume of fuming sulfuric acid. Oxidation was completed with permanganate. Correct results were obtained with dinitrophenol, m-nitroaniline, and o-nitrophenol. Asboth (31) working with azobenzene, nitrobenzene, and picric acid, also used sucrose (one gram), with copper sulfate as a catalyst. When nitrates were present, benzoic acid was substituted for sucrose. A further modification introduced by Jodlbauer (116) was the substitution of benzoic acid for phenol which is more readily nitrated. The use of phenol, however, was for the determination of nitrogen in inorganic nitrates. A modification by the Association of Official Agricultural

Chemists included the use of salicylic acid, followed by a reduction with zinc dust. Later, Forster (117) substituted sodium thiosulfate for zinc dust as a reducing agent. The reaction of inorganic nitrates with salicylic acid in concentrated sulfuric acid may be represented as follows:

$$2\ MNO_3\ +\ H_2SO_4\ \longrightarrow\ M_2SO_4\ +\ 2\ HNO_3$$

Cope (118) in 1916 used salicylic acid for such compounds as mono-, di-, and trinitrotoluene, picric acid and o-, m-, and p-dinitrobenzene. It was not satisfactory for the analysis of tetranitroaniline, tetranitromethylaniline, or dinitronaphthalene. Two grams of salicylic acid were dissolved in 30 ml of concentrated sulfuric acid with gentle heating. After addition of the sample, 2 gm of zinc dust were added, the mixture kept at room temperature, and let stand over night. After heating gently until evolution of gas ceases the mixture is boiled for $1^1/_2$ to 2 hours, cooled, one gram of yellow mercuric oxide added, and again boiled for 1 to $1^1/_2$ hours. It is then cooled, 7.5 gm of potassium sulfate and 10 ml of concentrated acid added, and boiled $1^1/_2$ to 2 hours. After this digestion, it is distilled in the usual manner.

The reaction of salicylic acid with nitro compounds is not one of nitration. The nitration of a phenol, phenolic acid, or polyhydroxy compounds by a nitro compound is infrequent. Actually, the function of such compounds is to supply free carbon, which, on heating, reduces sulfuric acid to provide a source of sulfur dioxide as the active reducing agent. Salicylic acid, in combination with sodium thiosulfate has been used for many years. Generally, salicylic acid is dissolved in concentrated sulfuric acid such that the concentration is one gram per 30 or 35 ml of sulfuric acid. In practice, the usual procedure is to allow the sample to stand in contact with this mixture, either at room temperature or steam bath temperature for a short period of time. This is followed by reduction with sodium thiosulfate, prior to actual heating and digestion.

A mixture of salicylic acid and a nitro compound dissolved in concentrated sulfuric acid and subjected to steam bath temperature for 3 to 4 hours does not nitrate, and the components may be recovered quantitatively after this treatment. What does happen, however, is that a loose addition compound is formed (119). This is clearly shown by the ultraviolet curves. Figures 12 and 13 show the curves for salicylic acid, 3-nitrosalicylic acid, m- and p-nitrochlorobenzene dissolved in concentrated sulfuric acid. If nitration actually took place, the curves of mixtures of salicylic acid and a nitro compound should exhibit some characteristics of the curve for nitrosalicylic acid. In every mixture, however, (Fig. 14–17), a peak appears approximately to 215λ. Except for this peak, the curves retain the general characteristics of the curve for salicylic acid, except for some shifting of the peaks due

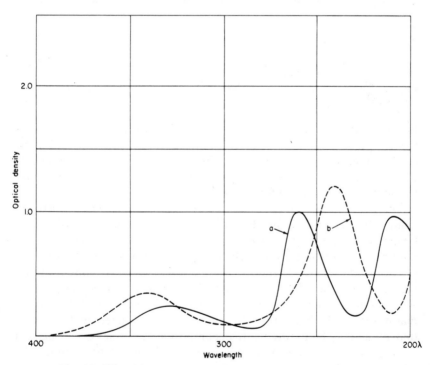

FIG. 12. Ultraviolet curves of a, salicylic acid; b, 3-nitrosalicylic acid.

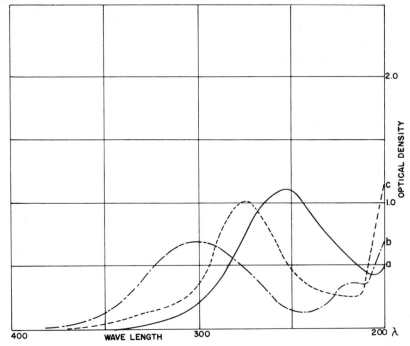

Fig. 13. Ultraviolet curves of a, *m*-dinitrobenzene; b, *p*-nitrochlorobenzene; c, *p*-dinitrobenzene.

to the presence of nitro compounds. The inference to be drawn from this is that salicylic acid does not contribute to the formation of more easily reducible compounds. Actually, as far as organic nitrogen compounds are concerned, it serves only as a source of sulfur dioxide on decomposition in hot sulfuric acid.

There are many so-called refractory compounds whose nitrogen cannot be determined by the salicylic acid-thiosulfate modification. Complete recovery of nitrogen is not obtained for several reasons: *(1)* total reduction is not accomplished on addition of sodium thiosulfate, at room temperature, and during the usual reaction time allowed (generally one-half hour): subsequent heating to produce carbonization of salicylic acid takes place at such a relatively high temperature that it is possible that part of the compound not reduced by the sodium thiosulfate may be pyrolytically decomposed; *(2)* losses can be caused by various compounds having a relatively high volatility under the influence of the existing temperature: this is generally true of mono-nitro compounds, although not entirely confined to them, *m*-nitrochlorobenzene, for example, can show a definite loss, which is evidenced both by odor and sublimation in the cooler part of the flask. A similar loss occurs with 2,4-dinitrophenol; *(3)* compounds such as pyridine, or containing the pyridine nucleus may be incompletely reduced, and in addition may not be digested at a sufficiently high temperature to assure thermal decomposition and complete conversion to ammonia.

Since the function of salicylic acid is to supply a source of sulfur dioxide, it is reasonable to assume that other compounds of similar structure, would act in the same manner. This is entirely the case. However, the reduction of many organic nitrogen compounds must take place at a temperature lower than that represented by the decomposition point of salicylic acid, which is relatively high. Otherwise, as has been pointed out before, losses can occur through volatilization and pyrolytic decomposition. It is fairly obvious, therefore, that for a general method, some compound whose decomposition point is low would be the best source of sulfur dioxide as the reducing medium.

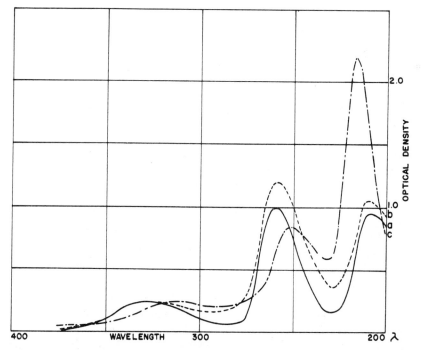

FIG. 14. Ultraviolet curves of a, salicylic acid; b, *m*-dinitrobenzene, zero time; c, *m*-dinitrobenzene, after 30 minutes.

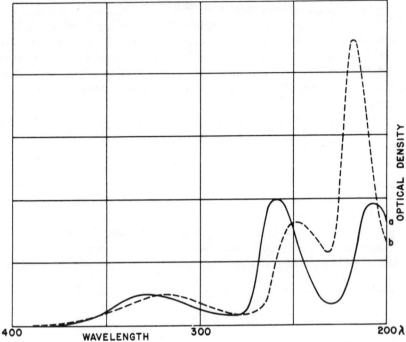

OPTICAL DENSITY

400   WAVELENGTH   300   200 λ

FIG. 15. Ultraviolet curves of a, salicylic acid; b, 3-nitrosalicylic acid after zero time and 30 minutes.

Table XVIII shows the temperature range of various compounds within which sulfur dioxide is liberated. Not all of the compounds shown in Table XVIII can be used successfully over a wide range of organic nitrogen compounds. However, many of them having low decomposition points greatly increase the scope of the method.

   McCutchan and Roth (120) have used thiosalicylic acid for the determination of nitrogen in nitro compounds and petroleum distillates. One gram of thiosalicylic acid is weighed into a Kjeldahl flask and 20 ml of concentrated sulfuric acid added. A weighed amount of sample (0.1–3.0 gm) is added and the neck of the flask washed down with an additional 20 ml of acid. The mixture is heated until boiling and spattering occur. After cooling to room temperature, 20 gm of potassium sulfate and 1.3 gm of mercury are added and the digestion completed in the usual manner, maintaining a digestion temperature of approximately 365°C. These authors also used thio-2-naphthol and thiophenol to determine the nitrogen in nitrobenzene and found 95% recovery with the former and 100% with the latter compound.

A comparison of the effect of some hydroxy compounds on the recovery of nitrogen from two so-called refractory compounds, *o*- and *p*-dinitrobenzene is shown in Table XIX (121). The following general digestion procedure was used: one gram of the hydroxy compounds was dissolved in 35 ml of concentrated sulfuric acid, the sample added and the mixture allowed to stand on the steam bath until solution took place. Five grams of sodium thiosulfate ($Na_2S_2O_3$ $5H_2O$) were added. After one-half hour of standing at room temperature, gentle heat was applied until carbonization took place. When cool, 18 gm of potassium sulfate and 0.1 gm selenium catalyst were added. After clearing of the digestion, boiling was continued for one hour. From the data shown in Table XIX it is apparent that a 1:1 mixture of 1-naphtholpyrogallol and sucrose show the greatest recovery of nitrogen. This is related, at least qualitatively, to the decomposition temperature of the hydroxy compound used. Tirouflet (122) in determining nitrogen in aromatic nitro compounds, used a digestion mixture of 20 ml of sulfuric acid, 1 gm of pyrogallol and 5 gm of a mixed

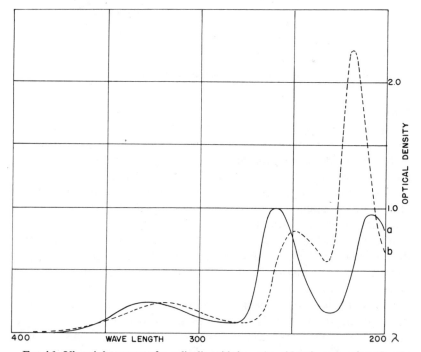

Fig. 16. Ultraviolet curves of a, salicylic acid; b, *p*-nitrochlorobenzene after zero time and 30 minutes.

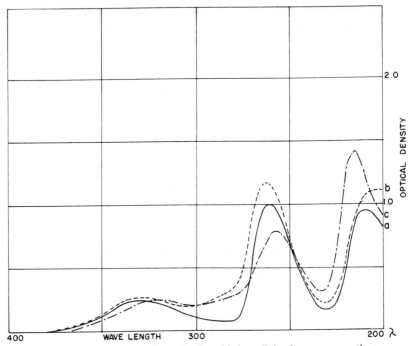

FIG. 17. Ultraviolet curves of a, salicylic acid; b, *p*-dinitrobenzene, zero time; c, *p*-dinitrobenzene, after 30 minutes.

mercury and selenium catalyst to promote reduction of the nitro groups. Sisley and David (**103** using a digestion mixture of 20 ml of sulfuric acid, 10 gm of potassium sulfate, and 0.3 gm of pyrogallol, were able to determine the nitrogen in many nitro and nitroso compounds. Takeda and Senda (**123**) found that with the addition of glucose, nitro nitrogen could be determined, although with volatile and relatively stable substances such as 2.5-dichloro-1-nitrobenzene recovery of nitrogen was not complete. Using the sealed tube digestion technique, Baker (**124**) found that the addition of 50 mg of either thiosalicylic acid or glucose promoted reduction of nitro compounds. Further use of glucose in the micro determination of nitrogen in petroleum fractions has been reported by Baibaeva and Orlova (**125**).

Sulfosalicylic acid has been used in place of salicylic acid, but since its decomposition point is as high as salicylic acid, there is no advantage in its use. Hydroxynaphthalene sulfonic acids, also, can be substituted for salicylic acid, but here again, high decomposition points preclude their use except in a very limited range and only

TABLE XVIII
DECOMPOSITION POINT OF VARIOUS OXYGENATED COMPOUNDS

Compound	Approximate T°C range for liberation of SO_2
Salicylic acid	230–240
Thiosalicylic acid	160–180
Sulfosalicylic acid	220–230
1-Naphthol	150–160
2-Naphthol	165–175
Pyrogallol	120–140
Inositol	150–155
Phenol	175–185
Benzoic acid	155–160
Sucrose	90–100
Dextrose	95–105
Resorcinol	130–140
Catechol	140–150
Phloroglucinol	145–155
Hydroquinone	140–150
Gallic acid	125–130

TABLE XIX
EFFECT OF HYDROXY COMPOUNDS ON THE RECOVERY OF NITROGEN FROM o- AND p-DINITROBENZENE

Compound	% N recovered o-Dinitrobenzene	% N recovered p-Dinitrobenzene	%N Calc.
Salicylic acid	14.48	15.49	16.68
1-Naphthol	15.00	16.03	16.68
2-Naphthol	14.95	15.88	16.68
Catechol	14.80	15.23	16.68
Resorcinol	14.00	15.49	16.68
Pyrogallol	16.49	16.59	16.68
Hydroquinone	15.12	14.77	16.68
Phloroglucinol	13.17	15.72	16.68
Gallic acid	15.65	15.76	16.68
Salicylic acid / Pyrogallol	13.89	16.13	16.68
Pyrogallol / 1-Naphthol	16.11	16.28	16.68
Pyrogallol / 2-Naphthol	15.77	15.38	16.68
Sucrose	16.59	16.54	16.68

where the compounds being analyzed have a higher decomposition point than the acid used.

Sucrose and other easily carbonizable compounds are generally excellent reducing agents for nitro, nitroso, azo compounds, and some heterocyclic ring nitrogen compounds. The fact that sucrose, for example, can be used successfully as a reducing agent for many compounds does not necessarily mean, however, that recovery of nitrogen will be quantitative, since this is dependent to some extent on other factors, e.g., high digestion temperatures and time of digestion. A comparison of sucrose with several other compounds does point out the advantage of a low reduction temperature. This is apparent from the results shown in Table XX. The digestion mixtures

TABLE XX

RECOVERY OF NITROGEN FROM AROMATIC NITRO COMPOUNDS USING SALICYLIC ACID AND SIMILAR REDUCING AGENTS

Compound	% N Calc.	Salicylic acid	1-Naphthol-pyro-gallol	Thio-salicylic acid	Pyro-gallol	Sucrose
o-Dinitrobenzene	16.68	14.48	16.11	16.38	16.49	16.59
m-Dinitrobenzene	16.68	16.68	16.66	16.72	16.71	16.59
p-Dinitrobenzene	16.68	15.49	16.28	16.47	16.59	16.54
2,4-Dinitrophenol	15.22	14.00	14.48	14.98	15.00	14.94
2,4-Dichloronitrobenzene	7.29	4.35	—	6.01	6.05	6.15
o-Chloronitrobenzene	8.89	—	—	—	8.97	8.93
m-Chloronitrobenzene	8.89	6.76	7.83	—	8.82	8.86
p-Chloronitrobenzene	8.89	8.07	8.80	8.42	8.83	8.79
o-Nitrophenol	10.07	10.00	10.03	—	10.01	10.07
m-Nitrophenol	10.07	10.02	—	—	10.02	10.03
p-Nitrophenol	10.07	10.05	10.06	10.06	10.04	10.10
o-Nitrotoluene	10.22	8.94	10.30	8.73	10.27	10.23
m-Nitrotoluene	10.22	9.38	10.15	—	10.21	10.18
p-Nitrotoluene	10.22	9.00	10.09	10.18	10.16	10.20
3-Nitrosalicylic acid	7.65	7.07	7.69	7.67	7.63	7.71
5-Nitrosalicylic acid	7.65	7.31	7.65	7.62	7.62	7.68
o-Nitrobenzoic acid	8.39	8.30	8.35	8.37	8.34	8.36
m-Nitrobenzoic acid	8.39	8.37	8.33	—	8.42	8.32
p-Nitrobenzoic acid	20.28	20.20	20.30	20.27	20.31	20.40
m-Nitroaniline	20.28	20.21	20.24	20.26	20.18	20.27
p-Nitroaniline	20.28	20.26	20.31	20.25	20.22	20.23
3,5-Dinitrobenzoic acid	13.21	12.62	13.26	13.22	13.16	13.24
2,6-Dichloro-4-nitrophenol	6.74	6.35	6.53	6.61	6.59	6.63
2,4-Dinitrochlorobenzene	13.82	13.57	13.84	13.88	13.86	13.81

had approximately the same acid index, so that essentially the same digestion temperatures were obtained in all cases.

With the combination of low reduction temperature (below the decomposition point of the compound being analyzed) and high digestion temperature the recovery of nitrogen in nitro compounds becomes quantitative in the majority of cases. These two factors also contribute to the recovery of nitrogen in other linkages such as nitroso, azo, thiazoles, and other heterocyclic compounds, examples of which are shown in Table XXI.

With the exception of the results obtained with thiosalicylic acid (McCutchan and Roth procedure), all others were obtained by the following procedure: 0.5 gm of the hydroxy compound is added to 35

TABLE XXI

RECOVERY OF NITROGEN FROM MISCELLANEOUS NITROGEN LINKAGES
USING SALICYLIC ACID AND SIMILAR REDUCING AGENTS

Compound	% N Calc.	Salicylic acid	1-Napthol- pyro- gallol	Thio- salicylic acid	Pyro- gallol	Sucrose
Azobenzene	15.36	15.28	15.36	15.33	15.37	15.34
p-Dimethylaminoazobenzene	18.65	18.42	18.51	18.53	18.53	18.63
Nitrosobenzene	13.08	12.69	12.77	12.88	12.73	12.96
o-Nitronitrosobenzene	18.42	17.25	18.02	18.15	—	18.46
Dimethylglyoxime	24.13	22.96	23.67	23.78	23.99	23.98
Cyclohexanoneoxime	12.38	11.67	—	12.17	12.04	12.37
Pyrrole	20.87	19.54	20.64	19.76	20.57	20.62
Piperine	4.69	3.05	4.63	4.30	4.47	4.62
Brucine	7.10	6.34	—	7.01	7.00	7.15
Theobromine	31.01	30.81	30.98	31.02	—	31.27
Isatim	9.59	9.05	9.37	9.40	—	9.42
Uric acid	33.25	32.18	33.13	33.06	33.11	33.09
Barbituric acid	21.81	21.72	21.78	21.76	—	21.79
Methylmercaptobenzo- thiazole	7.72	7.76	7.71	7.74	7.70	7.73
Betaine hydrochloride	9.12	8.00	8.92	9.02	9.03	9.15
Diacetylmonoxime	13.86	14.05	13.97	14.00	—	14.02
1-Aminobenzothiazole	18.64	18.07	18.53	18.59	18.57	18.70
Urea	46.68	46.59	46.52	46.60	46.47	46.60
Thiourea	36.81	36.47	36.76	36.68	36.76	36.75
N,N'-Diethyl-N,N'- diphenylurea	10.45	10.39	10.38	10.41	10.41	10.39
Guanidine hydrochloride	43.99	43.89	43.91	43.94	43.92	43.92
Diphenylguanidine	19.04	18.98	18.98	19.00	18.95	19.01
Nitroguanidine	53.85	52.77	53.29	53.53	53.47	53.56

ml of concentrated sulfuric acid in a 500 ml Kjeldahl flask and heated until a definite odor of sulfur dioxide is produced. After cooling to approximately room temperature, the sample is added and the flask allowed to stand on the steam bath for one hour with occasional shaking. After the reduction period, 18 gm of potassium sulfate and 0.1 gm of selenium are added and the mixture digested until clear. Boiling is continued for one hour. When cool, the digest is diluted, 140 ml of 35% caustic added and the ammonia distilled into 4% boric acid and titrated using methyl purple as an indicator.

A stock solution of salicylic acid in sulfuric acid keeps unchanged over a long period of time, but pyrogallol, 1-naphtholpyrogallol, and sucrose must be weighed out as needed, since carbonization takes place easily at room temperature. Reduction time in many cases may be shortened to one-half hour, and the amount of hydroxy compound e.g., sucrose safely reduced to 0.2–0.3 gm.

Catalysts

One of the drawbacks of Kjeldahl's original method was that it took considerable time to complete a digestion, particularly when natural products were involved and large samples necessary. The use of fuming sulfuric acid, and the addition of phosphorus pentoxide in sulfuric acid contributed somewhat in shortening digestion time by increasing the severity of the reaction and thereby widening the scrape of the method. The first published mention of the use of a catalyst appears to be by Wilfarth (126) who observed that the presence of copper salts appreciably reduced digestion time. Further investigation showed that oxides of lead, copper, mercury, manganese, bismuth, iron, and zinc reduced digestion time by varying degrees. While mercury was found to be the most effective, the total nitrogen could not be recovered on distillation because of the formation of a mercuro-ammonium complex. Wilfarth's researches, therefore, were confined to the use of copper oxide (CuO). In a second paper (127), a comparison of copper oxide and ferric oxide showed substantially no difference in digestion time.

During the following years various catalysts were examined and comparisons of their activity made. Ranedo (128) studying the effect of various elements on the Kjeldahl digestion, stated that those in the third and fourth groups of the Periodic System have considerable retarding effect which can be overcome by the use of positive catalysts. A systematic study of thirty-nine metals used as catalysts was made by Osborn and Wilkie (129). Determinations were carried out on gluten flour under controlled conditions. One gram samples were digested for 2 hours with 25 ml of sulfuric acid and 15 gm of sodium sulfate, with addition of 0.003 gm mole of metal or salt. A similar series of determinations was made stopping the digestion at the point of clearing. Of the elements examined, ten exhibited strong catalytic action as determined by the results of the shorter digestion. These are, in order, mercury, selenium, tellurium, titanium, molybdenum, iron, copper, vanadium, tungsten, and silver. If the amount of catalyst is increased to 0.03 gm mole, selenium, vanadium, and molybdenum are eliminated as catalysts, since the results show a low recovery of nitrogen.

Milbauer has made exhaustive studies of the mechanism of the Kjeldahl process and the relative activity of various elements as catalysts. Oxidation of sucrose (130) for example, in concentrated sulfuric acid at temperatures of 174° and 237°C showed palladium, mercuric sulfate, silver sulfate, platinum, vanadium pentoxide, selenium dioxide, tellurium dioxide, and copper sulfate to be positive catalysts, and their relative activities to vary depending on the temperature. Further results of studies (131, 132) on the oxidation of sucrose by concentrated sulfuric acid at elevated temperatures and with various catalysts are given in Table XXII. The speed of oxidation of 100 mg of sucrose in 100 ml of sulfuric acid was determined for selenium dioxide, mercuric oxide, copper oxide and tellurium. If the time of

TABLE XXII

ASCENDING ACTIVITY OF CATALYSTS

OXIDATION RATE OF SUCROSE BY SULFURIC ACID

237°C	302°C	Boiling point
Sb	Ni	No catalyst
Cu	No catalyst	Ni
Ag	As	As
V	Ag	Ag
Te	Pd	Pd
Pt	Sn	Sb
Hg	Sb	Pt
Pd	Pt	V
Se	Hg	Sn
	Cu	Te
	Te	Cu
	V	Hg
	Se	Se

oxidation of sucrose is taken as 1, the effective ratios for the different catalysts can be determined. These are shown in Table XXIII. The mixed catalysts SeO_2-$HgSO_4$(1:1) and SeO_2-$CuSO_4$(3:1) were most effective at 302°C, having an oxidation rate compared to sucrose alone of 1:49. In a later paper (133), it was stated that $HgSO_4$-Se is the most effective catalyst when the ratio Hg:Se is 4:1.

TABLE XXIII
OXIDATION RATE OF SUCROSE

Catalyst	302°C	Boiling point
No catalyst	1	1
14 mg SeO_2	1:26	1:49
374 mg HgO	1:6	1:43
100.4 mg CuO	1:7	1:38
161 mg Te	1:7	1:4

Baker and Shuttleworth (19) stated that in the digestion of leather the efficiency of the several catalysts examined was in the following descending order: mercury, selenium, copper, and manganese, and that the advantage gained by the use of mercury is offset by the subsequent operation to remove it prior to distillation. Baker (11) examined 21 metals as catalysts for the Kjeldahl micro digestion and found mercury to be the most effective.

Digestions of ammonium sulfate, benzylisothiouronium chloride, and nicotinic acid were made with 1.5 ml of sulfuric acid, 20–40 mg of catalyst, and concentrations of potassium sulfate varying from 0 to 3.0 gm/ml of acid, giving a temperature range of 329°–450°C. Digestions were carried out for 20 minutes at full heat, cooled, diluted, and distilled. Several catalysts apparently affect the recovery of nitrogen. At 387°C and above, loss of nitrogen occurs with selenium, with copper and titanium the critical temperature is 408°C. Selenious and selenic acid both promote decomposition of ammonia, the latter at relatively low temperature. Molybdenum, vanadium, and chromium oxides also cause loss of nitrogen, due to the fact that they probably act as oxidants rather than catalysts.

Many comparisons of the catalytic activity of mercury, selenium, and copper, alone or in combination have been made from the point of view of generalization or relation to specific compounds or types. This has resulted in considerable variance in the reported results, although it can be generally conceded that mercury more nearly approaches the ideal catalyst. Copper sulfate, while a satisfactory catalyst in a majority of cases, does not reduce digestion time sufficiently.

The most controversial of the catalysts is selenium. From the standpoint of speed of digestion, selenium is superior to mercury, with the added advantage that no further treatment is necessary prior to distillation. The data reported on the use of selenium as a catalyst are conflicting. Acceleration of the digestion is well demonstrated. However, loss of nitrogen through its use has been reported in many instances, and on this basis, has precluded its use as a general catalyst. On the other hand, if these data are examined from the standpoint of amount of catalyst used, digestion mixture, and types of compounds, some of the discrepancies credited to selenium can be eliminated. Various workers have used selenium in amounts of, and exceeding, 0.3 gm. Under this condition nitrogen can be lost during the digestion, since the allowable maximum appears to be between 0.2 and 0.25 gm. Further, the temperature at which the digestion is carried out influences the amount of recoverable nitrogen.

MERCURY

As a result of his experiments with various oxides as catalysts, Wilfarth at first discarded mercury because it formed an ammonium complex which was not broken up during distillation. The use of mercury, however, was continued since it was found that the complex could be destroyed by addition of alkali sulfide, thiosulfate, monosodium phosphate, potassium xanthate, or potassium arsenate. The amount of catalyst used varies somewhat from 0.5 to 1.2 gm of metal, oxide, or sulfate. In the analysis of pyridine zinc chloride, Phelps and Daudt (134) state that hydrolysis is complete only if 0.7 gm of mercuric oxide is present. Digestions were made under reflux conditions so that proportions of reagents would not vary. Samples of 0.3 gm pyridine zinc chloride were digested for 2.5 hours using a digestion mixture of 10 gm potassium sulfate, 25 ml concentrated sulfuric acid, and 0.7 gm mercuric oxide. Nolte (135), however, reported low results for nitrogen in uric acid and caffeine using 1.3 gm of mercury as a digestion catalyst. A similar loss occurred when ammonium sulfate was digested. When mercury was replaced with copper (foil), loss of nitrogen was also observed with uric acid and caffeine.

The addition of 250 mg of mercurous iodide (Hg_2I_2) instead of 1 gm of mercury, according to Sborowsky and Sborowsky (136), accelerates the oxidation of carbonized material. For example, the authors state that oxidation of 0.7 gm of sugar with 10 ml of concentrated sulfuric acid and mercurous iodide was accomplished as readily as the oxidation of 0.1 gm of sugar using mercury as the catalyst. Richards (137), also, reported a great saving in digestion time for coal and leather, using mercurous iodide. On the other hand, Hassig (138) found that digestion was not hastened by its use, and presented a distinct disadvantage, since iodine sublimed in the neck of the flask. In the digestion of fish meal, Potts, Parkam, and Schafer (139) found that the use of 0.7 gm of red mercuric oxide as against 0.2 gm of anhydrous copper sulfate tended to produce consistently higher results. Hiller, Plazin, and Van Slyke (140) state that only digestion mixtures using mercury as a catalyst will give nitrogen values for proteins corresponding to those obtained by the Dumas method. A comparison of selenium, copper sulfate, and mercuric oxide as catalysts was made by Louw (141) using a digestion mixture of 10 gm of potassium sulfate, 1.5 gm of catalyst, and 15 ml of concentrated sulfuric acid. A similar comparison made by Rozental (142) showed yellow mercuric oxide to be the most active catalyst, and giving highest recovery values. A digestion mixture of 7.5 gm of potassium sulfate, 20 ml concentrated sulfuric acid, and an optimum concentration of 1 gm of mercuric oxide is recommended.

COPPER

Copper and its salts have been used as catalysts since Wilfarth first discovered their effect on the time of digestion. In most cases, copper is a satisfactory catalyst, although slower than mercury, selenium, or mixed catalysts. Kurschner and Scharrer (143) used 1 gm of powdered copper in the digestion, both as reducing agent and catalyst.

A digestion mixture of 10 gm of potassium sulfate, 10 ml of concentrated sulfuric acid, 0.1 gm of sample, and 1 gm of copper is heated gently for 15 minutes and then strongly heated until clear. This is claimed to be sufficient for reduction and complete conversion to ammonia. It will be noted, also, that in this case the acid:salt ratio at the start of digestion is 1, so that close to maximum digestion temperature is possible throughout. The reduced copper is prepared by heating finely divided cupric oxide, and while hot, pouring into a dish containing 0.5 ml of methanol. Under the same digestion conditions, Mach and Lepper (144) found in the determination of protein in feed stuffs that the digestion time was the same for either copper sulfate pentahydrate or mercury. For the determination of crude protein in feed stuffs, Lepper (145) used a massive quantity of copper sulfate pentahydrate; the digestion mixture consisted of 5 gm of copper sulfate, 15 gm of potassium sulfate, and 20 ml of concentrated sulfuric acid. Digestion was complete in half an hour, and given an additional half hour boil period. Sandstedt's (146) comparison of copper, mercuric oxide, and selenium further confirms that the action of copper is much slower than either of the other two. Using a digestion mixture of 13 gm of potassium sulfate, 25 ml of acid, and 0.1, 0.7, and 0.1 gm, respectively, of copper, mercuric oxide, and selenium on samples of bran, digestion was complete in 45 minutes with selenium and mercuric oxide, and in 60 minutes with copper. If the digestion period is extended to 150 minutes, there is danger of loss of nitrogen when selenium is the catalyst. A comparison of these three catalysts by Nagosi and Nakagawa (147) on fertilizer and oil cake showed the catalytic activity to be in the following order: mercuric oxide, selenium, copper sulfate. Ashton (148), comparing copper sulfate and selenium as catalysts for total nitrogen in grasses, found that the same values were obtained by the use of either one. Clearing time with selenium was considerably less; however, a boil period of 2–3 hours was necessary in each case. With solids a total digestion period of 24 hours, using copper sulfate, and 3–6 hours using selenium gave constant values. The relative activity of the pentahydrate as compared to the anhydrous salt was examined by Beatty (149) who claimed some advantage in the use of the former.

SELENIUM

Since the first use by Lauro (150) in 1931, selenium and its salts, alone or in combination with other catalysts, have been the subject of many papers. Selenium has been, and still is, a controversial catalyst. Many workers have reported erratic results, incomplete recovery, or loss of nitrogen, and have recommended that its (Se) use be discouraged. It is true that losses of nitrogen can be caused by the use of selenium, especially when the amount of catalyst used is relatively large, i.e., greater than 0.25 gm, and through a prolonged boil period. There have been, however, cases in which large amounts of selenium, up to one gram, have been used in comparisons with other catalysts and similar results reported.

It is generally agreed that the clearing of a digestion is not necessarily indicative of complete decomposition and conversion of nitrogen to ammonia. However, Lauro, in his comparison of mercuric oxide, copper sulfate, and selenium oxychloride appears to have stopped the digestion at the point of clearing. Samples of flour, wheat, cottonseed meal, and cracklings were digested according to the official method of the American Oil Chemists Society (151) using 10 gm of potassium or sodium sulfate, 25 ml of acid, and catalyst. The results obtained with selenium oxychloride compared with those obtained with mercuric oxide, both of which were higher than results found with copper sulfate. The time of digestion was shortened considerably by use of selenium oxychloride or selenium.

Following Lauro's introduction of selenium as a catalyst, various investigators studied the mechanism of the reaction. Snider and Coleman (152) examined the effect of selenium and its compounds on the boiling point of Kjeldahl digests. They state that the function of catalysts is to raise the boiling point of the digest. While potassium sulfate is included in this category, it cannot be classified as a catalyst in the generally accepted sense. After establishing the temperature of 5–15 gm of potassium sulfate added to 20 ml of concentrated sulfuric acid, the further addition of 0.5 gm of mercuric oxide raised the boiling point of a mixture of 10 gm of potassium sulfate and 20 ml of acid only 2°C. Selenium (0.2 gm) added to the same mixture does not produce as high a temperature, although 0.5 gm of selenium gives a temperature comparable to mercuric oxide. If time-temperature curves are plotted, there appears to be a break in the curve, at which point the temperature of the boiling mixture rises sharply. This is designated as the critical point, and it is questioned as to whether loss of nitrogen occurs when the digestion is carried beyond this point. It was also noted that after addition of the sample (one gram of wheat), the maximum temperature of the digest during the oxidation rose 10°C above the same digest without sample. Samples of wheat (one gram) were digested with 20 ml of acid, 10 gm of potassium sulfate, and the following catalysts: 0.5 gm mercuric oxide: 0.075 gm, 0.1 gm, 0.25 gm selenium; 0.2 ml selenium oxychloride; 0.3 gm selenium dioxide + 0.05 gm copper; and 0.2 ml selenium oxychloride + 0.05 gm copper. A total digestion time of 30 minutes was allowed. In all cases where selenium was the catalyst, the results were slightly lower than those obtained using mercuric oxide.

Snider and Coleman note considerable difficulty with the distillation due to excessive frothing and the odor of hydrogen selenide, when zinc was used in the distillation. It is not necessary to add zinc when selenium is the catalyst, and this may be a contributory cause as to why the results obtained with selenium were lower. Snider and Coleman conclude that the action of mercury and selenium is for the most part catalytic, since the temperature rise, particularly with selenium is not sufficient to explain the rapid clearing of digests.

Crossley (153) using mercury, selenium, and selenium oxychloride, found the clearing time of coal and coke samples to be considerably less with selenium, although the boil period following clearing could not be reduced if maximum values were to be obtained. Approximately 40 minutes were necessary for clearing of the digest using selenium as compared with 87 minutes using mercury. Contrary to Lauro's findings, selenium oxychloride gave low results. As catalysts, 0.2 gm of selenium, and 1 gm of mercuric oxide were used.

An extensive investigation of the merits of mercury, copper, selenium, and their combinations, as catalysts has been made by Osborn and Krasnitz (154). Their results show that under the digestion conditions selenium alone has only a slight advantage over copper sulfate and none compared with mercury. Samples of natural products such as milk, meat, leather, coal, flour, and others were digested with 25 ml of concentrated sulfuric acid, 15 gm of sodium sulfate, and catalyst (mercuric oxide 0.7 gm, selenium 0.1 gm, copper sulfate pentahydrate 1.0 gm), for periods of 2 hours, and 1.5 times clearing time. A further comparison using 2 and 5 hour total digestion times was made and showed losses after a 5 hour digestion when selenium, and mercuric oxide-selenium were used as catalysts. It is stated that these losses on long digestion can be prevented by increasing the amount of acid to 37.5 or 50 ml. The effect of adding more acid naturally reduces the severity of the reaction, and it is understandable that a much longer digestion period will be necessary to obtain maximum results. With such a relatively large increase in the volume of acid, the digestion temperature is lowered considerably, so that the change of loss is reduced.

Davis and Wise (155), after evaluating selenium, concluded that it was not adaptable as a general catalyst and recommended that its use in combination with mercury or copper be discouraged. A series of determinations on flour using a digestion mixture of 10 gm of potassium sulfate, 25 ml of sulfuric acid, and varying amounts of selenium showed that after a 40 minute digestion, loss of nitrogen occurred when more than 0.2 gm of the catalyst was used. With an increase of sulfate to 16 gm/25 ml and a 40 minute digestion, low values were observed with both selenium and copper. Catalyst combinations of Hg-Cu and Cu-Se showed no loss at the higher concentrations. Mixtures containing Hg-Se, however, gave losses at low sulfate concentrations. Various other workers have not found this to be the case, either alone or in combination. Tennant, Harrell, and Stull (156) and Scharrer (157) confirm that selenium is a much better catalyst than copper, reducing total digestion time materially without loss of nitrogen. Taufel, Thaler, and Starke (158) digested both ammonium chloride and glycocol using 0.1 gm of selenium over a period of 20 hours without loss of nitrogen. When the amount of selenium was increased to 2 gm no loss of nitrogen occurred with either ammonium chloride, glycocol, or meal. However, in these cases, only sulfuric acid, catalyst, and sample were used.

Using the Kjeldahl-Gunning modification, Smith and Paterson (159), and Williams (160) found that 0.3 gm of selenium gave accurate results, but if more than this were used, losses occurred. Gonzales-Sanchez and Gomez Aranda (161) evaluated selenium and mercury as catalysts in the determination of nitrogen in coal. Using a digestion mixture of 30 ml of 98% sulfuric acid and 10 gm of potassium sulfate, the clearing time for selenium was 15–20 minutes, and for mercuric sulfate 20–25 minutes, using full heat. Boil periods as long as 10 hours showed no loss of nitrogen with either 0.25 gm or one gram of selenium, one gram of mercuric sulfate, or one gram of mixed catalyst.

The maximum amount of nitrogen is obtained after a total digestion period of 2.5 hours using selenium or mercuric sulfate-selenium (4:1), and 3 hours with mercuric sulfate. A comparison of selenium, and copper catalysts was made by Piper (162) on samples of grass, soil, and wheat using a digestion mixture of 35 ml of sulfuric acid and 10 grams of potassium sulfate plus catalyst (0.2 gm copper sulfate, and 0.2 gm selenium). Clearing time for selenium varied between 26 and 35 minutes, and for copper sulfate 43 and 65 minutes. An additional boil period of 2 hours was necessary to obtain maximum values using copper sulfate, while one hour was sufficient for selenium. Further experiments were made on a cereal grain using increasing amounts of selenium from 0.05 to 0.80 gm and a boil period after clearing of 40 minutes. A constant value of 2.36% was obtained in all cases.

If the proportions of salt to acid in the various digestion mixtures are examined, it will be noted that where the reported results show no loss of nitrogen even when relatively excessive amounts of selenium have been used and, in some cases, extremely long digestion periods, that the acid:salt ratio is high. Under such mild oxidizing conditions and comparatively low digestion temperatures, selenium apparently causes no loss of nitrogen. Conversely, in cases where selenium has been used on natural products (e.g., grass, grain, leather, etc.), according to specified procedures in which the acid:salt ratio is lower (25 ml acid/10 gm salt) and an extended boil period is generally necessary, losses of nitrogen have been observed. Since loss of acid occurs due to decomposition of the sample and by distillation over the entire digestion period, there is a subsequent rise in the digestion temperature. This would indicate a limiting time-temperature factor in the case of selenium. Using a digestion mixture of 35 ml of sulfuric acid containing one gram of salicylic acid, 10 gm of potassium sulfate, and subsequent treatment with 5 gm of anhydrous sodium thiosulfate, Bradstreet (163) found that digesting until clear and with an additional one hour boil period using amounts of selenium varying from 0.1 to 1.25 gm that definite losses occurred when more than 0.25 gm was used. Under controlled conditions the losses were random, and not proportional to the amounts of selenium used.

The action of selenium as a catalyst proceeds as shown below. The first reaction in hot concentrated sulfuric acid is the formation of selenious acid.

$$Se + 2\ H_2SO_4\ --------\blacktriangleright H_2SeO_3 + 2\ SO_2 + H_2O$$

The catalytic effect in the presence of organic material is represented as:

$$Se \rightleftharpoons SeO_2 \rightleftharpoons H_2SeO_3$$

and the reaction is reversible until all organic matter has been oxidized.

In a study of both selenium and tellurium as catalysts, Illarionov and Ssolowjewa (164) state that the catalytic effect of selenium is proportional to the amount used. If this were so, the more catalyst used, the shorter the digestion or clearing time. There is no straight line relationship between catalyst activity and the amounts used. If one gram samples of salicylic acid and varying amounts of catalysts are digested with 35 ml sulfuric acid and 18 gm of potassium sulfate, the clearing time of each catalyst decreases to a certain point, beyond which increased amounts of catalyst produce little if any effect. The curves in Fig. 18 show only the clearing times under specified conditions with specified amounts of catalysts and give no information as to whether total nitrogen recovery is possible under these conditions.

The loss of nitrogen occurring from the use of selenium has been stated by Illarionov and Ssolowjewa (164) to arise from the formation of ammonium selenite and subsequent decomposition:

$$3\ (NH_4)_2SeO_3 \cdot 9\ H_2O \longrightarrow 2\ NH_3 + 3\ Se + 2\ N_2 + 36\ H_2O$$

There is apparently no concrete evidence to substantiate this. However, if the above reaction does take place at some critical temperature, it would be expected that extended digestion would produce a more or less constant decrease in recoverable nitrogen, providing, of course, that the loss of acid over this period is not sufficient to cause an appreciable increase in temperature. A survey of literature results indicate losses over measured time periods to be random.

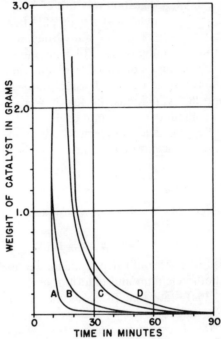

FIG. 18.   Clearing time of digests with various catalysts. A = Selenium, B = Selenium-Mercury, C = Mercury, D = Sulfate Copper.

The catalytic action of selenium has been thoroughly examined by Sreenivasan and Sadasivan (165). When 50 mg of selenium were heated for 15 minutes with 20 ml of sulfuric acid, only selenious acid was present. This was also true when copper selenite was used in place of selenium. However, when copper selenate was added both selenious and selenic acid were present. The addition of 0.5 gm of mercuric oxide to the above catalysts produced only selenic acid. The presence of mercury in hot concentrated acid, therefore, appears to oxidize any form of selenium to the highest oxide. When these experiments were repeated with organic matter, addition of selenium produced some selenious acid and deposited elemental selenium in the cooler part of the flask. The selenate was reduced to selenious acid and some selenium. With the addition of mercuric oxide only selenic acid was present. These authors conclude that the catalytic action of selenium in the presence of mercuric oxide can be represented as follows:

Selenium ⟶ Selenious Acid ⟶ Selenic acid

and in the absence of mercury, expressed as:

$$Se \rightleftharpoons H_2SeO_3$$

Selenium $\rightleftharpoons$ Selenious acid

Schwab and Schwab-Agallidis (166) state that when 0.8–8 mg of selenium as selenic acid are added to 3 ml of concentrated acid containing aniline (0.4 M) at temperatures ranging from 210° to 280°C a rapid initial reaction takes place accompanied by blackening of the mixture. This is followed by a slower, first-order reaction. Using 8 mg of selenium, the rate is independent of the temperature. However, with smaller amounts, it varies with temperature. The initial rapid reaction is assumed to be catalyzed by the formation of colloidal selenium which further aggregates to form fine droplets. At this stage, the reaction rate is limited by diffusion. The size of the drops calculated from reaction rate constants is 3.3×10^{-3} cm, as against a measured size of 0.07 mm. This is somewhat in contradiction of the findings of Sreenivasan and Sadasivan who reported the presence of only selenious acid with a trace of selenium when copper selenate was used. The concept of formation of colloidal selenium of measurable size does not appear tenable since selenium is easily soluble in hot concentrated sulfuric acid. Selenium should be expected to exist only momentarily and in molecular size. The oxidation-reduction system might then appear as

Selenium $\rightleftharpoons$ Selenious acid $\rightleftharpoons$ Selenic acid

The use of selenium in the form of its salts has been fairly well explored. Schwoegler, Babler, and Hurd (167) used copper selenite dihydrate $CuSeO_3 \cdot 2H_2O$ prepared by adding copper acetate to a hot solution of selenious acid (168). A comparison of copper sulfate and selenium showed an average clearing time of 13 minutes when 0.3 gm of the selenite was used with 25 ml of sulfuric acid and 12 gm of potassium sulfate. Addition of 20 mg/ml of acid of a mixture of one part mercuric selenite and 24 parts potassium acid sulfate was used on pure compounds by Dumazert and Marcelet (42). The results compared with the Dumas method were nearly identical. Dalrymple and King (168) made a comparison of selenium, and copper, calcium, and cadmium selenates. Various types of proteins were digested using an amount of catalyst equivalent to 0.10–0.15 gm of selenium. The relative effectiveness of these selenates is not too great and is of the order copper, calcium, and cadmium. The digestion times, on the proteins examined, were less than with selenium alone. However, loss of nitrogen occurs with prolonged digestion, so that with the use of these selenates the maximum digestion time should be known.

Mixed Catalysts

The function of a mixed catalyst is to promote greater activity than either component alone. In a majority of cases there is no significant advantage over a single catalyst. For the digestion of cereals and grains, Messman (169) used 20 ml of acid and a catalyst mixture of 8 gm composed of 9 parts of sodium sulfate, 7 parts of mercuric sulfate, 1.5 parts of copper sulfate, and 1.5 parts of metallic selenium for each gram of sample. Digestion was complete in 15–20 minutes, and satisfactory results obtained. Beet and Furzey (170) used 0.5 gm of mercuric oxide and 0.05 gm of selenium in the digestion of coal samples and found that the total digestion period was reduced from 45 minutes with selenium to 15 minutes with the mixed catalyst. In a later paper, Beet (171) modified this catalyst by substituting mercuric sulfate for the oxide. It is further reported (172) that at the point of clearing, the use of copper sulfate gave results which were 2% low, whereas with the mixed catalyst the deviation from maximum values was 0.5%. This loss, based on the total nitrogen, could be neglected in some cases. For the digestion of gram samples of oil cake, Nokajima and Ikedo (173) used 10 gm of a catalyst mixture consisting of 84.21% potassium sulfate, 13.16% mercuric sulfate, and 2.63% selenium. A comparison with copper sulfate showed that digestion time was reduced by half and with slightly higher results. Lloyd (174) claimed a 75% decrease in digestion time over copper sulfate and with higher results when a mercuric sulfate and selenium catalyst was used for the digestion of leather. In the analysis of several compounds of the camphor series, Vene (175) recommended a catalyst mixture containing by weight 32 parts potassium sulfate, 5 parts mercuric sulfate, and 1 part selenium. Close agreement with theory was reported. The use of iron in combination with selenium has been reported by Bradstreet (176). Equal parts of ferrous sulfate heptahydrate (0.25 gm) and selenium (0.25 gm) showed a slight improvement over copper sulfate and selenium, when used with a digestion mixture of 10 gm of potassium sulfate, 5 gm of thiosulfate, and 35 ml of sulfuric acid containing one gram of salicylic acid. A boil period of one hour after clearing gave results on pure organic compounds which agreed with the calculated values.

P. R. W. Baker (177) reported inconsistent results from use of a catalyst mixture of 9 gm mercuric sulfate and 2 gm selenium, and stated that loss of nitrogen was caused by decomposition of ammonia. The temperature of the digestion mixture is critical, and quantitative recovery can be expected only when the temperature does not exceed 420°C.

In a later paper, Baker (11) made a systematic investigation of single and mixed catalysts. Experiments were run on a micro scale using 20–30 mg of single catalysts, 40–20 mg mixtures of HgO-Se, HgO-CuSO$_4$, HgO-Te, and 20–20 mg of Se-CuSO$_4$, V$_2$O$_5$-Se. Digestions were carried out with ammonium sulfate using these catalysts and concentrations of potassium sulfate varying from 0 to 2.5 gm/ml of acid. Catalyst combinations with selenium indicate that losses occur at temperatures of 387°C and above, and that mixtures of mercury-selenium, or mercury-selenium-copper sulfate are no more efficient than mercury alone. The same is true for mercury-tellurium catalysts. It is evident from data reported in the literature that the successful use of selenium is due mainly to digestion conditions which give temperatures below the critical point. Lepper (178) noted a slight loss of nitrogen when copper sulfate and selenium mixture was used as a catalyst. For the determination of nitrogen in fertilizers, Allen (179) used 0.6 gm of a mixture of 5 parts copper sulfate pentahydrate, dried at 110°C and one part selenium. It is stated that this is a satisfactory catalyst, and is added at the start of the digestion. No potassium sulfate is used and the results are comparable to those obtained by the official AOAC method. With organic fertilizers the results were slightly lower.

Miscellaneous Catalysts

Aside from mercury and copper, platinic chloride, introduced by Ulsch (180), was one of the earliest catalysts. For one gram of material, a digestion mixture of 20 ml of acid containing 200 gm of phosphoric anhydride per liter, 0.05 gm copper oxide, and 5 drops of platinic chloride solution (0.04 gm platinum/ml). Digestion and clearing were much faster than with mercury, and satisfactory results were claimed. However, Osborn and Wilkie (129) established that there was a definite loss of nitrogen when platinum was used as a catalyst. Baker (177) also reported considerable loss with this catalyst.

The first reported use of vanadium as a catalyst appears to have been made by Riviere and Bailhache (181). The addition of vanadic, molybdic, and arsenic oxides, ferrous sulfate, and boric acid was, primarily, to raise the boiling point of sulfuric acid, thus shortening digestion time, rather than to investigate catalyst activity. Poor results were obtained with the oxides, and in cases where correct results were possible, extremely long digestions were necessary. Later, Oefele

(182) and Wunder and Lascar (183) reported on vanadic oxide. The latter digest the sample with a mixture of 5 ml of phosphoric acid, 25 ml of concentrated sulfuric acid, and 0.5 gm of ignited vanadic oxide. Prior to addition of acid, 3 gm of oxalic acid and 2 gm of sodium oxalate are added to the dry flask containing the sample. The digest is heated slowly until a green-yellow color is obtained. After cooling, 100–150 ml of water and 0.5–0.75 gm of fine iron filings are added, and the solution warmed for 30 minutes before distilling. Good agreement with theory is reported. Brill and Agcaoili (14) used vanadic acid unsuccessfully for the digestion of piperidine. Substitution of either bismuth or antimony oxide for the vanadium gave results of the same order. However, the results obtained in these cases are probably due to the low salt concentrations (5 gm/30 ml of acid), rather than to the catalysts used.

Crossley (184) investigated the efficiency of seven possible catalysts for the digestion of coal. Under the conditions specified in *Fuel Research Paper No. 44* (1940), one gram coal samples are digested with 9 gm of potassium sulfate, 30 ml of sulfuric acid, and 0.2 gm of selenium until clear, and given a further 2 hour boil period. Of the seven catalysts added to this mixture, potassium iodide, tungstic acid, bismuth oxide (Bi_2O_3), stannic oxide, chromic oxide, molybdic oxide, and vanadic oxide, only the last two effected complete recovery of nitrogen. When the boil period is reduced, complete recovery is not possible with molybdic oxide. Vanadium, alone, gave low results, but 0.5 gm of the oxide and 0.2 gm of selenium showed maximum recovery of nitrogen with one hour total digestion time at full heat.

Parri (185) reported on vanadium pentoxide, and a mixture of the oxide with copper oxide. For the digestion of one gram of flour, 20 ml sulfuric acid, 0.1 gm vanadium pentoxide, and 0.5 gm copper oxide were used. Total digestion time was 2.2 hours. With vanadium pentoxide alone, or with copper oxide, the necessary time was 6 hours. A comparison of the catalytic activity of mercuric sulfate-selenium, selenium, and selenium-vanadium pentoxide in the digestion of coal has been made by Edwards (186). Both mixed catalysts were satisfactory for semi-micro and macro digestions, while selenium could only be used for macro work. With catalyst mixtures of $32K_2SO_4$-$1Se$-$5HgSO_4$, and $90K_2SO_4$-$2Se$-$5V_2O_5$, the total digestion time was 25–35 minutes when the sample was digested with 2 gm of either catalyst and 4 ml of concentrated acid. The maximum temperature obtainable is 350°C. Baker (11) has stated that when the temperature of the digest is above 387°C, ammonia is lost if a selenium-vanadium pentoxide catalyst is used. Vanadium will definitely lower the temperature at which oxidation will occur. However, in these cases, the boiling temperatures are well below the critical temperature mentioned by Baker and may be the explaination as to why no losses occur under these conditions.

Illarionov and Ssolowjewa (164) studied the catalytic effects of the sulfur analogs, selenium and tellurium. They state that tellurous acid is a weaker oxidation catalyst than is selenious acid, and that no loss of nitrogen occurs when tellurium is used as a catalyst. On the other hand, Bradstreet (187) compared tellurium and selenium and found that with tellurium alone the calculated values for such compounds as acetanilide, anthranilic acid, p-nitroaniline, and m-dinitrobenzene were not obtained under controlled conditions using 35 ml sulfuric acid (containing one gram of salicylic acid), 10 gm potassium sulfate, and 5 gm sodium thiosulfate, with one hour boiling after clearing. In combination with copper sulfate or ferrous sulfate the results were slightly higher. An increase in the amount of tellurium used—from 0.1 to 1.00 gm—did not materially affect the results. This behavior differs from that of selenium, with which a definite loss (though apparently erratic) occurs. Further examination of sodium tellurite and tellurate gave results similar to tellurium. The fact that there is no recognizable loss, as such, and that the amount of tellurium that can apparently be used is relatively large might indicate that under proper conditions it could be a satisfactory catalyst. Illarionov and Ssolewjewa (164) and also Gressin (188) state that speed of decomposition is proportional to the amount used. Bradstreet did not find this to be true, under the conditions of digestion. Actually, the clearing times differed by only several minutes, the average being 30 minutes.

Since tellurium and selenium are analogs, it can be expected that the mechanism of their catalytic action will be similar, thus,

$$Te + 2 H_2SO_4 \longrightarrow H_2TeO_3 + 2 SO_2 + H_2O$$

$$Te \rightleftharpoons TeO_2$$

The possibilities of other elements such as molybdenum, titanium, and chromium have been well explored, and while a few have been used for specific purposes, none has been recommended for general use.

REFERENCES

1. P. A. W. Self, *Pharm. J.* **88**, 384–385 (1911).
2. E. Carpiaux, *Bull. soc. chim. Belges* **27**, 13–14 (1914).

3. R. B. Bradstreet, *Anal. Chem.* **29**, 944–947 (1957).
4. G. Middleton and R. E. Stuckey, *J. Pharm. and Pharmacol.* pp. 829–841 (1951).
5. J. W. Gunning, *Z. anal. Chem.* **28**, 188 (1889).
6. C. Arnold and K. Wedemeyer, *Z. anal. Chem.* **31**, 525 (1892).
7. C. Arnold, *Z. Anal. Chem.* **25**, 249 (1886).
8. C. L. Ogg and C. O. Willits, *J. Assoc. Offic. Agr. Chem.* **33**, 100–103 (1950).
9. H. A. McKenzie and H. S. Wallace, *Australian J. Chem.* **7**, 55 (1954).
10. G. R. Lake, P. McCutchan, R. Van Meter, and J. C. Neel, *Anal. Chem.* **23**, 1634–1638 (1951).
11. P. R. W. Baker, *Talanta* **8**, 57–71 (1961).
12. S. Dahl and R. Oehler, *J. Am. Leather Chem. Assoc.* **46**, 317–335 (1951).
13. W. L. Latshaw, *Ind. Eng. Chem.* **8**, 586 (1916).
14. H. C. Brill and F. Agcaoili, *Philippine J. Sci.* **12**, 261–265 (1917).
15. C. T. Dowell and W. G. Friedemann, *J. Ind. Eng. Chem.* **13**, 358 (1921).
16. I. K. Phelps and H. W. Daudt, *J. Assoc. Offic. Agr. Chem.* **4**, 72–76 (1920).
17. H. W. Daudt, *J. Assoc. Offic. Agr. Chem.* **4**, 366–373 (1921).
18. C. G. Harrel and J. H. Lanning, *Cereal Chem.* **6**, 72–78 (1929).
19. W. F. Barker and S. G. Shuttleworth, *J. Intern. Soc. Leather Trades' Chem.* **23**, 488–491 (1939).
20. L. P. Pepkowitz, A. L. Prince, and F. E. Bear, *Ind. Eng. Chem., Anal. Ed.* **14**, 856–857 (1942).
21. R. S. Alcock, *Analyst* **71**, 233–234 (1946).
22. A. E. Paul and E. H. Berry, *J. Assoc. Offic. Agr. Chem.* **5**, 108–132 (1921).
23. B. M. Margosches and E. Vogel, *Ber.* **55B**, 1380–1389 (1922).
24. B. M. Margosches, E. Scheimost, and M. Frissher, *Ber.* **58B**, 2233–2237 (1925).
25. H. C. Messman, *Cereal Chem.* **9**, 357 (1932).
26. W. H. Kitto, *Analyst* **59**, 733–735 (1934).
27. W. W. Umbreit and V. S. Bond, *Ind. Eng. Chem., Anal. Ed.* **8**, 276–278 (1936).
28. F. L. Ashton, *J. Soc. Chem. Ind.* **56**, 101–4T (1937).
29. Heffner, Hollrung, and Morgen, *Chem. Ztg.* **8**, 432 (1884).
30. Kulisch, *Z. anal. Chem.* **25**, 149 (1886).
31. A. Von Asboth, *Z. anal. Chem.* **26**, 240 (1887).
32. P. Fleury and H. Levaltier, *J. pharm. chim.* **29**, 137–147 (1924).
33. P. Fleury and H. Levaltier, *J. pharm. chim.* **30**, 265–272 (1924); cf. *Bull. soc. chim. France* **37**, 330–335 (1925).
34. O. Folin and L. E. Wright, *J. Biol. Chem.* **38**, 461–464 (1919).
35. H. Lundin and J. Ellburg, *Wochschr. Brau.* **46**, 133–137, 147–149 (1929).
36. H. W. Gerritz and J. L. St. John, *Ind. Eng. Chem., Anal. Ed.* **7**, 380–383 (1935).
37. H. Winkler, *Chem. Ztg.* **46**, 785 (1922).
38. H. Riehm, *Listy cukrovar.* **54**, 41–44; *Z. Zuckerind. czechoslov. Rep.* **60**, 156–159 (1935).
39. F. M. Stubblefield and E. E. DeTurk, *Ind. Eng. Chem., Anal. Ed.* **12**, 396–399 (1940).
40. H. G. Bennett and N. L. Holmes, *J. Soc. Leather Trades' Chem.* **3**, 24–27 (1919).
41. H. C. Goswami and M. R. Ray, *Sci. and Culture (Calcutta)* **3**, 180 (1937).
42. C. Dumazert and Y. Marcelet, *Bull. soc. chim. biol.* **20**, 201–211 (1938).
43. A. Soler, *Anales fis. y quim. (Madrid)* **41**, 789–797 (1945).
44. J. Kjeldahl, *Medd. Carlsberg Lab.* **2**, 1 (1883); *Z. anal. Chem.* **22**, 366 (1883).
45. J. H. Gibboney, *Proc. Assoc. Offic. Agr. Chem.* p. 76 (1906).
46. M. Siegfried and O. Weidenhaupt, *Z. physiol. Chem.* **76**, 238–240 (1911).

47. A. C. Fieldner and C. A. Taylor, *U.S. Bur. Mines Tech. Paper* **64** (1915).
48. W. Frear, W. Thomas, and H. D. Edmiston, *J. Assoc. Offic. Agr. Chem.* **3**, 220–224 (1919).
49. A. E. Beet, *Fuel* **13**, 343–345 (1934).
50. D. C. Cochrane, *J. Ind. Eng. Chem.* **12**, 1195–1196 (1920).
51. D. C. Cochrane *J. Ind. Eng. Chem.* **13**, 358 (1921).
52. I. K. Phelps, *J. Assoc. Offic. Agr. Chem.* **4**, 69–71 (1920).
53. E. Salkowski, *Z. physiol. Chem.* **57**, 523–526 (1907).
54. Kleeman, *Z. angew. Chem.* **34**, 625–627 (1921).
55. A. E. Beet, *Nature* **175**, 513–514 (1955).
56. R. Heuss, *Wochschr. Brau.* **40**, 73–74 (1923).
57. R. Heuss, *Z. ges. Brauw.* **6**, 44–46 (1922).
58. F. Skutil, *Chem. Listy* **16**, 173–177 (1922).
59. E. Rauterberg and H. Benischke, *Bodenk. u. Pflanzenernähr.* **26**, 97–105 (1941).
60. F. C. Koch and T. L. McMeekin, *J. Am. Chem. Soc.* **46**, 2066–2069 (1924).
61. R. H. Moore, *Botan. Gaz.* **100**, 250–252 (1938).
62. P. E. Portner, *Anal. Chem.* **19**, 502–503 (1947).
63. P. Saccardi, *Biochem. eterap. sper.* **14**, 252–255 (1927).
64. J. Cartiaux, *Ann. chim. anal. chim. appl.* **22**, 92 (1940).
65. I. Sarudi, *Z. Untersuch. Lebensm.* **82**, 451–454 (1941).
66. H. Leopold, *Z. Lebensm.-Untersuch. u. -Forsch.* **86**, 220–223 (1943).
67. F. Provvedi, *Atti accad. fisiocrit. Siena* [10] **3**, 423–425 (1928).
68. V. C. Meyers, *J. Lab. Clin. Med.* **17**, 272–273 (1931).
69. S. Liljevall, *Svensk Kem. Tidskr.* **34**, 187–189 (1923).
70. E. Gubarev, *Zhurn. Eksptl. Biol. i Med.* **6**, 261–265 (1927).
71. M. Carranza Marquez and G. Alliotta, *Tec. y econ. No.* **2**, 55–58 (1949).
72. B. Mears and R. E. Hussey, *J. Ind. Eng. Chem.* **13**, 1054–1056 (191).
73. J. G. Parker and J. T. Terell, *J. Soc. Leather Trades' Chem.* **5**, 380–384 (1921).
74. L. P. Pepkowitz and J. W. Shive, *Ind. Eng. Chem., Anal. Ed.* **14**, 914–916 (1942).
75. F. J. Koch, *Z. anal. Chem.* **131**, 426–427 (1950).
76. Le Tourneur-Hugon and Chambionnat, *Ann. fals. et Fraudes* **29**, 227–229 (1936).
77. J. de la Rubia Pacheco, F. B. Lopez-Rubio, and J. G. Marquez, *Inform. quim. anal. (Madrid)* **4**, 166–167 (1950).
78 L. F. Wicks and H. I. Firminger, *Ind. Eng. Chem., Anal. Ed.* **14**, 760–762 (1942).
79. I. I. Ribas Marques and F. L. Capont, *Anales real soc. españ. fís. y quím.*, Ser. B **44**, 483–492 (1948).
80. L. C. Scott and R. G. Meyers, *J. Am. Chem. Soc.* **39**, 1044–1051 (1917).
81. Huguet, *Repert. pharm.* **21**, 481 (1909); cf. P. LeMaire, *Bull. soc. pharm. Bordeaux* **50**, 306–311 (1909).
82. K. Steinitz, *Mikrochim. Acta* **3**, 110–112 (1938).
83. F. Rappaport, *Klin. Wochschr.* **16**, 1190–1191 (1937).
84. H. H. Willard and W. E. Cake, *J. Am. Chem. Soc.* **42**, 2646–2650 (1920).
85. S. Y. Wong, *J. Biol. Chem.* **55**, 427–430 (1923); cf. *J. Biol. Chem.* **55**, 431–435 (1923).
86. D. D. Van Slyke, *J. Biol. Chem.* **71**, 235–248 (1927).
87. A. E. Beet, *Fuel* **11**, 406–408 (1932).
88. R. L. Shirley and W. W. Becker, *Ind. Eng. Chem., Anal. Ed.* **17**, 437–438 (1945).
89. A. C. Andersen and B. N. Jensen, *Z. anal. Chem.* **67**, 427–448 (1926).
90. C. H. Perrin, *Anal. Chem.* **24**, 968–971 (1952).

91. G. J. van der Bie, *Mededeel. Ned.-Indisch Inst. Rubberonderzoek, Buitenzorg. No.* **64**, 8 pp. (1948).
92. W. L. Davies and H. C. Dowden, *J. Soc. Chem. Ind.* **55**, 175–9T (1936).
93. R. Jonnard, *Ind. Eng. Chem., Anal. Ed.* **17**, 246 (1945).
94. F. W. Dafert, *Land. Versuch.* **34**, 314 (1887).
95. C. Flamand and B. Prager, *Ber.* **38**, 559–560 (1905).
96. A. Eckert, *Monatsh.* **34**, 1957–1964 (1913).
97. V. I. Kuznetsov, *Zavodskaya Lab.* **9**, 1039 (1940); *Khim. Referat. Zhur.* **4**, No. 3, 62–63 (1941).
98. E. L. Rose and H. Zilliotto, *Ind. Eng. Chem., Anal. Ed.* **17**, 211–212 (1945).
99. G. Simek, *Chem. Listy* **25**, 322–325 (1931).
100. W. E. Schaefer and W. W. Becker, *Ind. Eng. Chem., Anal. Ed.* **19**, 307–310 (1947).
101. Z. Csuros, E. Fodor-Kenczler, and I. Gresets, *Magyar Chem. Folyoirat* **47**, 195–209 (1941); *Chem. Zentr.* **1943**, I, 545.
102. Z. Csuros and E. Fodor-Kenczler, *Magyar Chem. Folyoirat* **48**, 33–42 (1942); *Chem. Zentr.* **1943**, I, 545–546.
103. P. Sisley and M. David, *Bull. soc. chim. France* [4] **45**, 512–524 (1929).
104. S. M. Woods, D. Scheirer, and E. C. Wagner, *Anal. Chem.* **25**, 837–883 (1953).
105. G. Dorfmüller, *Z. Ver. deut. Zuckerind.* **80**, 407–412 (1930).
106. M. Weizmann, J. Yoff, and B. Kirzon, *Z. physiol. Chem.* **192**, 70–72 (1930).
107. V. B. Fish, *Anal. Chem.* **24**, 760 (1952).
108. W. E. Dickinson, *Anal. Chem.* **30**, 992–994 (1958).
109. A. Steyermark, B. E. McGee. E. A. Bass, and R. R. Kaup, *Anal. Chem.* **30**, 1561–1563 (1958).
110. A. Friedrich, E. Kuhaus, and R. Schurch, *Z. physiol. Chem.* **216**, 68–76 (1933).
111. N. N. Bezinga, T. I. Ovechkina, and G. D. Galpern, Zhur. Anal. *Khim.* **17**, 1027–1028 (1962).
112. J. Albert, *Mikrochem. J. Symp. Ser.* **2**, 527–534 (1962).
113. T. G. Lunt, *Analyst* **88**, 466–467 (1963).
114. A. Takeda and J. Senda, *Nogaku Kenkyu* (*Rept. Ohara Inst. Agr. Biol.*) **41**, 115–118 (1954).
115. Stebbins, *J. Am. Chem. Soc.* **7**, 108.
116. M. Jodlbauer, *Chem. Zentr.* [3] **17**, 433 (1886).
117. O. Forster, *Z. anal. Chem.* **28**, 422 (1889).
118. W. C. J. Cope, *Ind. Eng. Chem.* **8**, 592–593 (1916).
119. R. B. Bradstreet, *Anal. Chem.* **32**, 114 (1960).
120. P. McCutchan and W. F. Roth, *Anal. Chem.* **24**, 369 (1952).
121. R. B. Bradstreet, *Anal. Chem.* **26**, 235 (1954).
122. J. Tirouflet, *Bull. soc. sci. Bretagne* **23**, 129–131 (1948).
123. A. Takeda and J. Senda, *Nogaku Kenkyu* (*Rept. Ohara Inst. Agr. Biol.*) **41**, 97–108 (1954).
124. P. R. W. Baker, *Analyst* **80**, 481–482 (1955).
125. S. Baibaeva and N. Orlova, *Novosti Neftyanoi Tekh. Neftepererabotki, No.* **4**, 29–34 (1955).
126. H. Wilfarth, *Chem. Zentr.* **16**, 17 (1885).
127. H. Wilfarth, *Chem. Zentr.* **16**, 113 (1885).
128. J. Ranedo, *Anales soc. españ. fís quím.* **31**, 195–200 (1933).
129. R. A. Osborn and J. B. Wilkie, *J. Assoc. Offic. Agr. Chem.* **18**, 604–609 (1935).
130. J. Milbauer, *Bull. soc. chim. France* [5] **3**, 218–221 (1936); cf. *Chem. obzor* **11**, 183–185 (1936).

131. J. Milbauer, *Chem. obzor* **11**, 208–211 (1936).
132. J. Milbauer, *Chem. obzor* **11**, 238–240 (1936).
133. J. Milbauer, *Z. anal. Chem.* **111**, 397–407 (1938).
134. I. K. Phelps and H. W. Daudt, *J. Assoc. Offic. Agr. Chem.* **3**, 218–220 (1919).
135. O. Nolte, *Z. anal. Chem.* **55**, 185–189 (1916).
136. S. Sborowsky and L. Sborowsky, *Ann. chim. anal. chim. appl.* **4**, 266–267 (1922).
137. E. S. Richards, *Chem. Eng. Mining Rev.* **15**, 369 (1923).
138. M. Hassig, *Mitt. Lebensm. u. Hyg.* **14**, 101–102 (1923).
139. T. J. Potts, M. A. Parkam, and I. M. Schafer, *J. Assoc. Offic. Agr. Chem.* **30**, 648–651 (1947).
140. A. Hiller, J. Plazin, and D. D. Van Slyke, *J. Biol. Chem.* **176**, 1401–1420 (1948).
141. D. F. Louw, *J. S. African Chem. Inst.* **8**, 39–42 (1955).
142. L. Rozental, *Roczniki Panstwowego Zakladu Hig.* **9**, 183–197 (1958).
143. K. Kurschner and K. Scharrer, *Z. anal. Chem.* **68**, 1–14 (1926).
144. F. Mach and W. Lepper, *Landwirtsch. Vers.-Sta.* **109**, 363–366 (1929).
145. W. Lepper, *Landwirtsch. Vers.-Sta.* **111**, 155–158 (1930).
146. R. M. Sandstedt, *Cereal Chem.* **9**, 156–157 (1932).
147. T. Nagosi and I. Nakagawa, *J. Sci. Soil Manure, Japan* **11**, 433–438 (1937).
148. F. L. Ashton, *J. Agr. Sci.* **26**, 239–248 (1936).
149. C. Beatty, *Ind. Eng. Chem., Anal. Ed.* **15**, 476 (1942).
150. M. F. Lauro, *Ind. Eng. Chem., Anal. Ed.* **3**, 401–402 (1931); cf. *Oil & Soap* **10**, 149–150 (1933).
151. Am. Oil Chem. Soc. Official Methods of Chemical Analysis (1929).
152. S. R. Snider and D. A. Coleman, *Cereal Chem.* **11**, 414–430 (1934).
153. H. E. Crossley, *J. Soc. Chem. Ind.* **51**, 237–238 (1932).
154. R. A. Osborn and A. Krasnitz, *J. Assoc. Offic. Agr. Chem.* **17**, 339–342 (1934); cf. **16**, 110–113 (1933).
155. C. F. Davis and M. Wise, *Cereal Chem.* **10**, 488–493 (1933).
156. J. Tennant, H. L. Harrell, and A. Stull, *Ind. Eng. Chem., Anal. Ed.* **4**, 410 (1932).
157. K. Scharrer, *Z. Pflanzenerähr., Düng. u. Bodenk.* **41**, 203–207 (1935).
158. K. Taufel, H. Thaler, and K. Starke, *Angew. Chem.* **49**, 265–266 (1936).
159. A. M. Smith and W. Y. Paterson, *Analyst* **62**, 786–788 (1937).
160. D. Williams, *J. Am. Leather Chem. Assoc.* **34**, 261–263 (1939).
161. F. Gonzales-Sanchez and V. Gomez Aranda, *Combustibles* (*Zaragoza*) **17**, 176–187 (1957).
162. C. S. Piper, *Australian Chem. Inst. J. & Proc.* **5**, 312–316 (1938).
163. R. B. Bradstreet, *Ind. Eng. Chem., Anal. Ed.* **10**, 696 (1938).
164. V. V. Illarionov and N. A. Ssolowjewa, *Z. anal. Chem.* **100**, 328–343 (1935).
165. A. Sreenivasan and V. Sadasivan, *Z. anal. Chem.* **116**, 244–252 (1939); cf. *Ind. Eng. Chem., Anal. Ed.* **11**, 314–315 (1939).
166. G. M. Schwab and E. Schwab-Agallidis, *Naturwissenschaften* **36**, 254 (1949).
167. E. J. Schwoegler, B. J. Babler, and L. C. Hurd, *J. Biol. Chem.* **113**, 749–751 (1936).
168. R. S. Dalrymple and G. B. King, *Ind. Eng. Chem., Anal. Ed.* **17**, 403–404 (1945).
169. H. C. Messman, *Cereal Chem.* **9**, 357 (1932).
170. A. E. Beet and D. G. Furzey, *Fuel* **11**, 196 (1932).
171. A. E. Beet and D. G. Furzey *J. Soc. Chem. Ind.* **55**, 108–9T (1936).
172. A. E. Beet and D. G. Furzey, *J. Soc. Chem. Ind.* **55**, 108–9T (1936).
173. K. Nogajima and M. Ikeda, *J. Agr. Chem. Soc. Japan* **13**, 1208–1214 (1936).
174. D. J. Lloyd, *J. Intern. Soc. Leather Trades' Chem.* **23**, 275 (1939).
175. J. Vene, *Bull. soc. sci. Bretagne* **15**, 49–51 (1938).

176. R. B. Bradstreet, *Ind. Eng. Chem., Anal. Ed.* **10**, 696 (1938).
177. P. R. W. Baker, *Analyst* **78**, 500–501 (1953).
178. W. Lepper, *Z. anal. Chem.* **134**, 248–252 (1951).
179. H. R. Allen, *J. Assoc. Offic. Agr. Chem.* **38**, 185 (1955).
180. K. Ulsch, *Chem. Zentr.* **17**, 375 (1886); cf. *Z. anal. Chem.* **25**, 579 (1886).
181. G. Riviere and G. Bailhache, *Analyst* **26**, 267 (1901); cf. *Bull. soc. chim.* **16**, 806–811.
182. Oefele, *Pharm. Zentralhalle* **58**, 1121–1122 (1914).
183. M. Wunder and O. Lascar, *Ann. chim. anal.* **19**, 329–332 (1914).
184. H. E. Crossley, *Fuel* **20**, 144 (1941).
185. W. Parri, *Giorn. farm. chim.* **71**, 2530–2539 (1923).
186. A. H. Edwards, *J. Appl. Chem.* **4**, 330–340 (1954).
187. R. B. Bradstreet, *Anal. Chem.* **21**, 1012 (1949).
188. Y. D. Gresin, *Farm. Zhur.* 1937, *No.* **2**, 104–109 (1937).

CHAPTER III

Digestion Procedure

Since the inception of the Kjeldahl method in 1883, there have been many modifications, both general and specific. These are frequently referred to in the literature by name, e.g. Kjeldahl-Gunning, Kjeldahl-Gunning-Arnold, and refer to specific digestion mixtures and conditions. There are also well-defined methods of procedure known as the official methods of the various associations, one of whose functions is to establish standard methods of analysis.

The reactions of hot concentrated sulfuric acid on organic materials are complex, but are generally represented as complete conversion to carbon dioxide, water, and ammonia. Very little data exist regarding the actual intermediate degradation products. Bredig and Brown (1) and Schwab and Agallidis (2, 3) have studied the kinetics of the reaction of sulfuric acid and aniline. Their results indicate that this is a first-order reaction.

The decomposition of organic material takes place over a wide range of temperature, depending upon the structure of the compound involved and whether or not in the initial stages of digestion ring formation is possible, as in the case of some amino acids. The length of time to complete a digestion under a given set of conditions depends on these facts. If the decomposition point is low, nitrogen can be totally recovered, but if the compound forms a more stable intermediate or structurally has a high decomposition point nitrogen may not be recovered within the limits of the method used. Cases such as this usually require an extended boil period or higher digestion temperatures. It will be noted in the following procedures that where the boil period after clearing is relatively long, the acid:salt ratio is high, with a consequent low digestion temperature. Decomposition, under these conditions, proceeds slowly and may or may not be complete even on extended boiling.

Natural Products

FERTILIZERS

Fertilizers may contain either or both inorganic or organic nitrogen. If total nitrogen in nitrate-free fertilizer is to be determined, the following procedure, according to the methods of analysis by the AOAC (4) is used: 25 ml of concentrated sulfuric acid, 15 gm of either potassium or sodium sulfate, 0.7 gm of mercuric oxide (or 0.65 gm of mercury), and 0.7–2.2 gm of sample. If the sample has a tendency to foam or froth, very gentle heat should be applied,* and if necessary, a small piece of paraffin added to reduce frothing. The digestion mixture is boiled briskly until clear, and then for an additional 30 minutes, or for 2 hours if the sample contained organic material. For fertilizers containing nitrates (5), 40 ml of acid containing 2 gm of salicylic acid are added to the sample. Mix thoroughly and let stand for at least 30 minutes with occasional shaking. Add 5 gm sodium thiosulfate pentahydrate, or 2 gm of zinc dust (impalpable powder). Shake and let stand 5 minutes. The mixture is now heated at a low heat until frothing ceases. Cool and add the required amounts of catalyst and salt (see above), and continue the digestion as outlined. The distillation, in both cases, is the same — 200 ml of distilled water are added to the digest, keeping the temperature below 25°C. Add 25 ml of either sodium sulfide or sodium thiosulfate solution (40 gm Na_2S or 80 gm $Na_2S_2O_3 \cdot 5H_2O$) to precipitate the mercury. A few zinc granules are added to prevent bumping, and enough sodium hydroxide solution (450 gm/liter) to make the digest strongly alkaline. The flask is connected to the distillation bulb and condenser, the contents swirled and then heated, distilling the ammonia into an excess of standard acid. At least 150 ml of distillate should be collected. Excess acid is back titrated with standard caustic using methyl red as an indicator. A blank determination should be run at the same time.

* If the foaming takes place to such an extent that the sample or carbonized material extends far up the neck of the flask, stop heating, and when cool wash the material from the neck with a minimum of sulfuric acid (no more than 5 ml). Continue heating. If foaming still takes place, constant agitation and removal and replacement from the source of heat will be necessary. With materials of high foaming tendencies, it is better to add the samples to the digestion mixture and allow to stand overnight, loosely stoppered. After this period, digestion is usually straightforward.

For total nitrogen in fertilizers containing organic, ammoniacal, and nitrate nitrogen, Dyer and Hamence (6) used phenol (Jodlbauer) in place of salicylic acid with satisfactory results. Allen (7) digested samples of fertilizer in sulfuric acid containing only 0.6 gm of a catalyst mixture of 5 parts of copper sulfate pentahydrate dried at 110°C and 1 part of selenium. No potassium sulfate was used and the catalyst was added at the start of the digestion. The procedure, modified for nitrates, is claimed to give results comparable to the official AOAC method. With fertilizers containing organic nitrogen, results are approximately 0.1% lower than those obtained using mercury and potassium sulfate.

LEATHER

As in the case of fertilizers, the determination of nitrogen in leather is generally made according to the official method of the American Leather Chemists Association. There have been, however, from time to time, various modifications. Parker and Terrell (8) weigh an 0.8 gm sample in metal boat and transfer it to a Kjeldahl flask, adding 15 ml of sulfuric acid, 1 gm of copper sulfate, and 6 ml of perchloric acid ($d = 1.12$). A small funnel is placed in the neck of the flask to promote better reflux and smaller loss of acid, and the mixture is heated over a low flame for 15 minutes. The heat is then increased until the digest clears. It is given an additional boil period of 45 minutes, after which the digest is cooled and diluted, 50% caustic solution added, the ammonia distilled into 50 ml of 3% boric acid, and titrated with 0.5 N sulfuric acid. Comparable results with the official method are reported, with a considerably shortened total digestion time.

Jany and Morvay (9) digest a one gram sample with 30 ml of concentrated sulfuric acid and one drop of mercury for 1 to 1.5 hours over a small flame, and boil vigorously for 2 hours. With a copper sulfate-selenium catalyst, a shorter digestion time was obtained, but the results were slightly lower than with mercury. Minimum digestion time and catalytic efficiency of various mixtures relative to leather samples, were determined by Barker and Shuttleworth (10). Although catalyst efficiency was of the following order: Hg-Se-Cu-Mn, these authors conclude that the small difference in digestion time using mercury was offset by the extra step of precipitation before distillation. They recommend a mixture of 10 parts anhydrous sodium sulfate, 5 parts copper sulfate pentahydrate, and one part sodium selenate with 30 ml of sulfuric acid. Digestion is complete in 30 minutes.

A thorough examination of catalysts, digestion mixtures, digestion time, and titration conditions has been made by Dahl and Oehler (11). Nitrogen was determined on vegetable-tanned heavy leather, chrome-tanned side upper leather, and the same leather degreased. No difference was found in the use of either potassium or sodium sulfate. Mercuric oxide gave the most rapid digestion and slightly higher results than when selenium was used as a catalyst. The results also showed a low precision when the samples contained a high grease content. The digestion of 0.5 gm of sample was made with 20 ml of sulfuric acid, and 10 gm of a mixture of 7 parts of yellow mercuric oxide and 100 parts of either potassium or sodium sulfate. Ammonia was absorbed in 50 ml of 4% boric acid and titrated using a mixed indicator containing 0.06% methyl red and 0.04% methylene blue in 95% ethanol.

A statistical study of the determination of hide substance in leather made by Merrill *et al.* (12) used the following four methods for a comparison:

1. Official A.L.C.A. method.
2. Method 1 modified by a 2 hour boil period after clearing.
3. Dahl and Oehler method (see above).
4. Dahl and Oehler method using 1.4 gm of sample.

The values obtained with the official method were lowest, and no significant differences were found with the other three methods. As a result of this study, it was recommended that the official method be revised to require a 2 hour boil period after clearing when copper sulfate was the catalyst, and to permit the use of yellow mercuric oxide as a catalyst. A further recommendation was made to permit the use of 0.5 gm sample providing that the leather was reground, and also to require the use of the mixed indicator suggested by Dahl and Oehler.

CEREALS, GRAINS, GRASSES, SOILS

One of the difficulties encountered in the digestion of plant material was the extremely long time of digestion, partly due to the relatively large amounts of sample used. In 1921, Kleeman (13) recommended the use of hydrogen peroxide. A sample of one gram of dried material, or 5 gm of fresh material, is treated with 25 ml of 30% peroxide, and 40 ml of concentrated sulfuric acid added slowly with agitation. By this means, approximately 80% of the nitrogen is converted into ammonia. After addition of 15 gm of potassium sulfate, the mixture is boiled for

20 minutes. As an alternative procedure for large samples of fresh plant material, one gram of mercury is added with the peroxide. After addition of 40 ml of acid, the mixture is heated for 20 minutes, 15–20 gm potassium sulfate added, and the digest boiled until clear. This usually takes 25–30 minutes, although a 45 minute period is recommended for complete conversion. Experiments with ammonium sulfate, using the same procedure, indicated no loss of nitrogen even after a prolonged digestion of 3 hours. Heuss (14) using Kleeman's procedure on barley, reported a reduction in digestion time from 90 to 45 minutes, and also that the quantities of reagents used could be reduced to 15 ml of 30% peroxide, 8 gm of potassium sulfate, and 20 ml of acid. Lunden and Ellborg (15) claim complete digestion of 1–2 gm samples of malt, wort, and similar material in 8–12 minutes. The sample is digested over a microburner with 10–20 ml of 30% peroxide and 10 ml of a mixture of sulfuric acid and 85% phosphoric acid (3:2 by vol.) added slowly with shaking. After the initial vigorous reaction, 7 gm of potassium sulfate are added and the digest boiled for 5 minutes. Copper wire (0.5 gm) is used as a catalyst.

In the case of plant solutions or soil solutions in which nitrate nitrogen is present, the salicylic acid-thiosulfate method is not directly applicable, since the method depends upon nitration of the salicylic acid in concentrated sulfuric acid. The nitrate nitrogen, therefore, can be lost through the great dilution of the acid since nitration will not take place. Ranker (16) used the following procedure for total nitrogen in such solutions: the sample or aliquot of the solution is placed in an 800 ml Kjeldahl flask and made neutral or slightly alkaline. Water present is evaporated, under vacuum, on a water bath. Thirty-five to forty milliliters of sulfuric acid containing 1 gm salicylic acid per 30 ml of acid are added and the mixture allowed to stand an hour with occasional shaking. When organic matter is present, the flask is stoppered and left overnight. After addition of 5 gm of thiosulfate the contents are heated for 5 minutes, cooled and 7–10 gm of anhydrous sodium sulfate and 0.2–0.5 gm of copper sulfate added. Heating is resumed and the mixture boiled for one hour after clearing. The cooled digest is diluted to 400 ml, 100 ml of saturated caustic, paraffin, and mossy zinc are added, and the ammonia is distilled into excess acid. A volume of 150–200 ml is distilled in one hour. While the results on dried plant material are in good agreement, low values are recorded for total nitrogen in plant solutions. Pucher et al. (17) developed a method for the determination of total nitrogen in aqueous extracts of plant tissue and also made a comparison with the salicylic acid-thiosulfate method used by Ranker. The method depends on the reduction of any nitrates present with iron powder. A preliminary survey of the amount of reduced iron powder to be used indicated that 3 gm were sufficient, 99.46% recovery from known concentrations of nitrate solutions was possible, while with 2 gm of iron, only 92.99% was recovered. An aliquot of the aqueous plant tissue solution added to the digestion flask, is diluted to 30–40 ml, 10 ml of 1:1 sulfuric acid and 3 gm of reduced iron powder added, and the mixture shaken for 10 minutes. A funnel is placed in the neck of the flask, and the contents heated slowly and boiled for 5 minutes. After cooling, 30 ml of concentrated acid, 0.5 gm of mercury, 5 gm sodium sulfate, and boiling chips are added. The water is evaporated slowly, after which digestion proceeds normally, boiling for 1 to 2 hours after clearing. At the end of the boil period, several crystals of potassium permanganate are added and the digest allowed to cool, after which 300 ml of water, 3–5 gm of thiosulfate, zinc, and paraffin are added and the ammonia is distilled into an excess of standard acid. These authors also point out that careful attention should be given to the prescribed volumes of water and acid, otherwise loss of nitrogen may occur. An adaptation and modification of the Pucher method to the micro-determination of nitrogen in powdered plant material has been reported by Moore (18). A sample of 10–50 mg is moistened with 1 ml of water, 0.29 ml of 1:1 sulfuric acid and 85 mg of iron powder added and shaken for 10 minutes in a micro-Kjeldahl flask. After heating for 5 minutes over a low flame 0.86 ml of concentrated acid, a small amount of a 1:3 mixture of potassium sulfate-copper sulfate, and boiling chips are added and digested until fumes appear. Hydrogen peroxide, 30%, is added dropwise until the digest clears, and then boiled for one hour. After cooling, 1 ml of water is added and distillation carried out according to Pregl.

A micro digestion procedure reported by Pepkowitz and Shive (19) involves the use of perchloric acid, and can be carried out in 20 × 150 mm test tubes. Total nitrogen was determined on soy bean, leaf tissue, tankage, fish scrap, and a number of pure organic compounds. A comparison of the perchloric acid micro method with the official AOAC method showed an average deviation of 0.058. A sample of 10–15 mg is weighed into a test tube, and 1 ml of concentrated acid and 0.5 ml of selenium oxychloride solution (12 gm per liter H_2SO_4) added. If nitrates are present, 1 ml of salicylic acid-sulfuric acid mixture (16) is added, and the mixture allowed to stand 30 minutes, after which time

3 drops of 33% sodium thiosulfate and 0.5 ml of selenium oxychloride solution are added. The digestion mixture is heated moderately for a minute to determine if frothing will occur, then vigorously for 10–15 minutes. At the end of this period the solution is generally a clear ruby color, although it may become yellow or green. The digest is thoroughly cooled. Two drops of 35% perchloric acid are added directly to the liquid — without allowing the acid to run down the sides of the tube — and the contents heated below the boiling point. Heating is continued until the digest is permanently clear and colorless. After cooling, several milliliters of water are added and distillation made with the Parnas and Wagner apparatus. The ammonia is collected in 2% boric acid using methyl red-bromocresol green indicator (20). This method was further varied by Pepkowitz, Prince, and Bear (21) to include macrodigestions. Work was done on a large number of organic materials such as soils, fertilizers, compost, plant materials, tankage scraps. Comparison with the official AOAC method showed an average deviation for 33 samples to be 0.09%. To a one gram sample of dried material, 25 ml of concentrated sulfuric acid, 10 gm of sodium sulfate (anhydrous), and 1 ml of selenium oxychloride solution (see above) are added. Heat strongly for 10 minutes. Changes of color of the digest will take place. Plant materials assume a reddish tint, fertilizers a brown tint. The digest is allowed to cool for 10 minutes and further cooled under running water. Ten drops (0.5 ml) of 35% perchloric acid are added directly to the digest (without touching the sides) and heating continued below the boiling point until the solution is clear and colorless — generally 10 — 15 minutes. It is recommended that with fresh compost samples, 1 ml of 35% perchloric acid be added to compensate for the water contained in the sample. Since there is generally very little organic material in soils, there is only a slight color change after addition of perchloric acid. Therefore a fixed time of heating — 15 minutes — is used. Also, the use of sodium sulfate is unnecessary and, in fact, deleterious. Because of the rise in boiling point, the small amount of organic matter can be readily oxidized, and addition of perchloric acid in the absence of organic material will oxidize the ammonia. The digestion can be made in all cases without sodium sulfate, but the time involved is 40-45 minutes compared to 30 minutes with the sulfate. Kelley, Hunter, and Sterges (22) also used the method of Pepkowitz and Shive successfully on plant tissue, determining the nitrogen by Nesslerization. Koch (23) carried out the digestion of samples of grass, grain, and potato in a beaker containing 0.1-0.2 gm of sample

and 15 ml of concentrated acid. The sample carbonizes and foams. After foaming has ceased, 8-10 drops of perchloric acid are added from a pipette. A clear solution, on heating, is obtained in 5-10 minutes. The digest is then cooled, and distillation carried out in the usual manner.

Ashton (24) has made a comparison of several modifications of the Kjeldahl method as applied to the analysis of soil and grass from the standpoint of acceleration of the digestion. In this study, final oxidation with permanaganate, the use of selenium as catalyst, the mixed catalyst of Beet and Furzey (25) (1.32 gm mercuric sulfate, 0.26 gm selenium, and 8.42 gm potassium sulfate), and Subrahmanyan's dichromate oxidation method (26) were compared. For soils, all modifications gave comparable results, although the use of the mixed catalyst shortened digestion time considerably. Digestion of 10 gm of soil was made with 30 ml of sulfuric acid, 15 gm of catalyst mixture, and 40 ml of water. With grasses, the total digestion time using a one gram sample, 20 ml of sulfuric acid, and 10 gm of catalyst mixture was reduced from 90 to 20 minutes. Subrahmanyan's method depends on oxidation with potassium dichromate in dilute sulfuric acid solution. The sample and solution are refluxed for half an hour. It is claimed that at the end of this period, digestion is complete. When chlorides are present in soils, silver sulfate must be added and nitrates first extracted with water. In Ashton's comparison, the method gave low results with grasses.

The total nitrogen results obtained on soils, according to Sreenivasan (27), are generally low by the usual digestion methods. Higher and more concordant results are obtained by first wetting the sample (5 gm) with 20 ml of water, adding concentrated sulfuric acid, and allowing the mixture to stand overnight before proceeding with the digestion. A comparative study of the usual method and a modification using 1:1 acid and allowing the mixture to stand overnight (28) indicated that the presence of silicates acts as a protective agent when the silicate content is high. The direct action of concentrated acid is to form a protective coating of silica around the soil particles before the sample can be entirely wetted with the acid. This effect is avoided by treatment with the diluted acid, and silica is not formed until all the water has been evaporated. Sreenivasan (29) also reported that pretreatment of 5 gm of finely ground soil with 40 ml of 1:1 sulfuric acid and 3 gm of barium peroxide increased the rate of digestion, the barium sulfate thus formed acting as a boiling point raiser, and making it unnecessary to add potassium sulfate. Barium peroxide mixed with 0.5 gm of potassium permanganate is stated to be more effective when added in small quantities. When nitrates are present in the soil, satisfactory results can be obtained by reduction with ferrous sulfate, zinc, or Devarda's alloy in acid medium only if the amount of nitrate nitrogen is 40 parts per million or less (30). The salicylic acid method fails when water is present in the sample. However, total nitrogen may be determined in the presence of nitrates by a preliminary reduction with Devarda's alloy in a 3-4% alkaline solution. A 5 gm sample is treated with 20 ml of 4% potassium hydroxide and the alloy, and allowed to stand for 1.5-2 hours; the neck of the flask is plugged with glass wool soaked in 6% sulfuric acid. After reduction, 20 ml of sulfuric acid, 5 gm of potassium sulfate, and 0.5 gm of copper sulfate are added, and the digestion is completed as usual.

BIOLOGICAL MATERIALS, FOODS, AND PROTEINS

Much of the data available on the determination of protein nitrogen in natural products indicate, on the average, a long digestion period somewhat shortened by the use of various single or mixed catalysts. In many cases, the digestion conditions are mild, the amount of salt addition ranging from none to 10-15 gm per 30-40 ml of acid. The simple constituted amines and amides even under these conditions generally give little or no trouble from the standpoint of digestion. With naturally occurring amino acids in proteins containing more than one functional group, initially, at least, the possibility exists that ring closure can take place. As a matter of fact Sorensen and Andersen (31) indicated that lysine, which they found difficult to decompose, formed a stable piperidine carboxylic acid, at the same time splitting off ammonia [Eq. (1)].

$$H_2N-CH_2-CH_2-CH_2-\underset{\underset{NH_2}{|}}{CH}-COOH \longrightarrow \quad + NH_3 \quad (1)$$

The first reaction taking place in concentrated sulfuric acid will be dehydration. For example, glycine, with the loss of two moles of water forms a diketopiperazine [Eq. (2)].

$$2 \text{ CH}_3-\text{CH}_2-\underset{\underset{\text{NH}_2}{|}}{\text{CH}}-\text{COOH} \longrightarrow \quad + \ 2 \text{ H}_2\text{O} \qquad (2)$$

Acids having amino groups on a γ- or δ-carbon atom will form lactams. The tendency of β-amino acids is to split off ammonia on heating, with the formation of an unsaturated acid. The decomposition of six-membered heterocyclic rings such as piperidine requires a high digestion temperature. Five-membered rings of the pyrrole type are more easily attacked. Also, acids containing aromatic ring structures, or both aromatic and hetercocyclic rings can result in end products resistant to attack by hot concentrated acid. Since the decomposition points of many of these intermediate compounds are high, it is not surprising that long digestions are reported, particularly when the acid:salt ratio is high.

Gerritz and St. John (32) reduced the time of digestion by the use of dibasic potassium phosphate. Experiments were carried out on mixed feeds, wheat products, fish and soybean meal, dried blood, and high protein materials. Results obtained by the phosphate modification and the official A.O.A.C. method agreed closely. Low results were obtained when either sodium or potassium sulfate was entirely replaced with phosphate. The recommended mixture contained 64% of anhydrous dipotassium phosphate and 36% of anhydrous sodium sulfate (or potassium sulfate). Ten grams of this mixture are added to the sample, with 0.7 gm yellow mercuric oxide and 0.3 gm of copper sulfate. After addition of 25 ml of concentrated sulfuric acid, strong heating is applied. Using 2 gm samples, digestion is complete in 25 minutes. With smaller samples (0.7-1.0 gm) of meals, 15 minutes were sufficient. Goswami and Ray (33) using a semi-micro method for lymph, milk, whey, and various other proteins reduced digestion time to 15 minutes. The sample (2 ml of liquid or 0.1-0.5 gm of solid) is added to a digestion mixture of 10 ml of sulfuric acid, 5 gm of potassium acid sulfate, 0.5 gm of copper sulfate, 0.05 gm of selenium, and 0.1 gm of mercuric oxide. Gentle heat is applied for 5 minutes and full heat for 10 minutes or until the mixture clears. For the semi-micro determination of nitrogen in casein, albumin globulin, proteose-peptone, non-protein nitrogen in milk, Rowland (34) used a digestion mixture of 5 ml of acid, 2 gm of potassium sulfate, 0.2 gm of copper sulfate, and 2 drops of selenium oxychloride solution. The sample is digested at low heat and after clearing heating is continued for 15 minutes. Cartiaux (35) claimed good results on a variety of natural products such as mustard, corn, oil cake, tobacco. The sample, 0.7–3.0 gm, is moistened with 5 ml of acid and allowed to stand at room temperature for 15 minutes, then heated for several minutes with frequent shaking. After cooling, 10–20 ml of 3% hydrogen peroxide are added in small portions, and the mixture heated until gas evolution ceases. This treatment is repeated until the digest is clear. Boiling is continued until the volume of solution is about 50 ml, cooled, neutralized with caustic solution, and the ammonia distilled. This procedure is similar to that of Jelinek (36) who digested 2 gm of protein material with a mixture of 25 ml of sulfuric acid, 20 ml of 30% peroxide, and 1 gm of mercuric sulfate. Using gentle heat, digestion was complete in 30 minutes. Jonnard (37) reported a micro method for total nitrogen in proteins and their hydrolyzates according to Hotchkiss and Dubos' (38) procedure in which 1 ml of 57% hydriodic acid was substituted for perchloric acid. Further modification was made by adding 1 ml of 1.2% solution of selenious acid in sulfuric acid after the first hour of digestion. Digestion is usually complete between 2 to 5 hours. Proteins hydrolyzates and some amino acids require up to 16 hours for complete digestion. It is stated that this procedure is satisfactory in the presence of precipitating agents such as sodium tungstate and phosphotungstic acid.

Chibnall *et al.* (39) have stated that reported results of protein nitrogen are generally low due to insufficient digestion time, and recommended a boiling period of 8 hours to insure complete recovery. Using a micro method, Miller and Houghton (40) investigated digestion conditions for proteins and amino acids. Mercury was selected as a catalyst since a digestion period of 7 hours with copper sulfate as a catalyst was not sufficient to recover the nitrogen of lysine and β-lactoglobulin, whereas when mercuric oxide was the catalyst, calculated values could be obtained with a 6 hour boil period. Differences in results are attributed to the difference in catalytic activity when the rate of heating and total heating period were the same. In the final established procedure, samples containing 0.4–1.4 mg of nitrogen in 1–2 ml aliquots are digested with 500 mg of potassium sulfate, 50 mg of mercuric oxide, and 1.5 ml of sulfuric acid, first at low heat to evaporate the water, and then at full heat. After 5 hours, the digestion is stopped, and when cool, one drop of ethanol is added (Clark) and digestion continued for one hour. It is of interest to note that the salt:acid ratio of many of these procedures is relatively low — in the order of 0.33–0.5 gm per milliliter of acid. It is therefore not surprising, under these mild digestion conditions, that digestion must be extended for many hours since some of the amino acids have a tendency toward ring closure and the formation of intermediates more resistant to decomposition than the parent compound.

Mihashi and Tatsumi (41) use a modified micro-Kjeldahl apparatus for decomposition and distillation consisting of an 80 ml flask with an elongated neck of 16 centimeters and having an inside diameter of 2.5 centimeters. For the determination of proteins in foods, a sample representing 2–3 mg of nitrogen is digested with 3–5 ml of concentrated acid, and, if necessary, treated with 1 ml of 30% peroxide. After dilution and addition of caustic, the ammonia is steam distilled into 20 ml of 0.02 N sulfuric acid which is back-titrated with 0.2 N sodium hydroxide using 3 drops of methyl red-methylene blue indicator. For the microdetermination of protein in cereal products, Robinson and Shellenberger (41a) use the following method: a sample of 10–20 mg is weighed into a micro-Kjeldahl digestion tube, 2 ml of sulfuric acid and a small crystal of copper sulfate added. After a short digestion, the mixture is cooled and 1 gm of potassium persulfate added. It is digested until clear, diluted, and transferred to a distillation flask. Distillation is continued for 5–8 minutes, and the ammonia determined by back titration using methyl red as an indicator. In selecting optimum conditions for nitrogen content of proteins in foods and the amino acids in hydrolyzates, Wagner (42) recommends the following digestion mixture: 25 ml of sulfuric acid, 1 gm of copper sulfate, and 15 gm of potassium sulfate to be added after the mixture has been heated for 15 minutes. A boil period of half an hour is sufficient for total recovery. Slusanchi et al. (43) working on whole and deproteinized blood serum found that the presence of deproteinizing agents, e.g. trichloroacetic acid, metaphosphoric acid, or phosphotungstic acid, exerted no significant influence on the accuracy of the nitrogen determination. Both macro and micro determinations were made with ammonium chloride, and urea, keeping the concentration of deproteinizing agents at approximately the same as found in deproteinized filtrates. The method of digestion was that of Andersen and Jensen (44) who used 20 ml of sulfuric acid, 10 gm of potassium sulfate, 1 gm of copper sulfate, and 0.75 gm of mercuric sulfate. Digestion proceeds with a gentle but steady boiling. After clearing, a 2–4 hour boil period is generally sufficient.

Coal, Fuels, Petroleum

Apparently the first workers to apply the Kjeldahl method to the determination of nitrogen in coal and coke were Bunte and Schilling (45) who digested the samples with sulfuric acid alone. Schmitz (46) and Lord (47) used sulfuric acid in conjunction with mercury as a catalyst. Schmitz digested a 1 gm sample for 3 hours with a final oxidation with 2 gm of potassium permanganate. Total digestion time, according to Lord, was 3 hours. Since coal and coke can be classified as refractory materials and since digestion was carried out under extremely mild conditions there is no indication that total nitrogen was recovered, even after a permanganate oxidation. The assumption that a clear digest indicates complete oxidation and conversion of nitrogen to ammonia is not a valid one, and, probably under the stated conditions, it was not possible to recover the total nitrogen. Margosches and Lang (48) digested samples of coal, coke, and various charcoals with 30 ml of sulfuric acid alone, and in combination with various catalysts, and potassium sulfate. The greatest reduction in digestion time was attained by use of a mixture of 30 ml of acid, 15 gm of potassium sulfate, 2 gm of a mixture of tungstic acid and asbestos, and 0.5 gm of copper oxide. Digestion time for coke samples was reduced from 17 to 1.5 hours. Bornstein and Petrick (49) have also examined the effects of various metals as catalysts and consider a mixture of platinized asbestos, manganese dioxide, and zinc to be the most efficient. They observe, however, that total nitrogen cannot be recovered by the Kjeldahl method, since results obtained by the Lambris (50) method (a modified Dumas method) are higher. On the other hand, precision by the Kjeldahl method is good. Baranov and Mott (51) found that the only satisfactory procedure was the Kjeldahl-Wilfarth-Gunning modification. Digestion of 1 gm samples is made using 30 ml of sulfuric acid, 10 gm of either potassium bisulfate or sulfate, and 1 gm of mercuric oxide. The mixture is digested at low heat gradually increasing to boiling, and the boiling is continued for 2 hours after clearing. Results agree closely with the Dumas method. Crossley (52) using selenium as a catalyst compared digestion times with the official method of the Fuels Research Board (England) which uses the Kjeldahl-Gunning-Wilfarth modification (mercuric oxide catalyst) with a 2 hour boiling period after clearing. After 120 minutes total digestion time, the maximum amount of nitrogen was recovered, and further boiling of the digest produced no change. When 0.2 gm of selenium was used as a catalyst, clearing time was reduced from 87 to 33–40 minutes. Crossley (53) further investigated the influence of rate of heating, temperature, and the boil period after clearing, using selenium as the catalyst, and established maximum conditions for digestion. This is carried out on 1 gm samples of coal, 30 ml of sulfuric acid, 20 gm of potassium sulfate, and 0.2 gm of selenium. The flasks are loosely stoppered with glass bulbs, and after clearing, the digests are boiled for 1 hour. The recommended rate of heating is such that clearing takes place at 30 minutes.

Beet (54) has made extensive investigations of the conditions under which the digestion of coal can be made with the greatest efficiency. The experiments were carried out on a "standard" coal, which was a composite of a number of coals from different sources and had a nitrogen content of 1.61%. Digestions were made using sulfuric acid (30 ml) alone, acid with potassium sulfate (10 gm), acid with catalysts (HgO, Se, and HgO-Se) in amounts to 1 gm, and acid, sulfate, and catalysts (single and mixed). Final results showed that a digestion mixture of 30 ml of sulfuric acid, 10 gm of potassium sulfate, and 1 gm of mixed catalyst (0.5 gm HgO and 0.5 gm Se) allowed complete recovery of nitrogen in as little as 45 minutes. Slow initial heating does not seem to be necessary. It is stated that the action of the acid on the coal starts around 190°C, and any rapid rise in temperature is prevented by the water formed in the reaction. A partial list of data taken from Beet's article appears in Table XXIV, giving total digestion time, digestion mixtures, and nitrogen recovery.

Beet (55) later modified the mixed catalyst by substituting mercuric sulfate for the oxide in the ratio of 5 parts mercuric sulfate to 1 part selenium. A semi-micro method for coal (56) using this catalyst has been reported. A 0.1 gm sample ground to 72 mesh (British Standard) is treated with 1 gm of catalyst mixture (32 parts of potassium sulfate, 5 parts of mercuric sulfate, and 1 part of selenium) and 3 ml of sulfuric acid in a micro-Kjeldahl flask. Clearing takes place within 10 minutes, and digestion is complete in 30 minutes. The ammonia is distilled into 4% boric acid for 5 minutes, and is distilled for an additional minute with the receiver below the tip of the condenser. A semi-micro method for coal, proposed by Beet (57), uses potassium permanganate for the final oxidation. A 0.1 gm sample of the coal is treated with 10 ml of concentrated sulfuric acid in a 30 ml Kjeldahl flask, or in a boiling tube 7 × 1 inches. The flame is adjusted so that the tip just touches the bottom of the flask. After 5 minutes of heating,

TABLE XXIV [a]

DETERMINATION OF NITROGEN in COAL:
COMPARISON OF DIGESTION CONDITIONS

Digestion time (hours)	T°C at end of digestion	Gm K_2SO_4 used	Grams of catalyst			% Nitrogen
			HgO	Se	mixed catalyst	
32.0	320	—	—	—	—	1.24
267.0	328	—	—	—	—	1.61
5.0	—	10	—	—	—	1.52
18.5	350	10	—	—	—	1.60
7.5	316	—	0.25	—	—	1.22
34.0	323	—	0.25	—	—	1.61
3.7	342	10	0.25	—	—	1.29
5.3	346	10	0.25	—	—	1.60
1.5	340	10	1.0	—	—	1.46
2.5	338	10	1.0	—	—	1.60
6.0	328	—	—	0.25	—	1.26
16.0	—	—	—	0.25	—	1.61
2.0	340	10	—	0.25	—	1.46
4.0	346	10	—	0.25	—	1.59
1.8	330	10	—	1.0	—	1.48
4.5	341	10	—	1.0	—	1.60
2.3	—	10	—	—	0.25[b]	1.49
3.8	—	10	—	—	0.25[b]	1.61
1.0	—	10	—	—	1.0[b]	1.58
1.3	342	10	—	—	1.0[b]	1.60

[a] Adapted from Beet (54).

[b] Equal parts by weight of each catalyst.

potassium permanganate is added at the rate of 50 mg per minute, shaking after each addition. After a further 5 minutes, depending on the amount of organic matter present, the surface of the acid will be covered with a slight froth. At this point, permanganate is added cautiously, and the color of the digest changes from dark brown to dark orange, lemon, and then is finally colorless. (Iron will tend to obscure this endpoint.) The digest is allowed to cool somewhat, and 0.2 gm of permanganate added over a 1 minute period. The digest is heated just to the boiling point and immediately cooled again. The mixture should be a dirty, sage-green color. After addition of 20 ml of water, it is distilled into 2 ml of boric acid solution at a rate of 7–8 ml per minute for 5 minutes; then the receiver is lowered and distillation allowed to continue for an additional minute. The distillate is titrated with 0.01 N acid using methyl red-methylene blue indicator. The procedure shows close agreement with the official method.* A micro method (58) based on the above procedure has been developed. Samples containing 0.2–1.0 mg of nitrogen are digested in 8 × 1 inch tubes with 2 ml of concentrated acid for 5 minutes. After cooling slightly, successive small amounts of permanganate are added until a dirty, sage-green color is produced. After heating one minute longer, the digest is cooled, diluted, alkali added and distilled into 0.75% boric acid. Distillation is complete in 6 minutes.

Edwards (59) also has examined thoroughly the various factors influencing the digestion of coal and coke. The conclusions reached indicate that controlled conditions must prevail. For the semi-micro method, 0.1 gm sample is digested with 4 ml of sulfuric acid and 2 gm of catalyst-mixture. Heating is adjusted so that clearing takes place in 7 minutes, with a total digestion time of 30 minutes. Either of the following catalyst mixtures can be used: 32 parts of potassium sulfate, one part of selenium, 5 parts of mercuric sulfate, or 90 parts of potassium sulfate, 2 parts of selenium, 5 parts of vanadium pentoxide.

The criterion established for the rate of heating is that clearing time should be between 7 and 10 minutes. For the catalysts, mercuric sulfate-selenium, and Crossley's vanadium pentoxide-selenium mixtures were considered suitable. Under the conditions of digestion, selenium alone was considered unsatisfactory since low results were obtained. The catalyst mixtures contained (1) 32 gm of potassium sulfate, 1 gm of powdered selenium, 5 gm of mercuric sulfate, and (2) 90 gm of potassium sulfate, 2 gm of powdered selenium, and 5 gm vanadium pentoxide. A sample of 0.1 gm of coal and 2 gm of either catalyst mixture (see above) are well mixed in a Kjeldahl flask, and 4 ml of concentrated sulfuric acid are added. Heating is commenced and clearing must take place within 7 to 10 minutes. In order to achieve this, it may be necessary to run a preliminary digestion. After clearing, boiling is continued to give a total digestion time of 30 minutes. Any suitable steam distillation apparatus is adequate, and the ammonia is distilled into 10 ml of boric acid (60 gm in 1 liter of hot water; allow to stand 3 days before use) for 5 minutes at a rate of 4 ml per minute. The final volume is made up to 60 ml and titrated with 0.025 N hydrochloric acid using 5 drops of methyl red-methylene blue indicator.

*The official method of the fuels Research Board is as follows: 1 gm of coal is digested with 30 ml of sulfuric acid and 10 gm of a catalyst mixture containing 10 parts of potassium sulfate and 1 part mercuric oxide. The digest is boiled for 2 hours after clearing, followed by distillation in the usual manner.

Another semi-micro method using permanganate as the oxidizing agent is that of Badami and Whitaker (60). The sample of coal, 0.1 gm, is heated with 10 ml of concentrated acid for 5 minutes prior to addition of permanganate. Increments of 0.05 gm are added to the hot digest until it clears, after which it is given a final boil period of 20 minutes. It is stated that the same amount of manganese dioxide is as effective and that clearing time is shorter. Beet, who modified the method to the extent of using 1 gm samples, 50 ml of concentrated acid, and approximately 1 gm of permanganate, reported somewhat lower results compared with the official method.

A semi-micro method reported by Lange and Winzen (61) uses both a mixed catalyst and manganese dioxide. The sample, 0.1 gm, is digested with 1.5 gm of a catalyst mixture (containing 32 gm of potassium sulfate, 5 gm of mercuric sulfate), and 1 gm of selenium, 1.5 gm of manganese dioxide, and 8 ml of sulfuric acid. The mixture is boiled until clear and allowed to cool. One hundred milliliters of water and an excess of alkali solution containing sodium sulfide are added, the ammonia distilled into boric acid, and titrated. Satisfactory results are reported. However, Dermelj and Strauch (62) claim that correct results can be obtained only if a precise amount of manganese dioxide is added. This may be entirely possible since the use of permanganate or manganese dioxide does not involve a selective oxidation. That is to say, it is a preferential oxidation as long as free carbon or easily oxidizable material is present, after which ammonia can be oxidized. Their modification consists of eliminating manganese dioxide, and digesting a 0.1 gm sample with 9 gm of a catalyst containing 186 gm of potassium sulfate, 4 gm of mercuric sulfate, and 0.8 gm of selenium, and 8 ml of concentrated acid. The mixture is boiled gently until clearing, and vigorously for 10 minutes more. It is then cooled, diluted, the ammonia steam distilled into 25 ml of saturated boric acid solution containing 8 drops of methyl red-methylene blue indicator, and titrated with 0.02 N acid. The relatively short total digestion period is possible due to the low acid:salt ratio and consequent high digestion temperature.

Gonzalez-Sanchez and Gomez Aranda (63) have also examined the variables in the digestion procedure for coals. Their findings indicated that when mercuric sulfate (1.0 gm) or 1 gm of mercuric sulfate-selenium (5:1) as catalyst was used with 30 ml of 98% sulfuric acid and 10 gm of potassium sulfate, that complete recovery of nitrogen could be obtained in 2–2.5 hours using the mixed catalyst, and 2.5–3 hours with mercuric sulfate.

Mixtures of hydrocarbons such as those found in petroleum and petroleum fractions are fairly resistant to attack by hot, concentrated sulfuric acid. Since these fractions contain very small amounts of nitrogen compounds, this necessarily means a relatively large sample to be digested, if any accuracy is to be obtained. Where the expected nitrogen content is of the order of 0.05% or below, samples of up to 5 grams must be taken in order to obtain a reasonable precision. The chief difficulties connected with the digestion of samples of this size are the possibility of foaming, and the length of time of digestion.

Hale *et al.* **(64)** have reported a spectrophotometric method involving a semi-micro digestion and steam distillation using samples of 0.05–1.0 gm. The digestion is carried out in special 100 ml Kjeldahl flasks, each having an over-all length of 25 cm and fitted with a special joint for attaching to the distillation apparatus. Approximately 0.1 gm of salicylic acid, 0.1–0.2 gm of catalyst mixture of potassium sulfate, mercuric oxide, anhydrous copper sulfate, and selenium (5:2:1:1), and 7–8 ml of concentrated sulfuric acid are used for the digestion. The mixture is heated until clearing, usually from 0.5 to 2.0 hours, and the digestion is continued for 1 hour. After cooling, the digest is diluted with 5–10 ml of water and carefully neutralized with 50% alkali and 1 ml in excess added. During distillation the condensate is collected directly into a 50 ml volumetric flask. The exact volume is collected and the flask removed immediately. A 10 ml aliquot is taken and transferred to a 50 ml volumetric flask, which is then filled with water almost to the neck, 1 ml of Nessler solution added, and made up to volume.
After the solution stands at least 5 minutes but not over 1 hour, the absorbances at 450, 475, and 500 mμ are taken on a spectrophotometer and the amount of nitrogen determined from standard curves. Analyses of gas oils containing added type compounds such as amino, nitro, azo, nitroso, and ring nitrogen were determined, on an average, within ±10% in the concentration range of 0.002–1.0%.

The determination of trace nitrogen in petroleum fractions is of great importance because of the tendency of nitrogen compounds to poison the catalyst used, for example, in reforming, and also because many of these compounds promote gum formation, particularly on long storage. Noble **(65)** determined trace nitrogen by first using the conventional digestion and distillation and then determined nitrogen colorimetrically by the phenol-sodium hypochlorite method [see Determination and Distillation of Ammonia, p. 165 ref **(73)**]. He found, however, that the use of analytical reagent grade sulfuric acid and potassium sulfate gave high and variable blanks. Distillation of the sulfuric acid (10 to 80% cut) and recrystallization of the potassium sulfate (saturate 2 liters of boiling distilled water, allow to stand overnight, filter, wash with small quantities of distilled water). The blanks established by this procedure averaged four parts per million, 50 ml of acid showing two parts per million, and 10 gm of potassium sulfate, two parts per million.

The digestion of a 5-gm sample is carried out in the usual way with the exception that after clearing, heat is increased, and the volume of acid reduced to 25 ml. A 3 hour boil after this at a lower heat ensures complete conversion of nitrogen. For the determination of nitrogen in the range of 0 to 5 parts per million, Milner *et al.* (66) first extract with sulfuric acid, then digest, distill, and determine nitrogen colorimetrically by Noble's procedure. These workers found that much of the nitrogen present in reagent grade potassium sulfate was still retained after recrystallization. If, however, the salt were heated for 16 hours at 500°C, or fused, nitrogen was completely removed. Sulfuric acid was redistilled, from permanganate, and 50% sodium hydroxide solution (2 kg in 2 liters of water) treated while hot with 5 gm of powdered zinc, and blown with nitrogen (or helium) for 2 hours. The use of these repurified reagents gave blanks of 15 to 20 γ of nitrogen. The procedure allows relatively large samples to be used. A sample of 70 gm is extracted twice with 20 ml portions of 92% sulfuric acid, and the extracts are transferred to a Kjeldahl flask containing 20 gm of potassium sulfate and 1.3 gm of mercury. A reagent blank is run, using 100 ml of nitrogen free isooctane. The extract is heated to reflux until clear, then heated strongly to reduce the volume of acid to 25 ml. The heat is again reduced to reflux for an hour. Distillation is made by diluting the digest with 250 ml of redistilled water, and adding 80 ml of 50% caustic and 6 gm of powdered zinc. The distillate is collected in 15 ml of redistilled water and 10 ml of 0.0025 N sulfuric acid containing one drop of methyl red. When a total volume of 125 ml has been collected, the distillation is stopped, and the distillate evaporated to 20 ml. This is transferred quantitatively to a 50 ml graduated cylinder and the volume adjusted so that the final volume after addition of phenol and hypochlorite will be 50 ml. Nitrogen values are taken from a standard curve. If the stocks under examination contain large quantities of aromatics and/or olefins, it is best to reduce sample size by one half and replace it with isooctane, since the introduction of large amounts of organic material will prolong the digestion unnecessarily.

Another method for nitrogen in the range of one to ten parts per million is that of Bond and Harriz (67) which involves the use of an adsorption column. Nitrogen compounds are preferentially adsorbed on silica gel or similar substances. After percolation of the sample, the column is broken into a Kjeldahl flask, and digestion and distillation is carried out in the usual manner. The size of the sample is dependent upon the amount of nitrogen estimated to be present. When the nitrogen present is of the order of 1 to 10 parts per million, between 100 to 800 gm of sample should be taken, for 10 to 100 parts per million, 10 to 100 gm. For greater amounts, the sample size is reduced accordingly. The adsorption column is 4 feet long with 4 mm outside diameter standard wall borosilicate glass tubing drawn out at the end to a fine tip, and filled with 100–200 mesh silica gel to within 2 inches of the top. A reservoir having a 4 mm tip is connected to the column by means of Tygon tubing, and to an air line through a spherical joint at the top. The sample is added to the reservoir, and air applied so that the rate of flow through the column is 10–20 ml per hour. It is stated that for gasolines, naphthas, and kerosenes, a pressure of 10–20 lb per square inch is satisfactory. When all the sample has entered the gel, and before the air issues from the tip, the pressure is released. After percolation, the tube is cut in 1 inch sections and broken off into an 800 ml Kjeldahl flask containing 20 gm of potassium pyrosulfate, 1.3 gm of mercury, and 35 ml of concentrated sulfuric acid, wetting the entire neck of the flask. After introduction of the sample, an additional 20 ml of acid is used to wash down the neck of the flask. Low heat is now applied until frothing ceases. If no frothing occurs, it is recommended that the digest be held at low heat for 45 minutes. After intermediate heat for 10 minutes, the digest is boiled vigorously until clearing, and continued for an additional 2 hours. The flask should be removed *before* the heat is turned off, to avoid possible bumping and cracking of the flask. When cool, 400 ml of distilled water are added. After further cooling, 25 ml of sodium sulfide solution and a few pieces of zinc are added. Ice cold 50% sodium hydroxide (115 ml) is added in the usual manner. Ammonia is absorbed in 25 ml of boric acid containing 5 drops of methyl purple. Distillation is stopped when the volume of distillate is 130 ml. The volume is adjusted to 150 ml and titrated with 0.01 N sulfuric acid. A blank determination should be carried out at the same time, using an equivalent amount of silica gel. To prevent dangerous bumping when the blank is run, the flask should contain a magnetic stirring bar and be placed on a thin electric heater on a tripod with the magnetic stirrer underneath. It will be necessary to remove the cover of the stirrer in order to shorten the distance between the bar and stirrer.

A micro method for the nitrogen in petroleum in concentrations of 0.01–0.10% has been reported by Barbaeva and Orlova (68). A 20 to 200 mg sample is weighed into a flask and digested with 4.5 ml of concentrated sulfuric acid, 200 mg of sucrose, 200 mg of potassium sulfate, 40 mg of copper sulfate, and 40 mg of selenium for 1.5 hours at 400°–420°C. After cooling, the digest is treated twice with 2 ml of 0.1 N permanganate, heating for 30 minutes after each addition. Distillation is made using the Parnas-Wagner apparatus. Reproducibility is claimed to be 0.01% for nitrogen concentrations from 0.01 to 0.10%.

MISCELLANEOUS

The determination of total nitrogen in beet products and beet juices presents some difficulty due to foaming and the fact that the betaine which is always present is not easily decomposed by the usual Kjeldahl digestion. Riehm (69) has reported a procedure which eliminates foaming, reduces digestion time, and allows complete recovery of nitrogen. The size of sample used depends on the estimated amount of nitrogen, and Riehm recommends the following: beet pulp 10 gm, raw juice 20 ml, pressed juice 10 ml, heavy liquor 5 gm, raw sugar 5 gm, and molasses 1 gm. To the sample is added 0.5 gm of copper sulfate, 0.8 gm of mercuric sulfate, 10–20 ml of hydrogen peroxide and 20 ml of a 60–40 mixture by volume of sulfuric acid-phosphoric acid. The mixture is shaken, and, after the initial reaction, is heated over a low flame until evolution of sulfur dioxide occurs. The mouth of the flask is covered, and heating is continued for 6–10 minutes or until the digestion mixture turns green. Fourteen grams of potassium sulfate are added, and boiling is continued for exactly 6 minutes. After cooling, the digest is diluted with 180 ml of water, and 80 ml of 40% caustic and 5 gm of thiosulfate are added. Distillation is carried out for exactly 8 minutes, and the ammonia absorbed in 30 ml of 0.1 N sulfuric acid. Davies and Dowden (70) report that when betaine is present, 15 gm of potassium sulfate should be added to the digest when it has become fluid, and that an hour boil period after clearing is necessary. According to Volochamenko (71), complete digestion of a 1–2 gram sample of beet pulp can be made in 20 minutes by the use of 1 gm each of copper sulfate and mercuric oxide, 5 gm of potassium sulfate, and 30 ml of sulfuric acid. Materials having a tendency to foam, such as sugar cane juice, are treated by Davidson (72) in the following manner. A 25 ml sample of juice is heated with 35 ml of sulfuric acid, and with 10 gm of a mixture of 20 parts of potassium sulfate, one part of copper sulfate, and one part of ferrous sulfate, either to boiling or until foaming starts. The mixture is allowed to stand overnight and digestion is completed the following morning.

The determination of nitrogen in rubber, i.e. natural rubber, presents somewhat the same difficulties as found with petroleum, inasmuch as the amount of nitrogen is small, and the use of relatively large samples is necessary, involving long digestion. For compounded rubbers whose nitrogen is usually much higher, the salicylic acid-thiosulfate method is generally applicable. A micro method for the nitrogen in rubber hydrocarbon on the order of 0.01% is described by Tristram (73). A sample of 100 mg is added to 5 ml of hot sulfuric acid. After carbonization, and when fuming begins, 0.1–0.2 gm of a mixture of 15 parts of sodium sulfate, 2 parts of copper sulfate, and one part of sodium selenate is added. After digestion, ammonia is steam distilled into $N/140$ hydrochloric acid and the excess acid titrated with sodium hydroxide (carbonate free). The acid is prepared by making to one liter a mixture of 0.72 ml of 10 N hydrochloric acid, 200 ml of 95% ethyl alcohol, and 10 ml of indicator solution (0.2 gm of methyl red, 0.05 gm of methylene blue, and 250 ml of ethyl alcohol). It is standardized by distillation of pure ammonium sulfate containing 2.36 mg per 5 ml. Before distillation, the system is steamed for 30 minutes, and carbon dioxide must be excluded. Using this procedure, titrations must be extremely accurate, the reagent blanks should not exceed 0.04 ml of acid, and the back titration should not be more than 0.1 ml of alkali. Under these rather stringent conditions, it would seem more practical to determine nitrogen colorimetrically. Van der Bie (74) heated a 1 gm sample, finely divided, in a mixture of 20 ml of sulfuric acid, 9.4 gm of potassium sulfate, 0.5 gm of mercuric sulfate, and 0.1 gm of selenium, gradually to the boiling point and then boiled it for 10 minutes after clearing. The results obtained by this procedure were comparable to those obtained by the ter Meulen method.

Although all high polymers cannot be classified as natural products, they will be treated under this heading. A wide variety of nitrogen linkages appear in the various polymers, and the same limitations of the method apply here as well as to monomeric compounds containing the same linkages. Cole and Parks (75) have applied successfully a semi-micro method to organic materials including various butadiene-acrylonitrile copolymers, butadiene-vinyl pyridine copolymers, nylon, and others. The sample, 15–50 mg, is digested with 4 ml of sulfuric acid and 1.5 gm of a catalyst mixture of 150 gm of potassium sulfate, 5 gm of selenium, and 10 gm of mercuric oxide. Digestion is started at low heat which is increased until the digest boils briskly. Boiling is continued for 25 minutes after clearing. The ammonia is steam distilled into 4% boric acid. Skoda and Schurz (76) digest a 0.3–0.4 gm sample in 40 ml of sulfuric acid with 9 gm of sodium sulfate and a mixed catalyst of copper sulfate (1 gm) and mercury (0.5–0.7 gm) for 1 hour. Bartels (77), made a comparison of various digestion mixtures and catalysts, and reported that with polyacrylonitriles, the best results were obtained with sulfuric acid, potassium sulfate, and copper sulfate. The total digestion time was between 2 and 3 hours. Here again, it will be noted that digestion conditions are mild, and also that the type of nitrogen linkage, with the possible exception of polymers containing the pyridine ring, is easily ruptured. The adverse effect of such conditions is to prolong the total digestion period unnecessarily.

The official method of the American Oil Chemists Society (78) is used for the determination of nitrogen in products such as oil meals, peanuts, soybeans, soybean flours, oil cakes. The appropriate amount of sample is digested with 25 ml of sulfuric acid, 15 gm of either potassium or sodium sulfate, and 0.65 gm of mercury (or equivalent of mercuric oxide). The mixture is heated below the boiling point for 15 minutes, or until frothing ceases, boiled until clearing; boiling is continued for an additional 30 minutes. Ammonia from the distillation is absorbed in an excess of 0.5 N acid, and the solution back titrated with 0.25 N sodium hydroxide. Either methyl red or Alizarin Red S may be used as indicator. In cases of high fat content, it is recommended that 30 ml or more of acid should be used. Paul and Berry (79) in 1921 made a thorough study of digestion conditions for cottonseed meal. The digestion mixture contained 30 ml of sulfuric acid, 5 – 10 grams of either potassium or sodium sulfate and 0.5 – 0.7 gm of mercuric oxide. The time of clearing took 1.0 to 1.5 hours, and the digest was given a boil period of 3 hours. The mild digestion conditions here are in contrast to the more severe conditions of the official method. On the same type of material, the total digestion time is considerably shortened from 4.5 hours. A procedure having a very short total digestion time is proposed by Perrin (80). The materials used included fish meal, cottonseed meal, casein, and feed stuff. Nicotinic acid, as a highly refractory compound, was also included in the evaluation. The sample is first mixed with 12 gm of potassium sulfate, 1.3–1.5 gm of mercuric oxide, and six boiling stones are added. After addition of 15 ml of sulfuric acid, it is digested for 5 minutes at low heat, or until frothing ceases, then boiled at full heat until digestion is complete. This is determined when the appearance of the mixture remains unchanged from 3–5 minutes. The usual time of clearing is between 10 to 14 minutes. Further work (81) on the procedure using 1 gm samples of oil meals with a digestion time of 15 minutes gave results slightly higher than those obtained by either the AOAC or AOCS official method.

The determination of organic nitrogen in water, sewage, and waste is given in detail in the standard methods of the APHA (82). For water, 500 ml are treated with 10 ml of phosphate buffer; the buffer solution, pH 7.4, is prepared by dissolving 14.3 gm of anhydrous monobasic potassium phosphate and 68.8 gm of anhydrous dibasic potassium phosphate and diluting to 1 liter with ammonia-free water. A blank should be run on the buffer solution. After cooling, 10 ml of concentrated sulfuric acid and 1 ml of 10% copper sulfate are added. The mixture is evaporated to fumes, and digested for 20 to 30 minutes. Ammonia is determined colorimetrically with Nessler's solution. The standard procedure for sewage recommends the use of 20 ml of acid, 5 gm of either potassium or sodium sulfate, 1 ml of 10% copper sulfate, and several selenized granules if the organic material is hard to destroy. However, in most cases, the sulfate and selenium are not necessary. The sample (100 ml) is diluted to 300 ml, neutralized to pH 7, 25 ml of phosphate buffer added, and then boiled to expel any free ammonia. The digestion is carried out the same way as for water (see above). If total nitrogen is required, no treatment with buffer solution is necessary, and the acid and catalyst are added directly to the sample. Distillation is made in the usual way using either boric acid or an excess of standard acid. With industrial wastes, where organic matter is relatively high, it is necessary to use 20 ml of acid, 5 gm of sulfate and selenized granules. Total nitrogen on sludge (1.0 gm of dried sludge or 1–5 gm of dried mud) is determined by digestion with 20 ml of acid, 5–10 grams of potassium sulfate, 1 ml of 10% copper sulfate, and several selenized granules. The digest is boiled for 30 minutes after clearing. The residue from the ammonia determination is used for organic nitrogen and is digested in the same manner as for dried sludge. Free ammonia is determined on a 20 gm sample, diluting to 250 ml and distilling 10 ml into boric acid. Kiker (83) has simplified the Kjeldahl method for water, sewage, and waste by the use of three stock solutions: (1) sulfuric acid containing sulfate and catalyst; (2) sodium hydroxide and thiosulfate; and (3) boric acid and indicator.

Organic Materials

Amino Nitrogen

The ease with which amino compounds are digested depends to some extent on the initial reaction, or reactions, in concentrated sulfuric acid—up to the point of carbonization. Under a given set of conditions, e.g. acid:salt ratio and total digestion time, the recovery of nitrogen is dependent upon the temperature at which the compound, or its reaction products, decompose. If this is at or near the digestion temperature, decomposition and conversion to ammonia will be slow, and possibly not complete within the specified limits of the method used.

With aliphatic monoamines containing no other functional group, the point of attack will be somewhere between the amino group and the terminal carbon. Increase in temperature promotes sulfonation and elimination of hydrogen as water. Exhaustive sulfonation and further increase in temperature results in thermal decomposition with consequent formation of free carbon. This, in turn, reacts with sulfuric acid to form sulfur dioxide, reducing the amine to ammonia.

$$C + 2H_2SO_4 \rightarrow 2H_2O + 2SO_2 + CO_2$$

The presence of a secondary or tertiary carbon atom in the chain provides an initial point of attack, and rupture of the molecule will probably occur at this point. In the case of diamines, or polyamines, the possibility of ring closure exists, particularly where the amino groups are in the 1,4 or 1,5 positions. This structure is conducive to the formation of stable five- and six-membered heterocyclic rings [Eq. (3)].

(3)

When functional groups in addition to amino are present in the chain, substituted pyrrolidine and piperidine are formed. The piperidine ring is extremely stable to oxidation, which may explain, for example, why lysine requires a long digestion time unless high digestion temperatures are used [Eq. (4)].

$$H_2N-CH_2-CH_2-CH_2-\underset{\underset{NH_2}{|}}{CH}-COOH \longrightarrow \text{[piperidine ring]} + NH_3 \quad (4)$$

The pyrrolidine ring is not too difficult to decompose, but piperidine is resistant to attack except at temperatures in excess of 360°C. It is a strong base, and if it is not decomposed during the digestion period, it can be distilled over with the ammonia and titrated as such. An indication that this has happened is the slow and uncertain indicator change (e.g. with methyl red) at the endpoint.

Monoamino aliphatic acids react in several ways on heating, depending upon the position of the amino group. Similar reactions might be expected to take place in sulfuric acid under mild heating conditions, i.e. at the start of the digestion [Eqs. (5)–(7)].

$$2\ CH_3-CH_2-\underset{\underset{NH_2}{|}}{CH}-COOH \longrightarrow \text{[ring]} + 2\ H_2O \quad (5)$$

$$CH_3-\underset{\underset{NH_2}{|}}{CH}-CH_2-COOH \longrightarrow CH_2=CH-CH_2COOH + NH_3 \quad (6)$$

$$CH_3-\underset{\underset{NH_2}{|}}{CH}-CH_2-CH_2-COOH$$

$$\downarrow \qquad\qquad (7)$$

$$CH_3-CH-CH_2-CH_2-C=O \quad +H_2O$$
$$\underset{N}{\underset{H}{\rule{1.5cm}{0.4pt}}}$$

The condensation of two moles of an α-amino acid (1) gives a 2,5-diketopiperazine. β-Amino acids (2) split off ammonia with formation of an unsaturated acid, and γ-amino acids (3) form lactams. Generally, the presence of keto groupings as in (1) and (3), represents the weakest part of the molecule and the first point of attack. It would be expected that in the case of ring structures such as the 2,5-diketopiperazines and pyrrolidines, thermal decomposition would not be difficult. Leucine, for example, which forms a diketopiperazine on heating, carbonizes around 220°C. The presence of hydroxyl groups also expedites thermal decomposition, since the initial reaction is that of dehydration.

In general, aliphatic amino compounds that are highly oxygenated, those forming ring structures containing carbonyl groupings, or secondary or tertiary carbon atoms, will be thermally decomposed without difficulty. Compounds forming a stable ring, e.g. pyrrolidine and piperidine, decompose with difficulty, and usually require a high digestion temperature for complete conversion.

The initial reaction of sulfuric acid on the amino compounds of benzene and its homologs is sulfonation. With the monoamines, this takes place at a relatively low temperature, roughly up to 200°C. In the case of aniline, sulfanilic acid is formed [Eq. (8)].

$$\text{(8)}$$

Actually, an intermediate product, benzenesulfaminic acid is first formed which isomerizes to sulfanilic acid. An increase in temperature promotes further sulfonation and finally thermal decomposition and reduction of the amino group to ammonia.

The benzene nucleus is fairly resistant to oxidation and with acyl derivatives of the amines (e.g. acetanilide), and amino grouping in side chains (benzylamine) rupture of the molecule will first occur at the carbonyl or at the carbon to carbon linking the aliphatic group to the benzene ring. Digestion temperatures for aromatic compounds, in general, are higher than for simple aliphatic amino compounds.

NITRO COMPOUNDS

The extension of the Kjeldahl method to include materials other than the use for which it was originally intended led to many difficulties particularly with compounds containing nitrogen in an oxidized form, alkaloids, pyridine and quinoline derivatives and some amino acids. Arnold (84), Gunning (85), and Arnold and Wedermeyer (86) worked with nitro compounds, pyridine, and quinoline, and it is interesting to note that these latter compounds and their derivatives were successfully digested by use of the following digestion mixture: 15–25 gm potassium sulfate; 1 gm mercuric oxide; 1 gm cupric sulfate; and 30–50 gm sulfuric acid. One of the probable reasons for success is the low acid:salt ratio and consequent high digestion temperature.

Considerable amount of work on the determination of nitrogen in nitro aromatics was done by Margosches et al. (87-91), who tried to develop a correlation between the recovery of nitrogen and the position of substituent groups in mononitro compounds. Using a digestion mixture of 20 ml of sulfuric acid and 10 gm of potassium sulfate, it was found that only the nitrogen in those compounds having a nitro group in the ortho position, e.g. o-nitrophenol, o-nitrobenzaldehyde, and o-nitrobenzoic acid, could be determined. By the addition of 1 gm of salicylic acid, meta-nitro compounds could be determined, but not the para-nitro. The fact that nitrogen in a nitro group ortho to a hydroxyl, aldehyde, or carboxyl group was easily determined, without the use of salicylic acid or other reducing agents, suggested a possible means of determining whether or not one of these groups was present.

The determination of nitrogen in nitro aromatics depends on the successful reduction of the nitro group, either as a separate operation or combined with the digestion procedure. Methods of reduction have been discussed in the section on reducing agents.

The nitrogen of many nitro aromatics previously considered as refractory compounds can be determined by proper reduction conditions and subsequent digestion procedure. The failure to recover all the nitrogen in a compound has been generally attributed to loss as nitrogen. This is not necessarily the case. The primary factors influencing incomplete recovery of nitrogen are (1) insufficient reduction, in which case the nitro groups will eventually be oxidized to nitrogen, and (2) too high a reduction temperature. The end result of this is twofold—the compound may volatilize before reduction is complete, or the thermal decomposition point may be below the temperature of reduction. (3) The digestion temperature is not high enough to decompose the reduction product within the specified limits of the procedure. If reduction is not a separate operation, but is carried out directly in sulfuric acid prior to the actual digestion, care must be taken regarding the temperature of reduction. Many mononitro compounds are volatile and can be lost to an extent dependent on their vapor pressures at the ambient temperature. Halogenated compounds, particularly chlorinated nitro derivatives, volatilize and are deposited as crystals in the cooler portion of the neck of the flask.

A general method of treatment and digestion of nitro compounds, or samples of unknown composition that may contain nitrogen in an oxidized form, is to dissolve the sample first in 35 ml of concentrated sulfuric acid containing 1 gm of salicylic acid. Five grams of sodium thiosulfate ($Na_2S_2O_3 \cdot 5H_2O$) are added, and the mixture allowed to stand for half an hour with occasional shaking. After this period it is heated until carbonization, cooled, and 10 gm of potassium sulfate and catalyst added. Full heat is applied until clearing, and boiling continued for one hour.

While many nitro compounds can be determined by this procedure, the scope of the method can be increased in several ways. It can be realized from the above conditions that the maximum digestion temperature is not high (ca. 335°C), since the acid:salt ratio at the start of digestion (after converting thiosulfate to sulfate) is 2.6 and subsequently dropping to approximately 1.86. By increasing the potassium sulfate to 18 gm, the acid:salt ratio changes from 1.63 to 1.16. This advantage of higher digestion temperature makes possible complete recovery of the nitrogen of many additional compounds, and improvement of nitrogen recovery in others. A change from salicylic acid to 1-naphthol-pyrogallol (92) and 18 gm of potassium sulfate gives further evidence that the scope of the method can be increased. Lowering the temperature of reduction by the use of sucrose or pyrogallol (93), eliminating the thiosulfate, and increasing the acid:salt ratio, allows a wide range of nitro compounds to be determined by the following procedure. The sucrose (or pyrogallol), 0.5 gm, is first carbonized in 25 ml of sulfuric acid and heated strongly enough to produce sulfur dioxide. When the acid has cooled to ca. 50°C, 0.1–0.2 gm of sample is added, the flask is loosely stoppered with an alundum crucible, and reduction is carried out for 1 hour within the decomposition range of the reductant. For sucrose this is approximately 90°–100°C, and reduction may be carried out on the steam bath. The reduction period of 1 hour is arbitrary, since in many cases half an hour is sufficient. When reduction is complete 18 gm of potassium sulfate and a suitable catalyst are added, and the mixture is digested at full heat until clear. Boiling is continued for 1 hour.

McCutchan and Roth (94) using thiosalicylic acid as a reductant give the following procedure which can be used for nitro compounds, although the method was originally designed for small amounts of nitrogen in petroleum fractions. One gram of thiosalicylic acid is dissolved in 20 ml of sulfuric acid and a sample of 0.1–3.0 gm added. Any sample adhering to the neck of the flask is washed down with an additional 20 ml of acid. The mixture is heated to boiling, giving a temperature of 274°–288°C. It is cooled to room temperature, and 20 gm of potassium sulfate and 1.3 gm of mercury are added. Digestion is continued until clearing and given an additional boil period of 1 hour. The digestion temperature is stated to be approximately 365°C.

Elek and Sobotka (95) describe a micromethod for nitro, azo, and similar compounds. A sample of 3–10 mg is digested in a mixture of 50–100 mg of glucose, 1 gm of potassium sulfate, a small crystal of copper sulfate, and 3 ml of sulfuric acid. Harte (96) adapted this method to the semi-micro determination of nitro and azo nitrogen, using a 100 ml flask having a restriction half way up the neck. The sample, containing 2–5 mg of nitrogen, is digested with 300 mg of dextrose, 1–1.5 grams of potassium sulfate, 20 mg of copper sulfate, and 4 ml of concentrated sulfuric acid. Several pieces of well-washed alundum are added, and the mixture is digested with the flask in a nearly horizontal position. As soon as the digest has become homogeneous, a drop of selenium oxychloride is added. Heating is continued for 15–20 minutes after clearing.

White and Long (97) used a sealed-tube digestion on a variety of compounds including heterocyclics and p-nitroacetanilide, and reported low results for the nitro compound. The sealed-tube technique had been previously used by Levi and Gimignani (98) who carried out the digestion with fuming sulfuric acid at 330°C for several hours. In the method described by White and Long, a 5–10 mg sample is weighed into a 17.5 cm long borosilicate thick-walled Carius tube, 40 mg of mercuric oxide and 15 ml of concentrated sulfuric acid are added, and the tube is sealed. This is placed in an inclined position on an aluminum shelf in a welded steel box constructed to fit closely into a muffle furnace. The furnace is preheated to 560°C, and after the box is closed and in the furnace the temperature is reset to 470°C. This differential allows the sample to come to temperature within 15 minutes. After 15 minutes at 470°C the box is withdrawn and cooled. The tube is removed and opened, 2–3 ml of water added, and the contents washed into a beaker with 8–10 ml of water. When cool, the solution is washed into the distillation unit containing 8 ml of 40% sodium hydroxide and 5% sodium thiosulfate, and the ammonia distilled and titrated.

After the Carius tube has cooled, the tip is heated, while still in the box, to drive out any condensed acid. The lower half of the tube is immersed in ice water and a small narrow flame applied to the tip until it opens due to a difference in pressure. The top portion can then be removed by marking with a file. Baker (99) using the sealed-tube procedure found that by addition of 50 mg of either thiosalicylic acid or glucose, nitro compounds could be easily reduced.

The reduction of *m*-dinitrobenzene and *p*-nitroaniline by chromous chloride has been reported by Belcher and Bhatty (100). A sample of 4–5 mg is dissolved in 1 ml of sulfuric acid in a Kjeldahl flask and a small piece of solid carbon dioxide added to expel the air. Two to two and a half milliliters of chromous chloride solution are now added, swirling continuously. The flask is well shaken, and the excess water removed by boiling. One-half gram of potassium sulfate and 7.5 mg of mercuric sulfate are added, and digestion and distillation are completed in the usual manner. The chromous chloride solution is made by dissolving 15 gm of the chloride in 100 ml of 2.5 N sulfuric acid. This is transferred to a 250 ml bottle, and mercury containing 2% of zinc is added. Light petroleum fraction is added to a depth of about 5 cm. The bottle is shaken occasionally during a period of 30 minutes. A blue solution should be obtained. Both nitro compounds gave results very close to theory. A low result, however, was obtained with azobenzene.

A semi-micro method has been described by Ma and co-workers (101) covering a wide range of mono- and polynitro aromatics. From 3 to 8 mg of sample are weighed in a charging tube and transferred to the bottom of a 30 ml flask. This is dissolved in 1 ml of glacial acetic acid, and 100 mg of zinc and 1.5 ml of methanol are added. Reduction is started by addition of 0.1 ml of concentrated hydrochloric acid. A total of 0.4 ml of acid is needed, and toward the end of the reduction, low heat must be applied to ensure a steady evolution of hydrogen. After reduction, two drops of concentrated sulfuric acid are added, and the mixture boiled to remove the solvents. When cool, 1.5 ml of sulfuric acid are added and heat applied until the digest darkens. The contents of the flask are cooled again, and 700 mg of potassium sulfate, 25 mg of selenium, and 0.5 ml of sulfuric acid are added. After clearing, boiling is continued for 1 hour.

Ashraf, Bhatty, and Shah (102) effect reduction of nitro, nitroso, and azo compounds in two ways: by pretreatment with zinc in methanol and hydrochloric acid, and by addition of glucose directly to the digestion mixture. Reduction, digestion, and subsequent titration of

ammonia are carried out in the same flask. For the semi-micro procedure, a 250 ml round bottom flask with a tapered point, fitted with a
15 cm long tube is used, and for the micro procedure a 100 ml flask
is used. Reduction of 4–6 mg of sample is essentially the same as that
of Ma *et al.*, except that the hydrochloric acid is added a few drops at
a time, boiling for 2 minutes after each addition, until a total of 2 ml
have been added. The tube is then attached and most of the volatile
material is evaporated. Sulfuric acid, 1.5 ml, is now added, and the
solution boiled to remove the remainder of volatile matter. After
cooling, 0.7 gm of mercuric sulfate and 1 ml of sulfuric acid are added. Digestion is carried out for 2 hours. The determination of nitrogen
is made by diluting with four volumes of water, adding 60% sodium
hydroxide dropwise with shaking until the appearance of the yellow
precipitate of mercuric oxide. The solution is cooled and neutralization completed with sodium bicarbonate. Two grams of potassium
bromide are added, and the flask is shaken until an almost clear solution is obtained. An excess of 0.02 N sodium hypochlorite is added,
until the solution is pale yellow. After 5 minutes, a known excess of
0.01 N arsenious oxide is added, and the excess titrated with
hypochlorite, using aqueous tartrazine as an indicator. Reduction
with glucose is carried out with the same amount of sample and
catalyst mixture, but with the addition of 0.2–0.3 gm of glucose and 3
ml of sulfuric acid. The mixture is heated gently for 30 minutes and
then digested at boiling temperature for 2 hours. Both methods gave
good results on various mononitro and several dinitro compounds.
They are not applicable to such compounds as *p*-nitrophenylhydrazine,
or 2,4-dinitrophenylhydrazine.

Up to this point, the methods referred to have been developed for
nitroaromatics. The nitroaliphatics, while not as numerous, are perhaps more troublesome. Their reduction can be brought about by a
separate pretreatment. However, in concentrated sulfuric acid, the
reactions are complex, and when the nitro group is attached to either
a secondary or tertiary carbon, complete recovery of nitrogen is not
possible. The nitrogen of the primary nitroaliphatics can be determined by first reducing with sucrose in sulfuric acid (**92**) (see above)
for 1.5 hours at room temperature or slightly above. With secondary
and tertiary nitroaliphatics, the compounds decompose before
complete reduction. The initial products of the reaction of a primary
nitroaliphatic with concentrated sulfuric acid might be represented as
follows:

$$CH_3CH_2NO_2 + H_2SO_4 \rightarrow CH_3COOH + NH_2OH + H_2O + SO_2$$

the nitrogen being converted first to hydroxylamine (sulfate). In the presence of sucrose as a reductant, there is probably partial reduction to amine. The secondary and tertiary nitro compounds decompose to form possibly ketones and nitrous oxide, the latter apparently being further oxidized, since red fumes of nitrogen trioxide, N_2O_3, are generally present when reduction with sucrose in sulfuric acid is followed by digestion.

PYRIDINE AND DERIVATIVES

One of the most refractive groups is that of pyridine and its derivatives. Frequently the success of a modification of the digestion procedure is based on the ability to recover quantitatively the nitrogen of nicotinic acid. Regardless of whether or not reduction is carried out as a separate procedure or as an integral part of the digestion, probably the most important factor is the digestion temperature.

The reduction product of pyridine, for example, is piperidine, in itself an extremely stable compound having a high decomposition point. If the digestion temperature is not at or above this point, it is possible that an equilibrium such as shown in Eq. (9) is established.

$$\text{(9)}$$

Under these conditions, the reaction goes slowly from left to right, and an extended boil period will frequently result in higher recovery values. However, under fixed conditions, both pyridine and piperidine will be present at the end of the digestion, and on subsequent distillation are carried over with the ammonia and titrated. Since they are strongly basic, this is possible, although the endpoints are generally poor, and frequently an odor of pyridine is detectable.

Shirley and Becker (103) using the official method of the AOAC (104) report satisfactory results for nicotinic acid and pyridine. The most efficient catalysts were found to be mercury (0.6 gm), and mercury-selenium oxychloride (0.6–0.15 gm). In a study of digestion time, 3 to 4 hours were required for complete recovery. A semi-micro method for heterocyclic, nitro, nitroso, and azo nitrogen is reported by Belcher and Godbert (105). As a general method, 20–50 mg of sample are weighed into a dry flask, a small amount of red phosphorus and 5 ml of hydriodic acid added. The mixture is boiled gently for 45 minutes to effect reduction. Diazo compounds must first be coupled with phenol before reduction. During the period of boiling there should be no more than a slight loss in volume. After reduction, 20 ml of water and 1 ml of sulfuric acid are added and the mixture boiled vigorously to remove iodine. Two grams of catalyst mixture (32 gm of potassium sulfate, 5 gm of mercuric sulfate, and 1 gm of selenium) are added with 4 ml of sulfuric acid. Once the catalyst mixture has dissolved in the acid, digestion is continued for 45 minutes regardless of time of clearing. Ammonia will be lost if digestion is continued for more than 75 minutes. The authors also state that no reduction is necessary if the sample contains no nitrogen-oxygen linkage.

A semi-micro and micro procedure reported by Ogg, Brand, and Willits (106) for heterocyclic compounds can be applied successfully as a general method. The digestion procedure does not differ greatly from the macro method of Shirley and Becker. A 15–30 mg sample is weighed into a 30 ml Kjeldahl flask, and 0.65–0.70 gm of catalyst mixture (150 gm of potassium sulfate, 10 gm of mercuric oxide, and 3 gm of selenium), 3 or 4 boiling chips, and 2 ml of sulfuric acid are added. The mixture is heated slowly until carbonization occurs or danger of frothing is past. Heat is increased until the acid mixture refluxes a distance of two thirds up the neck of the flask, and digestion is continued for 4 hours. This digestion period is apparently sufficient for most heterocyclic compounds, although nicotyrine requires 6 hours. On the other hand, digestion of nicotine is complete in 3 hours.

Willits, Coe, and Ogg (107) in a study of the application of the Kjeldahl procedure to refractory compounds, used nicotinic acid as a representative type. The factors influencing complete recovery of nitrogen, e.g. salt concentration, catalysts, and digestion time, were examined. Of the two catalysts used, mercury and selenium, it was found that selenium required a specific time of digestion, and might cause incomplete recovery of nitrogen (see section on Selenium, p. 73). When mercury is used as a catalyst, the amount of potassium sulfate, catalyst, and time of digestion are not critical, as far as loss of nitrogen is concerned. The recommended digestion mixture is 25 ml of sulfuric acid, 15 gm of potassium sulfate, and 0.6 gm of mercury with a total digestion time of 3 hours.

Cole and Parks (108) examined a wide range of nitrogen compounds including pyridine, other ring structures, and high polymeric materials using a semi-micro method. A sample of 15–50 mg is weighed into a 100 ml Kjeldahl flask, and 4 ml of sulfuric acid and 1.5 gm of a catalyst mixture (150 gm of potassium sulfate, 5 gm of selenium, and 10 gm of mercuric oxide) are added. Digestion is started with low heat, gradually increasing until the digest boils briskly, and continued for 25 minutes after clearing which generally takes place within 10 minutes. For compounds such as pyridine, boiling is continued for an hour after clearing. It is claimed that this procedure is satisfactory for most organic compounds with the exception of those containing nitrogen to nitrogen, or nitrogen to oxygen bonds.

The determination of nitrogen in pyridinium compounds by Crane and Fuoss (109) is based on a series of reactions with alkaline peroxide resulting in aliphatic cleavage products which are easily converted to ammonia by Kjeldahl digestion. The ratio of peroxide (Na_2O_2) is about 2.2 gm per millimole of nitrogen. An appropriate sample (2–6 mg of nitrogen) is weighed into a 100 ml Kjeldahl flask. A borosilicate tube (3×1 cm) containing 2–3 grams of peroxide is placed carefully in the flask, avoiding spillage. The flask and apparatus are assembled for the usual steam distillation, the receiver containing 0.025 N sulfuric acid. Ten milliliters of water are added through the funnel to wet or dissolve the sample. An additional 20 ml are added, and the flask tipped to allow mixing. After standing, with occasional swirling, for 20 minutes, the flask and contents are slowly heated to 80°C, and steam distillation is started and continued until 150 ml of distillate have been collected. This is now evaporated to 40 or 50 ml. After the Kjeldahl flask has cooled, the solution is neutralized with concentrated acid and an excess of 7–12 ml added. Most of the water is evaporated over a microburner, and heated until frothing ceases. If the pyridinium compound is an iodide, the iodine is first carefully evaporated, and 5–10 mg of catalyst (1 part red mercuric oxide and 3 parts selenium) are added. Digestion proceeds in the normal way at 300°–350°C for at least one hour. The actual digestion time should be experimentally determined since in some cases one hour is not sufficient. Ammonia is distilled into the receiver containing the concentrated solution from the first distillation. The quantity of peroxide used is in great excess of the theoretical amount. However, one reason for this is that reaction speed is greatly increased, and there is also some loss due to evolution of free oxygen. It is stated that this initial reaction and distillation accounts for about 75% of the total nitrogen.

Further work on a semi-micro method for pyridinium halides and oxyhalides has been reported by Fish and Collier (110). Samples are weighed into small tin foil cups having an average weight of 140 mg, and digested with 1.5 gm of Cole and Parks' (see above) catalyst mixture and 4 ml of concentrated sulfuric acid for 2 hours after clearing. This boil period may be reduced to 45 minutes if the material is not a refractory compound. Distillation is completed in the usual manner. In the absence of tin, and when samples are weighed on cigarette paper, low results are obtained with pyridinium iodide compounds with the exception of 1-methylpyridinium iodide. If stannous chloride is added to the digestion mixture, the results are comparable to those obtained by weighing into tin foil cups. The loss observed when tin is not used may possibly be attributed to formation of hydrogen iodide which is oxidized to iodine in hot concentrated sulfuric acid. Formation of free iodine in the digestion mixture could conceivably lead to oxidation of the ammonium salt already present, to nitrogen.

Marzadro (111) has approached the estimation of ring nitrogen (pyridine and compounds containing the pyridine nucleus) by difference. Total nitrogen is first determined by the Dumas-Zimmermann procedure. Any nitrogen in side chains is first reduced, if necessary, followed by digestion and distillation. The difference between total nitrogen and side chain nitrogen is assumed to be ring nitrogen. Under the digestion conditions, pyridine nitrogen is not attacked, and only the side chains are converted to ammonia. If reduction is necessary, a 2–4 mg sample is treated with 3 mg of red phosphorus and one ml of hydriodic acid and then is boiled gently for half an hour. After cooling, 7–8 ml of distilled water and 2 ml of concentrated sulfuric acid are added and the mixture boiled until free of hydriodic acid and iodine. Digestion is carried out at a vigorous boil for 30 minutes after addition of 10 mg of mercuric acetate and 70 mg of potassium sulfate. There appear to be two exceptions to this procedure: 2-bromopyridine and 2-aminopyridine. In both cases the calculated amount of nitrogen is recovered.

It can be generally accepted that the amounts of selenium or its compounds used as catalysts are closely related to the amount of acid used, and to the acid:salt ratio. For successful use of selenium under a given set of conditions, the maximum amount of this catalyst should first be determined. Selenium lowers the temperature of digestion somewhat, and although it allows a fast conversion of nitrogen to ammonia, if the maximum amount is exceeded, prolonged digestion will result in loss of nitrogen. The conditions under which selenium can be used, therefore, must be strictly adhered to.

In direct opposition to this, Dupuy (112) in a systematic study of the influence of selenium oxychloride and potassium sulfate, stated that the nitrogen of pyridine could be completely recovered by digesting 0.15 gm of sample with 0.5 gm of selenium oxychloride, 40 gm of potassium sulfate, and 25 ml of sulfuric acid for 1 hour. Following Dupuy's procedure, Moreau (113) was unable to obtain reproducible results for quinoline and quinaldine. Using relatively large amounts of selenium oxychloride, he obtained calculated values with the following procedure: From 0.2 to 1.0 gm of selenium oxychloride were mixed with 0.15 gm of quinoline and allowed to stand for 15 minutes. The reaction is highly exothermic, and when cool, the mixture is solid. This is treated with 25 ml of sulfuric acid and 40 gm of potassium sulfate, and boiled for 1.5 hours. Correct results were obtained when either quinoline or quinaldine was reacted with 0.2 gm of selenium oxychloride and digested 1.5 hours. Larger amounts or less digestion time gave variable lower results.

According to Ribas and Vazquez-Gesto (114) refractory heterocyclic compounds can be digested in 30 minutes by using 3 gm of potassium sulfate, 0.05 gm of mercuric sulfate, 1 ml of 0.5% selenium in sulfuric acid, and 2 ml of sulfuric acid, for each 10 mg of sample.

The use of sulfuric acid-phosphoric acid as a digestion medium (93) in conjunction with potassium sulfate produces appreciably higher temperatures than the use of sulfuric acid alone. Compounds containing a pyridine nucleus can be first reduced with 0.5 gm of sucrose and subsequently digested in a mixture of 25 ml of acid (70% sulfuric acid-30% phosphoric acid, v/v), 18 gm of potassium sulfate, and 0.1 gm of selenium. The sucrose is first carbonized in the acid, the sample added, and the reduction carried out for 1 hour at steam bath temperature. After addition of sulfate and catalyst, the mixture is digested until clear, and boiling is continued for one hour.

HETEROCYCLIC NITROGEN

Essentially, the methods described in the previous section will apply to heterocyclic compounds containing ring structures other than that of pyridine. Based on the older modifications of the method, many such compounds were considered refractory, and the nitrogen incapable of recovery. There are, presently, various types of compounds that cannot be determined by any modification of the conventional Kjeldahl method, that is, by reduction in concentrated sulfuric acid followed by the usual digestion. Examples of these are the triazoles, pyrazolones, aminopyrine, and antipyrine.

Fleury and Levaltier (115) examined a large number of compounds containing heterocyclic rings such as uric acid, piperazine, skatole, and some of the alkaloids. The sample, 0.5 gm, is digested in a mixture of 5 ml of sulfuric acid, 15 ml of phosphoric acid, and 5 gm potassium sulfate. Heating is continued for 10 minutes after clearing.

A semi-micro procedure based on Clark's method (116), and used by Kaye and Weiner (117) on a wide variety of compounds, gave excellent results on ring nitrogen with the exception of antipyrine and semicarbazone. In Clark's procedure, 10 mg of sample are weighed on a piece of cigarette paper, 15 × 25 mm, and added to 40 mg of mercuric oxide, 0.5 gm of potassium sulfate, and 1.5 ml of sulfuric acid. The digestion mixture is heated gently until frothing ceases. The temperature is increased until the contents of the flask boil vigorously, and acid vapors rise to within 5 cm of the mouth of the flask. Total digestion time is one hour, and the digestion mixture should be colorless for the last half hour. A longer digestion time, however, does no harm. When the digest is cool, one drop of alcohol is added, and the mixture reheated until it is again colorless. For substances containing azo, nitro, nitroso, or other linkages necessitating separate reduction, the Friedrich (118) method is used. The sample is treated with 1 ml of constant boiling hydriodic acid and refluxed for 45 minutes, after which approximately 0.7 ml of the acid is distilled carefully. One ml of water, 1.5 ml of sulfuric acid, and 0.5 gm of potassium sulfate are added, and the mixture heated until most of the water is driven off. Treatment with water is repeated until all traces of iodine are removed. After cooling, 40 mg of mercuric oxide are added and digestion carried out as above. Kaye and Weiner use 175 mm test tubes for the digestion procedure, and weigh the sample on aluminum foil.

Esafov (119) states that the successful digestion of heterocyclic compounds depends on very slow decomposition in the presence of a large amount of potassium bisulfate — 4 grams per milliliter of sulfuric acid. The scope of the method is increased by the addition of glucose as a reductant.

MISCELLANEOUS NITROGEN LINKAGES

As stated in the preceding section, many of the digestion procedures applicable to pyridine and its derivatives, and to heterocyclic compounds, can be used as general methods.

Fleury and Levaltier (115) modified their procedure to include benzonitrile, benzophenone oxime, acetoxime, and azobenzene. A sample of 0.5 gm is weighed into a warm mixture of 1.5 gm of benzoic acid in 20 ml of sulfuric acid and heated gently for 30 minutes. The temperature is increased somewhat and heating is continued for 5 minutes. After cooling, 40 ml of phosphoric acid and 10 gm of potassium sulfate are added, and the mixture is strongly heated for 15 minutes. (Clearing is presumed to take place by the end of this period.) Semicarbazide and semicarbazone are given a treatment with a mixture of 3 gm of benzoic acid and 20 ml of sulfuric acid (as above), followed by a further addition of 2 gm of powdered zinc, 10 ml of water, and 10 ml of 95% alcohol. This is heated gently for 30 minutes, and given a final treatment at high heat for 15 minutes with 40 ml of phosphoric acid and 10 gm of potassium sulfate.

Sisley and David (120) working with nitro, nitroso, and azo compounds first tried a preliminary sulfonation at 100°–120°C with 20 ml of 30% oleum and 10 gm of potassium sulfate, followed by digestion. Very few compounds could be determined by this procedure. Using a digestion mixture of 20 ml of acid and 10 gm of potassium sulfate, a large number of organic compounds decomposable at relatively low temperatures to give sulfur dioxide, were tried using picric acid as a type compound. Pyrogallol proved to be the most satisfactory, and when 0.3 gm was used with 0.5 gm of sample, many azo and nitroso compounds could be determined. On the other hand, many of the azo dyes examined, e.g. Brillant Croceine, Benzopurpurin, Orange II, p-nitrobenzeneazonaphthylamine, gave low results by this procedure. By using a reducing pretreatment with sodium hydrosulfite (see section on Reduction), the nitrogen of azo dyes, azo, nitroso, and nitro compounds was quantitatively recovered.

Phelps and Daudt (121) treat azo compounds with alcoholic stannous chloride. The sample is dissolved in 20 ml of ethanol, and 5 ml of stannous chloride solution containing 40 gm in 100 ml of concentrated hydrochloric acid are added. This is boiled under reflux for about half an hour. After cooling, an equal volume of water and 30 ml of concentrated sulfuric acid are added. The mixture is carefully heated until the water and alcohol have been expelled and foaming ceases. Ten grams of potassium sulfate and 0.7 gm of mercuric oxide are added and digestion continued. The method gave satisfactory results with simple azo compounds and azo dyes such as methyl red, Congo Red, and Ponceau 4R.

The digestion of azo compounds and the conversion of nitrogen to ammonia are to some extent dependent on substituent groups in the benzene nucleus. The simplest azo compound, azobenzene, is first reduced to hydrazobenzene, and in the presence of concentrated sulfuric acid goes through the benzidine transformation as the principal reaction [Eq. (10)].

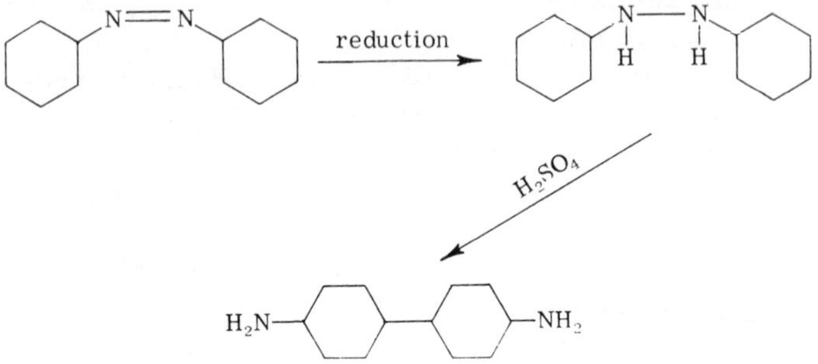

reduction

H_2SO_4

(10)

H_2N- —NH$_2$

A secondary reaction is also possible, resulting in the formation of
4,2'-diaminodiphenyl (phenyline). A substituent in *para* position will
result in further transformations. In addition to benzidine (and phenyline), semidines are formed [Eq. (11)].

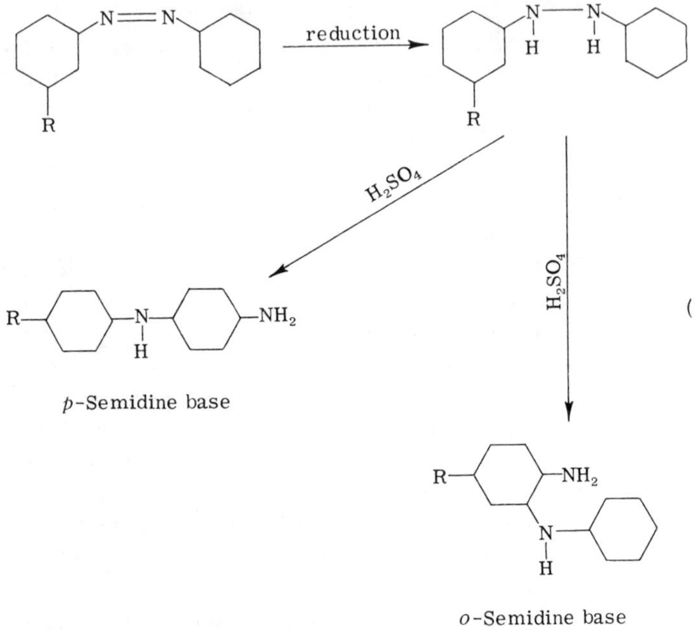

reduction

R

R

H_2SO_4

H_2SO_4

(11)

$R-$ —N— —NH$_2$
          H

p-Semidine base

$R-$ —NH$_2$
        N—
        H

o-Semidine base

This is known as the semidine transformation. If reduction is complete,
and digestion temperature high enough, there should be no difficulty in
the conversion of the amino groups to ammonia. In the case of azo
dyes, these transformations are prevented by the number and position
of the constituents. When reduction is carried out in concentrated

sulfuric acid, the possibility exists that hydrazines may, in part, be formed. Azo compounds, on reduction by pretreatment will be reduced to hydrazo, and finally to amines. When the *para* substituent in the ring is an amino or nitroso group, reduction follows another direction [Eq. (12)].

In a study of the Friedrich micro-Kjeldahl method, Secor *et al.* (122) found that with —NO, —NO$_2$, =N—N=, and —N=N— linkages, an increase in the salt:acid ratio resulted in lower nitrogen values. When the Friedrich reduction (with and without red phosphorus) and the prescribed micromethod of the AOAC (123) were used, (0.33 gm of potassium sulfate per milliliter of sulfuric acid), correct values for 2-nitroso-1-naphthol, 4-nitrosodimethylaniline, 4-nitroacetanilide, methyl orange, *s*-diphenylcarbazone, and aminopyrine were obtained. When the amount of sulfate was increased to 0.67 gm per milliliter, somewhat lower results were found. With an established digestion time of 70–80 minutes, ammonium sulfate pretreated in the same manner as a sample showed losses of the same order with the higher salt concentration. However, repeated boiling to remove hydriodic acid and iodine, followed by determination of nitrogen, showed no loss with either concentration. The presence of red phosphorus does not prevent or cause loss of nitrogen, nor does the hypophosphorous acid used as a preservative for hydriodic acid, at higher concentrations of sulfate. Reported results indicate the maximum salt concentration to be 0.5 gm per milliliter, if the Friedrich reduction is used as a pretreatment.

The following method was used by Phelps and Daudt (121) for the reduction of hydrazine sulfate and hydrazine derivatives. An alcoholic solution of the sample is treated with formaldehyde, zinc dust, and hydrochloric acid and boiled under reflux for at least 30 minutes. After refluxing for 15 minutes, a few drops of stannous chloride solution (40 gm in 100 ml of concentrated hydrochloric acid) is added. This serves to increase the action of the acid on the zinc. After reflux, the sample is treated in the same manner as for azo compounds (see page 127). If reduction of the aldehyde-nitrogen complex to amino nitrogen is complete, results compare with the calculated values. The method fails, however, with semicarbazide and oxamazide.

Perrot and Barghow (124) found that complete recovery of nitrogen from hydrazines, semicarbazides, and guanidines was not possible by the usual Kjeldahl procedure, and could be obtained only when a reductive pretreatment (Friedrich) was used. While a few of these compounds can be reduced by refluxing with hydriodic acid, the majority must be reduced (either with or without red phosphorus) in a sealed tube at 300°C, followed by digestion with 10 ml of sulfuric acid, 2 gm of potassium sulfate, and 0.5 gm of copper sulfate. Digestion of 0.1–0.4 gm samples with the foregoing mixture, without pretreatment, gave consistent results amounting to one third or one half the total nitrogen. Examples of these are shown in Table XXV.

TABLE XXV

RECOVERY OF NITROGEN FROM HYDRAZINES, CARBAZIDES, AND GUANIDINES

Compound	% N Calc.	% Nitrogen recovered		
		33.3%	50.0%	K_2SO_4 CuSO₄	Reduction at 300°C

Compound	% N Calc.	33.3%	50.0%	K_2SO_4 CuSO₄	Reduction at 300°C
Hydrazine sulfate	21.53	—	—	0.27	21.35
s-Diphenyl hydrazine	15.22	—	—	15.0	15.3
Diphenyl carbazide	23.14	—	—	16.7	23.4
Semicarbazide hydrochloride	37.69	12.56	—	12.8	37.6
Phenyl-1-semicarbazide hydrochloride	22.41	7.47	—	7.52	—
Aminoguanidine hydrochloride	50.68	—	25.34	25.40	50.7
Aminoguanidine carbonate	41.17	—	20.58	20.3	40.9

It can be seen from this table that not all of these type compounds respond to this treatment. However, in cases where a specific fraction of total nitrogen is recovered, it would appear that the hydrazine portion of the molecule is split off in the form of nitrogen.

A semimicro procedure for hydrazones, semicarbazones, oximes, and azines is described by Fish (125), in which the substance is given a reductive pretreatment with zinc and hydrochloric acid. A sample of appropriate size is weighed into a tin foil cup (made of cutting circles from tin foil with a No. 15 cork borer and shaping over a rod) and placed carefully in a flask. One milliliter of glacial acetic acid is added to the cup to dissolve the sample, warming if necessary. When cool, 1.5 ml of methanol, 200 mg of powdered zinc, and 4 drops of concentrated hydrochloric acid are added. The mixture is warmed slightly to promote reduction. Quantities of 4 drops of acid are added consecutively until a total of 16 drops has been used. Heat is increased slightly to remove volatile matter, care being taken not to bring the mixture to near dryness, since possible loss of nitrogen may occur. After cooling, 3 ml of concentrated sulfuric acid are added and the contents of the flask boiled to remove water. It is cooled again, 1.5 gm of catalyst mixture (150 gm of potassium sulfate, 10 gm of mercuric oxide, and 5 gm of selenium) and 1 ml of sulfuric acid added, and boiling continued until colorless. A further boil period of 30–45 minutes is recommended for nonrefractory, and 2 hours for refractory compounds, although with the latter, 1.5 hours is frequently sufficient. In the micromethod of Rose and Zilliotto (126) for nitriles, the sample is reduced by addition of 1.5 gm of potassium iodide and 30 ml of sulfuric acid. This is heated on the steam bath for 45 minutes, with occasional shaking. After addition of 10 gm of potassium sulfate, 0.3 gm of copper sulfate, and 0.1 gm of selenium, the mixture is first heated gently and then boiled vigorously, continuing the boiling for one hour after clearing. The procedure was checked by the Friedrich sealed tube method, and the salicylic acid modification and found to compare favorably. The method is applicable to both aliphatic and aromatic nitriles, but cannot be used for hydrazines and pyridine.

Generally speaking, the nitriles are readily decomposed by acid, and also easily reduced. Reduction will give an amine:

$$RCN \xrightarrow{\text{reduction}} RCH_2NH_2$$

The action of sulfuric acid on a nitrile goes through several steps, probably with the formation of an imido sulfuric acid, amide, and finally ammonia. The relative ease with which nitriles are decomposed would indicate that reduction before digestion might not be necessary. Vanetten and Wiele (127) have explored this possibility. Using Clark's (29) micro and semimicro procedure, both aliphatic and aromatic nitriles were analyzed. An average recovery of 98.96% was obtained.

Among the structures most resistant to reduction and digestion (oxidation) is the pyrazolone ring and its derivatives. Antipyrine, pyramidon, and 1-phenyl-3-methylpyrazolone are examples of highly refractory compounds whose nitrogen cannot be quantitatively recovered by reduction in concentrated sulfuric acid and subsequent digestion.

Antipyrene   Pyramidon   1-Phenyl-3-
                                                           methylpyrazolone

Reduction, and subsequent thermal decomposition will rupture the ring at the carbonyl group with probable formation of a mixed hydrazine, which on further decomposition of the organic portion of the molecule will give possibly a mixture of ammonia and hydrazine. Conversion of hydrazine to ammonia is not complete because of partial oxidation to nitrogen.

The triazoles are further examples of great ring stability, and 1,2,3-benzotriazole is a typical compound.

1, 2, 3- Benzotriazole

Using various reduction and digestion procedures, only a portion of the total nitrogen is recovered. The interesting fact is that, apparently, by whatever digestion procedure used, one third of the total nitrogen is recovered. The results in Table XXVI illustrate this. The relative consistency of these results would indicate that the effect of reduction and progressive thermal decomposition is to first rupture the triazole ring with formation of amino and hydrazine groups and consequent loss of the latter as nitrogen.

TABLE XXVI
NITROGEN RECOVERY FROM 1,2,3-BENZOTRIAZOLE

| Method | % Nitrogen | |
(using 18 gm K_2SO_4+25 ml H_2SO_4)	Found	Calc.
Salicylic acid—thiosulfate	11.56	35.26
Sucrose	11.87	35.26
Thiosalicylic acid	11.71	35.26
Sucrose and H_2SO_4-H_3PO_4	11.79	35.26

Compounds containing the pyrazole ring in which there are adjacent nitrogens are generally difficult to reduce, and even if reduction is carried out as a separate operation, the calculated amount of nitrogen is usually not completely recoverable. As in the case of the 1,2,3-triazoles, nitrogen is probably lost due to formation of a hydrazine. Reduction, progressive digestion, [Eq. (13)]

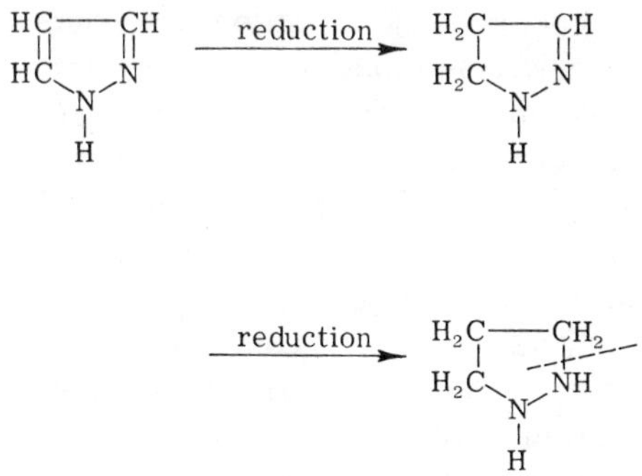

$$HC{=\!\!=}CH \xrightarrow{\text{reduction}} H_2C{-\!\!-}CH$$

(13)

$$\xrightarrow{\text{reduction}} H_2C{-\!\!-}CH_2$$

and oxidation of a CH_2 group adjacent to a nitrogen to $\rangle C{=\!\!=}O$ possibly lead to rupture of the ring at this point with formation of the hydrazine. Hydrazines, both aliphatic and aromatic, are powerful reducing agents. Hydrazine (sulfate) digested with concentrated sulfuric acid is oxidized almost completely to nitrogen, and it is reasonable to assume that under the digestion conditions at least part of the hydrazine grouping will oxidize to nitrogen.

The nitrogen of urea, thiourea, guanidine, and their derivatives can generally be determined without a separate pretreatment. Digestion procedures using salicylic acid, sucrose, or similar compounds are applicable providing that the salt concentration is at least 0.5 gm per milliliter. Concentrations below this level do not result in high enough digestion temperatures for complete conversion. This applies, similarly, to the oxazoles, imidazoles, and thiazoles. The aromatic hydroxylamines, where possible, isomerize to form the aminophenols, [Eq. (14)]

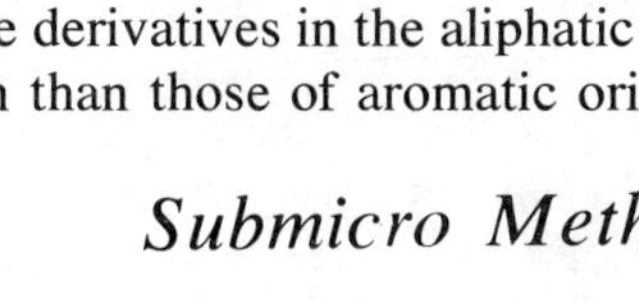

NHOH   NH₂

(14)

                      OH

the OH group migrating to the *para* position. Generally, the hydroxylamine derivatives in the aliphatic series are more resistant to decomposition than those of aromatic origin.

Submicro Methods

The necessity of determining nitrogen in microgram quantities in biological materials, for example, has led to the development of special methods and techniques. The digestion procedure is, basical-ly, much the same as for micro and macro quantities, although greatly reduced in size of sample and apparatus. Total nitrogen is generally determined by diffusion followed by titration. Other methods of es-timation have included steam distillation (128), aeration (129, 130), nesslerization (131), and electrometric titration (132).

In 1933 Conway and Byrne (133) devised a diffusion vessel for the absorption of volatile substances which Conway (134) used for the determination of urea and ammonia in body fluids. The principle of the method is the absorption of volatile material placed in one section of a closed system by an absorbing liquid in another section. It is stated that 99.5% of the ammonia content of 1 ml samples is absorbed within a maximum period of 1.5 hours at room temperature. The cells are made of either glass or plastic, such as Lucite, and are construc-ted so that there is an inner and outer chamber with a tight fitting cover. Bentley and Kirk (135) also developed a diffusion unit consisting of a small, conical, flat-bottomed flask with a ground glass stopper to which a small glass hook was attached to support the diffusion cup.

Some of the earlier difficulties primarily involving digestion and subsequent transfer of the digest to a diffusion vessel have been over-come by the use of an apparatus in two parts by which the entire operation can be conducted without transfer of the digest. Needham and Boell (136) describe a digestion-diffusion unit in which the diges-tion tube has two bulbs and a ground glass connection at the top to which the diffusion tube is attached. Manipulation of the unit requires a fair amount of technique; moreover, it requires considerable time for completion, and is liable to error if not handled properly. A diges-tion-diffusion vessel somewhat similar to Needham and Boell's de-signed by Tompkins and Kirk (137) has one large bulb and a much smal-ler one at the end of the digestion tube. Both bulbs are flattened on one side to allow the apparatus to lie in a horizontal position. The small bulb and its neck are inclined slightly to allow complete drainage of the neutralized digest into the larger bulb. A short glass rod with a cup or depression, having a volume of 0.1–0.2 ml at the end, to hold the drop of standard acid is inserted in a rubber stopper which in turn fits the neck of the digestion section. For vacuum diffusion, the digestion tube is fitted with a grooved ground glass joint grooved at the lower half, and closed with a hollow plug drilled to connect with the groove.

For samples containing 1–20 μg of nitrogen, Needham and Boell digest the sample with 50 to 60 μl (50–60 λ) of a mixture of 300 ml of concentrated sulfuric acid, 3 gm of copper sulfate, 1 gm of potassium sulfate, and 0.1 gm of selenium dioxide, first drying in an oven for 3 hours at 120°C to remove water. After addition of two glass beads, the digest is heated by a moving flame until it becomes straw colored — usually in about 3–5 minutes. Heating is continued for one half to one hour over a fine flame 2 mm high using a submicro burner. The digest is diluted with 0.7 ml of distilled water and neutralized by tilting the digestion unit and placing 300 mg (3 pellets) of sodium hydroxide in the first bulb. The interior of the diffusion tube is coated with wax. 70 λ of distilled water placed near the opening and 7 λ of 0.294 N hydrochloric acid added to the drop. The apparatus is assembled, the digest neutralized carefully, avoiding excess heat of reaction, and cooled in water. Care must be taken so that none of the acid is left on the inside surface. It is then placed in a rocker, at 37°C, left overnight and titrated the following morning with 0.102 N sodium hydroxide.

The method of Tompkins and Kirk is less complicated, and the time of diffusion greatly reduced. Digestion of samples containing 0.5–20 μg of nitrogen is conveniently made in a sand bath, using 0.1 ml of the digestion mixture. This is prepared by diluting concentrated sulfuric acid with an equal volume of water saturated with potassium sulfate and adding 0.1% copper selenite (made by adding concentrated copper sulfate solution to a solution of sodium selenite and filtering off the copper selenite). The sand bath is maintained at a bottom temperature of 300°C. Prior to actual digestion, the tube is placed at an angle of 10° to 20° from the horizontal to allow the water to evaporate, then placed upright deep in the sand bath. After clearing, heating is continued for an hour. This is a somewhat arbitrary time limit, since some materials containing proteins or amino acids such as tryptophan and lysine require longer heating periods. If clearing is prolonged, 5 λ of 10% hydrogen peroxide may be added to accelerate the oxidation. After the digest is cool, 0.5 ml of distilled water is added, and the mixture again cooled. The caustic solution — 0.3 ml of a half saturated solution — is added below the surface of the diluted digest by means of a capillary pipette the tip of which has a film of Vaseline on it to prevent adherence of any solution. The rim of the absorption cup is also greased, and 30–50 λ of 0.025 N sulfuric acid containing methyl red indicator is added to the cup. The upper part of the digestion unit is warmed gently with a flame, avoiding any mixing of the two layers, the flame withdrawn, and the cup inserted firmly, creating a slight vacuum when the unit is cool. The assembly is tilted and rotated slowly, mixing the reactants, and continuing until the entire inside surface has been wet by the alkalinized solution. It is now transferred to an oven kept at 37°–50°C, and absorption is allowed to continue for 3 hours. After this time, the tube is removed and cooled, the cup withdrawn, and the solution titrated with 0.02 N sodium hydroxide. The procedure for diffusion under vacuum is the same except that before mixing the two layers, the unit is cooled in ice water and evacuated to a pressure of 20 mm of mercury. The absorption takes place at room temperature and is complete for 10 μg of nitrogen in slightly more than an hour. The precision of the method in determining amounts of nitrogen as low as 1 γ is 0.3%, with a probable absolute error of 1%.

The method of Brüel *et al.* **(138)** is lengthy and requires a high degree of technique; however, the accuracy is of the order of 0.5%. Digestion and diffusion are carried out in separate small tubes. Before actual digestion but after addition of a digestion mixture containing 1 gm of copper sulfate, 10 gm (5) of potassium sulfate, 0.2 gm of sucrose, and 5 ml of sulfuric acid per 100 ml of solution, the tube with sample is placed in a vacuum desiccator at 150 mm pressure for 24 hours, and for 24 hours longer at 0.1 mm in order to remove all water. Selenium catalyst in sulfuric acid is added and the sample digested for 6 hours in a sulfuric acid bath held at 295°C. The digest is diluted with half a drop of water, and the tube washed with another half drop, the diluted digest and washings finally being transferred to the absorption tube. After addition of 18 N caustic solution, the tube is sealed with two drops of water and standard acid is added to the water seal. The tube is capped and immersed halfway in a water bath at 40°C for 1.5 hours. An excess of standard disodium hydrogen phosphate containing indicator is added and back titrated with standard acid. While this method is precise and accurate, particularly for very small quantities of nitrogen, it is not adaptable to routine control work.

A procedure based on the method of Brüel *et al.* is that of Doyle and Omoto **(139)**. The digestion is carried out in tubes 6 × 50 mm. The digestion mixture is divided into two parts: *(1)* 1 gm of copper sulfate, 10 gm of potassium sulfate, 5 ml of sulfuric acid made up to 100 ml with water, and a final addition of 0.2 gm of sucrose; *(2)* equal volumes of sulfuric acid and water. Samples containing 1 γ of nitrogen are digested with 5 λ of solution *(1)* above, and 10 λ of 1:1 sulfuric acid. Heating is first conducted in an aluminum block at 90°, the temperature being slowly raised to 130°C to expel water. When the tubes are free of all condensed water, they are transferred to another heating block maintained at 245° ± 5°C and digested for 2 hours. The amount of heat should be such that a ring of condensate does not rise higher than 10 mm above the surface of the block. (*Note:* the overall dimensions of the heating blocks are 7.5 × 7.5 × 5 cm deep set with 15 mm holes.) After 2 hours the digests are removed to a cool block and 5 λ of 30% hydrogen peroxide added, with a final addition of 10 λ of saturated potassium persulfate. After each addition, water is expelled by heating in the low temperature block, finally heating at the higher temperature for 30 minutes. The tubes used for diffusion are 6 × 25 mm and are coated with a 5% solution of G.E. Dri-film 9987 in chloroform. The film is set by heating for 2 hours at 110°C. Using a pipette, 50 λ of water are spotted as three drops of unequal size on a clean Teflon strip. The same pipette is used to transfer the digest to the diffusion tube. The digestion tube is washed with each drop starting with the smallest, and each washing is carefully transferred to the diffusion tube without touching the sides. To the solution are added 20 λ of 13 N sodium hydroxide to form two layers. A liquid seal of 100 λ of 0.05 M potassium dihydrogen phosphate containing 0.103 mg of bromocresol green is made about 5 mm above the surface of the digest. After mixing the acid and alkali layers, the tube is closed and allowed to stand from 8 to 15 hours at 25°C after which time, the seal is titrated with 0.05 M hydrochloric acid. Unless jarred severely, the seal will not drop into the alkaline digest.

Amounts of nitrogen in the order of 1 to 15 μg have been determined by Grunbaum, Schaffer, and Kirk (140) using a sealed tube digestion followed by diffusion. Digestion of the sample is carried out in borosilicate tubes, 7 mm in outside diameter and 45 mm long, which previously have been cleaned with chromic acid, thoroughly washed with water, and dried. After sealing one end, an appropriate amount of sample is added. If liquid, it is first dried in a vacuum desiccator, after which 10 λ of redistilled sulfuric acid are added and the open end of the tube sealed by pressing the edges together with hot forceps, then annealing in the gas flame. The sealed tube is now placed in a brass block, set at a slight angle and preheated to 450°C for 30 minutes after which the hot tube is withdrawn and centrifuged at once using an asbestos pad at the bottom of the centrifuge cup. This serves to cool the tube and force the sulfuric acid to the bottom. The tube is cut into two pieces and the parts placed in an oven at 90°C to free the digest of dissolved gases. The digest is then transferred to the diffusion vessel, both parts of the digestion tube are washed with a total amount of 50 λ of water, which are also transferred to the diffusion cell. The diffusion unit is in two sections and connected with a ground glass joint. Both the upper and lower bulbs are coated with Desicate, washed with water, and dried at 100°C. After the digest has been transferred, the upper bulb of the unit is charged with 50 λ of 2% boric acid containing the mixed indicator of Ma and Zuazaga (141), which is a 5:1 mixture of 0.1% solution of bromocresol green and 0.1% of methyl red in 95% alcohol. The boric acid is placed so that the neck of the bulb is sealed about 2 mm from the rim. A thin layer of Vaseline is spread on the neck of the lower bulb, a 5 mm stirring bar is added, and a 2 to 2.5 times excess of caustic (saturated solution free from carbonate) is added at a point slightly above the bottom of the vessel. The two bulbs are then connected and held over a magnetic stirrer to mix the two layers, while the assembly is rotated and tipped to wet the wall of the lower bulb with the alkaline solution. Stirring is continued during the diffusion period of 90 minutes. The upper bulb is disconnected, wiped free of Vaseline, the opening covered with a small piece of Parafilm; the bulb is then centrifuged, forcing the boric acid to the bottom of the bulb. After addition of a 3 mm stirring bar, the solution is titrated with 0.01 hydrochloric acid.

Belcher, West, and Williams (142) have also used a sealed tube digestion for submicro quantities of organic material (as differentiated from natural products and biological fluids). Digestion of 50 γ samples is carried out in borosilicate glass tubes (7 cm long and 11 mm inside diameter). These are soaked overnight in chromic acid, rinsed well and dried at 120°C, and then stirred in a desiccator over phosphoric anhydride. The sample is treated with 10 λ of concentrated sulfuric acid; the tube is sealed off about 2 cm from the open end and placed in a heating block at 420°–430°C for 30 minutes. After this period the tube is cooled and centrifuged for 5 minutes, then opened about 1.5 cm below the seal and heated in an oven at 90°C for 5 minutes to remove any dissolved gases. The main section of the tube is carefully washed down the inside with 0.5 ml of water, the shorter section is washed with two portions of 0.25 ml of water transferring each to the diluted digest by means of a capillary pipette. Titration of ammonia is made with sodium hypochlorite solution at a pH of 7.5–9.6. In order not to exceed the pH range, one drop of 2% mercuric sulfate solution (143) is added prior to titrations with 2 N sodium hydroxide to indicate the approach of the end point. Addition of caustic should be rapid until the first appearance of turbidity, at which point it is added slowly until both stirrer and burette tip are completely obscured. At this point caustic is added very slowly and when the appearance of crystalline material is noted, just enough solution is added (at fairly long intervals) to obtain clearing of the turbidity. One drop of 5% sodium bicarbonate, and two drops of 30% potassium bromide are added immediately. If the solution has been overtitrated, which is indicated by a precipitate of mercuric oxide, a further addition of bicarbonate and bromide is helpful. A known volume (150% of the theoretical) of 0.04 N sodium hypochlorite is added with stirring, and the tube and contents are placed in a desiccator for 5 minutes. After this period, the tube is removed and the solution titrated with 0.04 N sodium thiosulfate after the addition of one drop of 30% potassium iodide and one drop of 4 N sulfuric acid. The hypochlorite solution is standardized using ammonium sulfate or a previously standardized thiosulfate solution.

Belcher, Bhasin, and West (144) extended the sealed tube method to include heterocyclic, azo, hydrazo, and nitro compounds. When either iodine or bromine is present, the digestion is carried out at $350 \pm 5°C$ for 30 minutes. For heterocyclic compounds 100–200 γ of mercuric sulfate are added as catalyst. When azo, hydrazo, or nitro linkages are present, an additional 20 λ of sulfuric acid (in place of glucose) are added to the digestion mixture which is heated for 30 minutes at 420°C. Later (145) this procedure was modified using mercuric sulfate as a catalyst and digesting at 380°C for 30 minutes regardless of the type of nitrogen linkage. Compounds containing iodine or bromine are first digested with acid before sealing the tube in order to expel the halogens. Reduction with glucose or red phosphorus and hydriodic acid is also carried out in the open tube, after which the catalyst is added, the tube sealed, and digestion completed at 380°C.

Exley (146) has extended the procedure for submicro quantities of nitrogen to the range of 20–100 μmg. Digestion is made in Pyrex tubes (45 mm long and 2.5 mm inside diameter) calibrated at 30, 100, and 200 λ. They are fitted with ground glass joints to take either a stopper or an acid trap 20 mm long containing a glass wool plug soaked in 10 N sulfuric acid. After transference of the sample to the digestion tube, and addition of 0.1 λ of digestion mixture, it is stoppered and centrifuged at 3000 g for 5 minutes, the stopper replaced by the acid trap and the assembly placed in an oven at 100°C for 1 hour to remove water. The stopper is replaced and the tube is again centrifuged for 5 minutes. The heating unit consists of a 3 cm square copper block heated with a micro burner, on top of which rests a digestion bath of sulfuric acid 2.5 cm high and 1.5 cm in diameter with a constriction at a height of 1 cm. When the bath is at $300° \pm 5°C$, the tube with the acid trap is placed in it and allowed to digest for 1 hour. The acid trap is replaced with a stopper and the tube is centrifuged for 5 minutes, after which 50 λ of water, 0.5 λ of methyl orange (0.04%), and 0.5 λ of manganese catalyst (0.002 M Mn_2SO_4) are added, and the tube again centrifuged for 5 minutes. After placing the tube in crushed ice, the digest is neutralized with 5 N sodium hydroxide at the rate of 2 λ per minute for the first 6 λ. Further additions of caustic in 0.5 λ quantities are made until the color matches that of a comparison tube containing indicator and 8 λ of the digestion mixture. By keeping the tube cold during titration, no ammonia is lost even if the solution is overtitrated to a pH limit of 12. Nitrogen is estimated by the phenol-hypochlorite method, and the color intensity measured in a spectrophotometer at 625 mμ. Sodium phenoxide is prepared by adding 0.5 ml of water to 1 gm of phenol, cooling in ice, adding 2.0 ml of 5.4 N sodium hydroxide with stirring, and making the final volume to 4.0 ml. The calcium hypochlorite solution, once prepared, is stored at 0°C. It is recommended, however, that the sodium phenate solution be prepared fresh daily. Both solutions are cooled before adding to the sample. After addition of 10 λ of sodium phenate and 5 λ of hypochlorite, the tube is stoppered and placed in a boiling water bath for exactly 5 minutes. and transferred to an ice bath. When cool, the volume is made up to either 100 or 200 λ depending on the color concentration, stirred, and centrifuged for 15 minutes. It is then transferred to a 100 capillary cell with 1 cm light path made of Fluon or Teflon (147).

In this range of nitrogen, the purity of the water is critical. Ammonia-free water for the several solutions is prepared from distilled water by distilling twice over dilute sulfuric acid and permanganate, and finally passing through a 10 cm column of Permutit. Water containing more than 0.05 μg of ammonia per milliliter is rejected. Russel (148) found that iron, chromium, and manganese acted as catalysts for the color development, while copper inhibited the reaction. In this case, 50 ± 10 λ of 0.003 M manganese sulfate were used as a catalyst. Exley, however, has shown that at this concentration and the existing pH (ca. 12–13) of the final solution, the possibility exists that manganese hydroxide may be precipitated. This is avoided by the use of 0.002 M manganese sulfate.

Methods other than diffusion and titration with hypochlorite have been used for the recovery and estimation of nitrogen. Sisco, Cunningham, and Kirk (149) for example, have applied the formal titration to the drop analysis of ammonia. A description of two aeration units is given by Sobel, Hirschman, and Besman (129) for the recovery of nitrogen in ranges of 10–200 and 1–10 μg. For the larger amounts aeration is conducted in Pyrex test tubes 125 mm × 15 mm wide with sealed-in side outlets and bubbling tubes constricted to 1 mm. In the lower range, 5 ml conical centrifuge tubes connected with rubber stoppers holding the outlets and bubbling tubes are used. Digestion can be carried out in an aeration tube, and after addition of alkali, the tube is placed in series with a trap and receiver tube. Air is first drawn through a trap containing 1.5 ml of 2% boric acid, passing into the digestion tube, and finally goes to the receiver containing 1.5 ml of 2% boric acid. The flow rate is adjusted to a moderate stream of bubbles so that all tubes are aerating at the same rate. A period of 20–40 minutes is required for aeration at room temperature. Precision and accuracy are good, with a reported deviation of ±0.03 for 2, ±0.05 for 5, and ±0.1 for 10 μg of nitrogen. Day, Bernstoff, and Hill (150) modified the aeration tube of Sobel et al. by setting the side arm at an angle of 45° to the bubbler tube. They found, however, that discordant results were obtained by the Sobel method, but if aeration were conducted at 70°C, complete recovery was possible. This is in keeping with Davis (151) and Dillingham (152), both of whom stressed the importance of using higher than room temperature for macro aeration.

REFERENCES

1. G. Bredig and J. W. Brown, *Z. physik. Chem.* **46**, 502 (1903).
2. G.-M. Schwab and E. Agallidis, *J. Am. Chem. Soc.* **73**, 803–809 (1951).
3. G.-M. Schwab and E. Agallidis, *Angew. Chem.* **65**, 418–421 (1953).
4. Assoc. Offic. Agr. Chem., "Methods of Analysis," 9th ed., p. 12, para. 2.036 (1960); cf. *J. Offic. Agr. Chem.* **38**, 56 (1955).
5. Assoc. Offic. Agr. Chem., "Methods of Analysis," 9th ed., p. 13, para 2.037 (1960).
6. B. Dyer and J. H. Hamence, *Analyst* **63**, 866–870 (1938).
7. H. R. Allen, *J. Assoc. Offic. Agr. Chem.* **38**, 185 (1955).
8. J. G. Parker and J. T. Terrell, *J. Soc. Leather Trades' Chem.* **5**, 380–384 (1921).
9. J. Jany and A. Morvay, *Z. anal. Chem.* **114**, 120–125 (1938).
10. W. F. Barker and S. G. Shuttleworth, *J. Intern. Soc. Leather Trades' Chem.* **23**, 488–491 (1939).
11. S. Dahl and R. Oehler, *J. Am. Leather Chem. Assoc.* **46**, 317–335 (1951).
12. H. B. Merrill, S. Dahl, R. M. Lollar, H. L. Ellison, and A. N. Kay, *J. Am. Leather Chem. Assoc.* **47**, 15–40 (1952).
13. Kleeman, *Z. angew. Chem.* **34**, 625–627 (1921).
14. R. Heuss, *Wochschr. Brau.* **40**, 73–74 (1923).
15. H. Lundin and J. Ellburg, *Wochschr. Brau.* **46**, 133–137, 147–149 (1929).
16. R. Ranker, *J. Assoc. Offic. Agr. Chem.* **10**, 230–251 (1927).
17. G. W. Pucher, C. S. Leavenworth, and H. B. Vickery, *Ind. Eng. Chem., Anal. Ed.* **2**, 191–193 (1930).
18. R. H. Moore, *Botan. Gaz.* **100**, 250–252 (1938).

19. L. P. Pepkowitz and J. W. Shive, *Ind. Eng. Chem., Anal. Ed.* **14**, 914–916 (1942).

20. T. S. Ma and G. Zuazaga, *Ind. Eng. Chem., Anal. Ed.* **14**, 280 (1942).

21. L. P. Pepkowitz, A. L. Prince, and F. E. Bear, *Ind. Eng. Chem., Anal. Ed.* **14**, 856–857 (1942).

22. O. J. Kelley, A. S. Hunter, and A. J. Sterges, *Ind. Eng. Chem., Anal. Ed.* **18**, 319–322 (1946).

23. F. J. Koch, *Z. anal. Chem.* **131**, 426–427 (1950).

24. F. L. Ashton, *J. Soc. Chem. Ind.* **56**, 101–4T (1937).

25. A. E. Beet and D. G. Furzey, *Fuel* **13**, 343–345 (1934); cf. *J. Soc. Chem. Ind.* **55**, 108–9T (1936).

26. Y. V. Yarayanaya and V. Subrahmanyan, *Proc. Indian Acad. Sci.* **2B**, 213–235 (1935); cf. **3B**, 35 (1935); *Current Sci.* **3**, 423 (1935).

27. A. Sreenivasan, *Indian J. Agr. Sci.* **2**, 525–530 (1932).

28. A. Sreenivasan and V. Subrahmanyan, *Indian J. Agr. Sci.* **3**, 646–657 (1933); cf. A. Sreenivasan, *Indian J. Agr. Sci.* **4**, 320–326 (1934).

29. A. Sreenivasan, *Indian J. Agr. Sci.* **4**, 546–553 (1934).

30. A. Sreenivasan, *J. Indian Inst. Sci.* **18A**, Pt 6, 25–38 (1935).

31. S. P. L. Sorensen and A. C. Andersen, *Z. physiol. Chem.* **44**.

32. H. W. Gerritz and J. L. St. John, *Ind. Eng. Chem., Anal. Ed.* **7**, 380–383 (1935).

33. H. C. Goswami and M. R. Ray, *Sci. and Culture* **3**, 180 (1937).

34. S. J. Rowland, *J. Dairy Research* **9**, 42–46 (1938).

35. J. Cartiaux, *Ann. chim. anal. chim. appl.* **22**, 92 (1940).

36. B. Jelinek, *Bull. anciens élévés École franc. meunerie*, pp. 233–234 (1937).

37. R. Jonnard, *Ind. Eng. Chem., Anal. Ed.* **17**, 246–249 (1945).

38. R. D. Hotchkiss and R. J. Dubos, *J. Biol. Chem.* **141**, 155–162 (1941).

39. A. C. Chibnall, M. W. Rees, and E. F. Williams, *Biochem. J.* **37**, 354–359 (1943).

40. L. Miller and J. A. Houghton, *J. Biol. Chem.* **159**, 373–383 (1945).

41. Y. Mihashi and M. Tatsumi, *Ann. Rept. Tokyo Coll. Pharm.* **3**, 189–191 (1953).

41a. R. J. Robinson and J. A. Shellenberger, *Ind. Eng. Chem., Anal. Ed.* **4**, 243 (1932).

42. J. Wagner, *Kühn-Arch.* **21**, No. 1, 1–74 (1957).

43. H. Slusanschi, M. Suteanu, and A. Lozinschi, *Acad. rep. populare Romine, Inst. biochim., Studi ceretari biochim.* **2**, 385–393 (1959).

44. A. C. Andersen and B. N. Jensen, *Z. anal. Chem.* **67**, 427–448 (1926); cf. **83**, 116–120 (1931); *Beretn. Forsøgslab.* (1923), 38–102; *Intern. Rev. Sci. Pract. Agr.* **2**, 458–459.

45. H. Bunte and E. J. Schilling, *J. Gasbeleucht.* **30**, 707 (1887).

46. Schmitz, *Z. anal. Chem.* **25**, 314 (1886).

47. Lord, *U. S. Geol. Survey Profess. Paper* **48**, 186.

48. B. M. Margosches and A. Lang, *Chem. Ztg.* **108**, 673–675 (1915).

49. E. Bornstein and A. J. Petrick, *Brennstoff-Chem.* **13**, 41–45 (1932).

50. G. Lambris, *Brennstoff-Chem.* **6**, 1–6 (1925); cf. **8**, 69–72, 89–93 (1927).

51. L. A. Baranov and R. A. Mott, *Fuel* **3**, 49–52 (1924); cf. **3**, 31–34 (1924).

52. H. E. Crossley, *J. Soc. Chem. Ind.* **51**, 237–238 (1932).

53. H. E. Crossley, *J. Soc. Chem. Ind.* **54**, 367–9T (1935).

54. A. E. Beet, *Fuel* **11**, 196–199 (1932).

55. A. E. Beet, *Fuel* **13**, 343–345 (1934).

56. A. E. Beet and R. Belcher, *Mikrochemie* **24**, 145–148 (1938).

57. A. E. Beet, *J. Appl. Chem.* **4**, 373–379 (1954).

58. A. E. Beet, *Nature* **175**, 513–514 (1955).

59. A. H. Edwards, *J. Appl. Chem.* **4**, 330–340 (1954).
60. G. N. Badami and J. W. Whitaker, *Fuel* **30**, 8–9 (1951).
61. W. Lange and W. Winzen, *Glückauf* **89**, 324–325 (1953).
62. M. Dermelji and L. Strauch, *Bull. sci., Conseil. acad. RPF Yougoslavie*, **2**, 104–105 (1956) (in German).
63. F. Gonzales-Sanchez and V. Gomez Aranda, *Combustibles (Zaragoza)* **17**, 176–187 (1957).
64. C. H. Hale, M. N. Hale, and W. H. Jones, *Anal. Chem.* **21**, 1549–1551 (1949).
65. E. D. Noble, *Anal. Chem.* **27**, 1413–1416 (1955).
66. O. I. Milner, R. J. Zahner, L. S. Hepner, and W. H. Cowell, *Anal. Chem.* **30**, 1528–1530 (1958).
67. G. R. Bond, Jr. and C. G. Harriz, *Anal. Chem.* **29**, 177–180 (1957).
68. S. Barbaeva and N. Orlova, *Novosti Neftyanoi Tekh. Nefteperabotki No.* **4**, 29–34 (1955).
69. H. Riehm. *Listy cukrovar.* **54**, 41–44; cf. *Z. Zuckerind cechoslov. Rep.* **60**, 156–159 (1935).
70. W. L. Davies and H. C. Dowden, *J. Soc. Chem. Ind.* **55**, 175–9T (1936).
71. L. E. Volochanenko, *Sovet. Sahkar* **9**, 44–46 (1936).
72. L. G. Davidson, *J. Assoc. Offic. Agr. Chem.* **23**, 171–172 (1940).
73. G. R. Tristram, *Trans. Inst. Rubber Ind.* **16**, 261–267 (1941).
74. G. J. van der Bie, *Mededeel. Ned.-Indisch. Inst. Rubberonderzoek, Buitenzorg No.* **64**, 8 pp. (1948).
75. J. O. Cole and C. R. Parks, *Ind. Eng. Chem., Anal. Ed.* **18**, 61–62 (1946).
76. W. Skoda and J. Schurz, *Z. anal. Chem.* **162**, 259 (1958).
77. U. Bartels, *Faserforsch. u. Textiltech.* **8**, 194–195 (1957).
78. Am. Oil Chemists Soc. Official Methods of Analysis, Method Aa 5—38 (Published in 1945, in loose leaf form, additions and revisions being made as needed).
79. A. E. Paul and E. H. Berry, *J. Assoc. Offic. Agr. Chem.* **5**, 108–132 (1921).
80. C. H. Perrin, *Anal. Chem.* **25**, 968–971 (1953).
81. C. H. Perrin, *J. Am. Oil Chemists Soc.* **34**, 409–411 (1957).
82. "Standard Methods for the Examination of Water, Sewage, and Industrial Wastes," 10th ed., 1955, pp. 156, 247, 249, 325, 351, American Public Health Association, Inc., New York (1955).
83. J. E. Kiker Jr., *Public Works* **88**, No. 12, 89–90 (1957).
84. C. Arnold, *Z. anal. Chem.* **26**, 249 (1886).
85. J. W. Gunning, *Z. anal. Chem.* **28**, 188 (1889).
86. C. Arnold and K. Wedemeyer, *Z. anal. Chem.* **31**, 525 (1892).
87. B. M. Margosches and E. Vogel, *Ber.* **52B**, 1992–1998 (1919).
88. B. M. Margosches and E. Vogel, *Ber.* **55B**, 1380–1389 (1922).
89. B. M. Margosches, W. Kristen, and E. Scheinost, *Ber.* **56B**, 1943–1950 (1923).
90. B. M. Margosches and W. Kristen, *Z. ges. Schiess- u. Sprengstoffw.* **18**, 39–40 (1923).
91. B. M. Margosches and W. Kristen, *Z. ges. Schiess- u. Spriengstoffw.* **18**, 73–76 (1923).
92. R. B. Bradstreet, *Anal. Chem.* **26**, 235–236 (1954).
93. R. B. Bradstreet, *Anal. Chem.* **32**, 114–117 (1960).
94. P. McCutchan and W. F. Roth, *Anal. Chem.* **24**, 369–370 (1952).
95. A. Elek and H. Sobotka, *J. Am. Chem, Soc.* **48**, 501–503 (1926).
96. R. A. Harte, *Ind. Eng. Chem., Anal. Ed.* **7**, 432–433 (1935).

97. L. M. White and Long, *Anal. Chem.* **23**, 262–265 (1951); cf. L. M. White and G. E. Secar, *ibid.* **22**, 1047–1049 (1950).
98. T. G. Levi and L. Gimignani, *Gazz. chim. ital.* **59**, 757 (1929).
99. P. R. W. Baker, *Analyst* **80**, 481–482 (1955).
100. R. Belcher and M. K. Bhatty, *Analyst* **81**, 124–125 (1956).
101. T. S. Ma, R. E. Lang, and J. D. McKinley, Jr., *Mikrochim. Acta* pp. 368–377 (1957).
102. M. Ashraf, M. K. Bhatty, and R. A. Shah, *Anal. Chim. Acta* **25**, 448–452 (1961).
103. R. L. Shirley and W. W. Becker, *Ind. Eng. Chem., Anal. Ed.* **17**, 437–438 (1945).
104. Assoc. Offic. Agr. Chem., "Official and Tentative Methods of Analysis," 5th ed. p. 25 (1940).
105. R. Belcher and A. L. Godbert, *J. Soc. Chem. Ind.* **60**, 196–198 (1941).
106. C. L. Ogg, R. W. Brand, and C. O. Willets, *J. Assoc. Offic. Agr. Chem.* **31**, 663–669 (1948).
107. C. O. Willets, M. R. Coe, and C. L. Ogg, *J. Assoc. Offic. Agr. Chem.* **32**, 118–126 (1949).
108. J. O. Cole and C. R. Parks, *Ind. Eng. Chem. Anal. Ed.* **8**, 61–62 (1940).
109. F. E. Crane and R. M. Fuoss, *Anal. Chem.* **26**, 1651–1652 (1954).
110. V. B. Fish and P. R. Collier, *Anal. Chem.* **30**, 151–152 (1958).
111. M. Marzadro, *Mikrochemie ver. Mikrochim. Acta* **36/37**, 671–678 (1951).
112. P. Dupuy, *Compt. rend.* **232**, 836–838 (1951).
113. C. Moreau. *Compt rend.* **233**, 1616–1617 (1951).
114. I. Ribas and D. Vazquez-Gesto, *Inform. quim. anal.* (*Madrid*) **7**, 29–42 (1953).
115. P. Fleury and H. Levaltier, *J. pharm. chim.* **30**, 265–272 (1924); cf. *Bull. soc. chim. France* **37**, 330–335 (1925).
116. E. P. Clark, *J. Assoc. Offic. Agr. Chem.* **24**, 641–647 (1941).
117. I. A. Kaye and N. Weiner, *Ind. Eng. Chem., Anal. Ed.* **17**, 397–398 (1945).
118. A. Friedrich, E. Kühaus, and R. Schnurch, *Z. physiol. Chem.* **216**, 68–76 (1933).
119. V. I. Esafov, *Zavodskaya Lab.* **21**, 1160–1163 (1955).
120. P. Sisley and M. David, *Bull. soc. chim. France* **4**, 312–324 (1929).
121. I. K. Phelps and H. W. Daudt, *J. Assoc. Offic. Agr. Chem.* **3**, 306–315 (1920).
122. G. E. Secor, M. C. Long, M. D. Kilpatrick, and L. M. White *J. Assoc. Offic. Agr. Chem.* **33**, 872–880 (1950).
123. Assoc. Offic. Agr. Chem. "Official and Tentative Methods of Analysis," 6th ed., Sections 41.5–41.6 (1945).
124. R. Perrot and A. Barghow, *Proc. 11th Intern. Congr. Pure and Appl. Chem.* **2**, 247–251 (1957).
125. V. B. Fish, *Anal. Chem.* **24**, 760–762 (1952).
126. E. L. Rose and H. Zilliotto, *Ind. Eng. Chem., Anal. Ed.* **17**, 217–12 (1945).
127. C. B. Vanetten and M. B. Wiele, *Anal. Chem.* **23**, 1338–1339 (1951).
128. P. L. Kirk, *Mikrochemie* **16**, 13–24 (1934).
129. A. E. Sobel, A. Hirschman, and L. Besman, *Anal. Chem.* **19**, 927–929 (1947).
130. H. G. Day, E. Bernstoff, and R. T. Hill, *Anal. Chem.* **21**, 1290–1291 (1949).
131. Levy, *Compt. rend. trav. lab. Carlsberg* **21**, No. 6 (1936).
132. H. Borsook and J. W. Dubnoff, *J. Biol. Chem.* **131**, 163 (1939).
133. E. J. Conway and A. Byrne, *Biochem. J.* **27**, 419–420 (1933).
134. E. J. Conway, *Biochem. J.* **27**, 430–434 (1933).
135. G. T. Bentley and P. L. Kirk, *Mikrochemie* **21**, 210–217 (1937).
136. J. Needham and E. J. Boell, *Biochem. J.* **33**, 149–152 (1939).

137. E. R. Tompkins and P. L. Kirk, *J. Biol. Chem.* **142**, 477–485 (1942).
138. D. Bruel, H. Holter, K. Linderstrom-Lang, and K. Rozits, *Compt. rend. trav. lab. Carlsberg, Ser. chim.* **25**, 289–324 (1946).
139. W. L. Doyle and J. H. Omoto, *Anal. Chem.* **22**, 603–604 (1950).
140. B. W. Grunbaum, F. L. Schaffer, and P. L. Kirk, *Anal. Chem.* **24**, 1487–1490 (1952).
141. T. S. Ma and G. Zuazaga, *Ind. Eng. Chem., Anal. Ed.* **14**, 280–282 (1942).
142. R. Belcher, T. S. West, and M. Williams, *J. Chem. Soc.* pp. 4323–4328 (1957).
143. R. Belcher and M. K. Bhatty, *Mikrochim. Acta* pp. 1183–1186 (1956).
144. R. Belcher, R. L. Bhasin, and T. S. West, *J. Chem. Soc.* pp. 2585–2587 (1959).
145. R. Belcher, A. D. Campbell, and P. Gouverneur, *J. Chem. Soc.* pp. 531–533 (1963).
146. D. Exley, *Biochem. J.* **63**, 496–501 (1956).
147. O. A. Bessey and O. H. Lowry, *J. Biol. Chem.* **163**, 633 (1946); cf. P. L. Kirk, "Quantitative Ultramicro Analysis" p. 72, Wiley, New York (1950); P. L. Kirk, R. S. Rosenfels, and D. J. Hanahan, *Anal. Chem.* **19**, 355–357 (1947).
148. J. A. Russel, *J. Biol. Chem.* **156**, 457–461 (1944).
149. R. C. Sisco, B. Cunningham, and P. L. Kirk, *J. Biol. Chem.* **139**, 1–10 (1941).
150. H. G. Day, E. Bernstoff, and R. T. Hill, *Anal. Chem.* **21**, 1290–1291 (1949).
151. R. O. E. Davis, *J. Am. Chem. Soc.* **31**, 556–558 (1909).
152. F. L. Dillingham, *J. Am. Chem. Soc.* **36**, 1310–1312 (1914).

CHAPTER IV

Distillation
and Determination
of Nitrogen

The recovery and determination of nitrogen as ammonia may be effected in various ways. Kjeldahl (1) diluted the digest with distilled water, added an excess of fixed alkali, and distilled into a known volume of standard acid. After distillation, the excess of standard acid was determined iodometrically.

$$5 \text{ KI} + \text{KIO}_3 + 3 \text{ H}_2\text{SO}_4 \longrightarrow 3 \text{ I}_2 + 3 \text{ K}_2\text{SO}_4 + 3 \text{ H}_2\text{O}$$

$$\text{I}_2 + 2 \text{ Na}_2\text{S}_2\text{O}_3 \longrightarrow 2 \text{ NaI} + \text{Na}_2\text{S}_4\text{O}_6$$

According to Wilson and Mattingley (2), since carbon dioxide is usually present in the distillate, it is advisable to boil the solution prior to the addition of standard iodide-iodate solution. For this reason, the method is seldom used. However, Michaelis and Maeda (3) state that the iodometric method applied to the microdetermination of nitrogen is to be preferred to the acidimetric method because of the danger of a shift in the endpoint by carbon dioxide absorption is much less.

The most common means of recovery of ammonia is by heat distillation. The digest is diluted with distilled water and cooled. Either solid sodium hydroxide or an excess of a concentrated solution (30%, 40%, 50%) is added to the diluted digest slowly so that two distinct layers are formed. This is necessary, since the heat of reaction of sulfuric acid and sodium hydroxide is great enough to cause loss of ammonia. It is important, therefore, to regulate the densities of the two solutions so that a minimum amount of mixing takes place. Under these conditions, any ammonia so formed will have to pass through the acid layer, thereby being converted again to the sulfate. After addition of the caustic, and without disturbing the layers, the flask is fitted with an efficient trap, and connected to the condenser whose exit tube dips below the surface of the absorbing liquid. The flask is swirled rapidly for complete mixing, and full heat is applied. The heaters should be on full before connecting the flask to minimize the danger of liquid sucking back through the condenser. Immediately after mixing, the flask containing the absorbing medium should be withdrawn momentarily to let the exit tube drain, and to equalize the pressure in the distilling flask. Distillation should be carried out under regulated conditions, i.e. to a specific volume or for a specified length of time. After distillation, the volumes are adjusted so that they are the same before titration. It is also good practice to use a reference solution for comparison of the end point.

The rate of distillation, naturally, is dependent upon the temperature. However, the greater portion of the ammonia will distill over during the first 5 or 10 minutes even with low heat. Fig. 19 shows the recovery of ammonia from simulated digests.

After the introduction of mercury as a catalyst, it was found that distillation of ammonia was incomplete by the sample addition of caustic, due to the fact that mercury formed a complex with am-

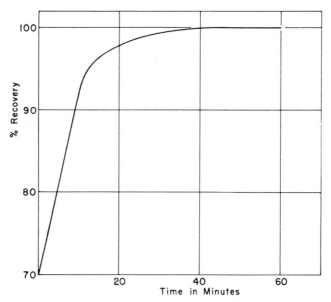

FIG. 19. Recovery of ammonia.

monia. A solution of potassium sulfide (4) added prior to the caustic destroyed the complex and allowed recovery of ammonia. The Official Agricultural Chemists (5), also, incorporated the addition of potassium sulfide (25 ml of a solution containing 40 gm of sulfide (liter) in the official modified procedure. The present official method (6) specifies 25 ml of potassium sulfide (40 gm per liter) or 25 ml of sodium thiosulfate (80 gm $Na_2S_2O_3 \cdot 5H_2O$ per liter) when 0.7 gm mercuric oxide or 0.65 gm of metallic mercury is used as a catalyst. Davis and Wise (7) found that for 1 gm of mercury, approximately 0.2 gm of $Na_2S_2O_3 \cdot 5H_2O$ are necessary when the precipitating agent is added with the alkali. When using sodium sulfide, a slight excess over the required amount is satisfactory, but apparently with sodium thiosulfate, a large excess is preferable. With the sulfide, a black precipitate indicates sufficient reagent. Thiosulfate gives a black precipitate with a brownish cast. If not enough reagent has been added, the precipitate is definitely brownish. The extent to which thiosulfate must be added to the diluted digest is shown in Table XXVII. Simulated digests were

TABLE XXVII
THIOSULFATE NECESSARY TO INACTIVATE MERCURY CATALYST

		% Nitrogen	
$Na_2S_2O_3 \cdot 5H_2O$ (ml)	$Na_2S_2O_3 \cdot 5H_2O$ (gm)	Found	Recovery
25	2	20.76	97.98
25	2	21.03	99.15
25	2	20.76	97.98
25	2	20.78	97.97
25	2	20.73	97.74
30	2.4	20.95	98.77
30	2.4	20.96	98.82
40	3.2	20.95	98.77
40	3.2	20.93	98.68
50	4.0	21.09	99.43
50	4.0	21.11	99.53

prepared containing 35 ml sulfuric acid, 20 gm potassium sulfate, 0.55 gm mercury, and 0.1000 gm of ammonium sulfate. These were diluted with 200 ml of distilled water. Varying amounts of thiosulfate and 170 ml of 35% sodium hydroxide were added. These diluted digests were then distilled into boric acid. The calculated percent of nitrogen in ammonium sulfate is 21.21%. It is apparent, therefore, that at least 4 gm of thiosulfate should be added to the diluted digest in order to effect complete recovery of nitrogen.

Salm and Prager (8) studying the influence of various reagents used in digestion and distillation reported that when mercury was used as a digestion catalyst, correct results could be obtained on distillation by addition of zinc powder. However, it is stated that the degree of fineness of the zinc affects the recovery of nitrogen; and that for maximum recovery, the zinc should be in the form of a very fine powder. When potassium sulfide is used, the addition of zinc shavings is sufficient. Hiller, Plazin, and Van Slyke (9) giving detailed digestion and distillation procedures for macro- and microanalysis of proteins, use mercuric sulfate as a catalyst, and zinc dust to reduce the mercuric oxide to mercury during distillation.

Mercury and salts of mercury are apparently the only commonly used catalysts that require a pretreatment before distillation.

The collection of ammonia from the distillation is frequently made by absorption in an excess of standard acid and determined by a back titration with a standard alkali solution using methyl red as an indicator. More common practice is the use of boric acid for the absorption of ammonia, which has the advantage that only one standard solution is necessary. It was first introduced by Winkler (10) who used a concentration of 5 gm/100 ml to absorb the ammonia with methyl orange or Congo red as indicators. This amount (100 ml) of solution will absorb up to 0.1 gm of NH_3. At ordinary laboratory temperatures, a saturated solution contains between 4 and 5% of the acid, and for the usual macro-Kjeldahl procedure, 25 ml is generally sufficient.

Scales and Harrison (11) confirmed Winkler's modification by comparison with results obtained using an excess of standard acid, and concluded that the accuracy was at least as great as that obtained with a back titration. Bromophenol blue was considered to be a better indicator than those previously employed. A comparative study of the two methods was also made by Markley and Hann (12), confirming previous studies. Experiments were also conducted to determine at what temperature the ammonium borate in the receiving flask would decompose. Samples of ammonia in boric acid heated at various temperatures for 30 minutes showed no appreciable loss at 50°C, 1.29% at 60°C, and 65.25% at 100°C. Spears (13) also found good agreement between methods. The ammonia was distilled into 50 ml of 4% boric acid using bromophenol blue as the indicator. For micro-Kjeldahl determinations, Staver and Sandin (14) absorb the ammonia in 4 ml of 2% boric acid and titrate with 0.014 N acid, using a mixed indicator of methyl red and tetrabromophenol blue.

Reith and Klazinga (15) believe that more accurate results are obtained with the boric acid modification, and use as an indicator a mixture of one part of 1% methyl red, three parts of 1% bromocresol green, and four parts of distilled water. The color change is from blue-gray to violet-red. An indicator recommended by Willits, John, and Ross (16) as the most satisfactory for use with boric acid — since it changes at the exact stoichiometrical point of 4.7 pH — is composed of a 4:1 mixture of methyl red-methylene blue at a concentration of 0.1% in alcohol. The color change is to gray at the neutral point.

Benzoyl auramine G has been suggested as an acid-base indicator by Scanlan and Reid (17). The color change is from intense violet at pH 5.0 to pale yellow at pH 5.6, passing through an intermediate gray at pH 5.4 when used in daylight. By artificial light, the change is from an intense red to pale red to pale yellow. The indicator is prepared by benzoylation of auramine G base. The indicator hydrolyzes in both acidic and basic solutions, and therefore should not be added until the solutions are ready for titration. It is used in a concentration of 0.25% in ethanol.

Green and Pellard (18) state that in the presence of bases, the buffering action of boric acid increases with its concentration at a rate that appreciably affects the end point of the ammonia titration. When solutions of high concentration are used, a greater transition period is observed for methyl red, methylene blue-methyl red, and bromocresol green. With a concentration not exceeding 1% of boric acid the foregoing indicators gave sharp end points. It might be pointed out, however, that the concentration of boric acid at the end of a distillation is normally in the range of ±1%, if 25 ml of 4% or saturated solution are used and 100–150 ml of distillate collected.

A method of titration using boric acid solution containing methyl red is suggested by Wagner (19). Each liter of 4% boric acid contains 2 ml of 0.05% methyl red prepared by dissolving the indicator in one part of methanol and adding two parts of water. It is stated that no sharp color change occurs during the titration with either 0.01 or 0.1 N acid, and that the maximum color is reached beyond the equivalence point. At the proper end point the intensity of the indicator color is the same as the boric acid-methyl red solution diluted to the same extent as the distillate being titrated. This is used as a reference solution. In a previous paper (20), it was pointed out that addition of an equivalent amount of an ammonium salt to the reference solution is not necessary since the salt effect is negligible. For the macro distillation 50 ml of 4% boric acid and 2–4 drops of 0.1 methyl red are used; for the microdistillation, 5 ml of 4% boric acid and 2 drops of 0.05% methyl red are used, maintaining a final volume of 35–40 ml.

The choice of an indicator is to some extent a matter of preference except that whatever indicator is used, its transition range must include the equivalence point. In the case of back titration of a distillate, the equivalence point will occur at pH 7, since this is the point of neutralization of a strong acid by a strong base. Any indicator, therefore, changing color at or close to pH 7 is suitable. The titration of boric acid distillates represents the neutralization of a weak base with a strong acid, the equivalence point appearing in the acid range, ca. pH 5. Consequently, an indicator changing in slightly acid solution at or near this equivalence point can be used. Titration of ammonia in boric acid solution using a mixed indicator is often advantageous. Generally the color change is sharper and the transition range shorter. When the pH interval is narrow, no reference solution need be used.

According to Yuen and Pollard (21) the buffer capacity of boric acid in the presence of bases increases with its concentration. In the micro-procedure, indicators such as methylene blue and methyl red, at the higher concentrations of boric acid, show a wide transitional range. Sharp end points, however, are obtained with the usual indicators at a concentration of 1%. This allows fixation of 5 mg of ammonia per 10 ml, and of 90 mg per 100 ml of 2% boric acid.

The stability of boric acid solutions has been examined by Eisner and Wagner (22). Freshly prepared 4% boric acid solutions were placed in clean bottles of lime glass and Pyrex. At regular intervals samples were talken, methyl red indicator added, and the color compared with a standard containing the same proportion of boric acid solution and indicator. No deterioration was noticeable after 197 days with the solution kept in Pyrex. The solution kept in lime glass, after the same length of time showed a measurable difference, and when used in a micro titration required 0.02 ml of 0.01 N acid to adjust the color to that of the standard.

Miller (23) points out that there is loss of ammonia during the first few minutes of distillation and proposed a delivery tube containing numerous small holes so that large bubbles would be easily broken up, and the ammonia more readily absorbed. However, in repeating these experiments, Speirs and Mitchell (24) did not duplicate Miller's findings.

The absorption of ammonia in distilled water alone, has been employed to some extent. Fridman and Komissaiova (25) neutralize the digest with 20% sodium carbonate until alkaline to methyl orange, dilute to 300 ml with distilled water, and add 3 gm of solid sodium bicarbonate. After 150 ml of distillate have been obtained, the solution is titrated with standard acid using 4–6 drops of a mixture of 0.1% dimethyl yellow and 0.1% methylene blue in ethanol. Schulek *et al.* (26) also confirm that milligram amounts of ammonia can be absorbed in water and titrated directly, without loss.

A procedure for the distillation of ammonia in a closed system has been described by Bradley (27). A suction flask is attached to the delivery tube and acts as the receiver. The side arm is fitted with a rubber balloon to equalize the pressure. Under these conditions, ammonia is distilled into the receiver and titrated directly using methyl orange as an indicator. From 70 to 200 mg of ammonia can be determined in this manner. A minimum of 99.9% recovery is reported. Chand (28) also used this closed system, but distilled the ammonia into both boric acid in freshly boiled water and standard sulfuric acid. The reported results were slightly higher than those from the usual procedure.

A diffusion technique for the micro-determination of nitrogen has been reported by Howes and Skavinski (29). The digestion is carried out in a Pyrex test tube, and the amount of digest is kept below 0.5 ml. This is diluted with 0.6 ml of water and cooled. Addition of 0.3 ml of 50% sodium hydroxide is made without mixing. The receiver is a platinum helix formed by five turns of 22 gage wire around a glass rod to which the ends are sealed. The glass rod is held by a rubber stopper which, in turn, fits the test tube. The helix is dipped in a 1.0 M solution of monobasic sodium phosphate and inserted in the test tube. The contents of the tube are mixed and the entire assembly left overnight on its side, during which time the ammonia diffuses and is absorbed by the phosphate. The receiver assembly is removed, placed in 1 ml of water and the solution titrated.

Kuck *et al.* (30) determining extremely small amounts of nitric acid esters in the atmosphere also used the diffusion method.

Another means of recovering ammonia, which at one time was given considerable attention, is by aeration. The method, devised by Kober (31) and shown schematically in Fig. 20, draws concentrated alkali into the cooled, diluted digest. Ammonia is liberated and absorbed in standard acid. Air is drawn through the system at the rate of 400–600 liters per hour. During the addition of alkali, the flask was cooled in a water bath. Good results were claimed. At the same time Sebelien *et al.* (32) published a paper on a procedure which was iden-

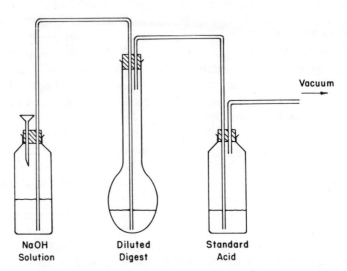

Vacuum

NaOH   Diluted   Standard
Solution   Digest   Acid

FIG. 20. Schematic diagram for aeration.

tical with Kober's. Further work with this method was done by Davis
(33) on cottonseed meal. Low results were obtained. However, if the
flask were insulated with asbestos, the solution after addition of alkali
remained warm throughout the period of aeration which took a
minimum of 1 hour. Heating of the flask and also addition of
aluminum was found necessary for complete recovery of ammonia.
Gill and Grindley (34) compared Kober's method with the official
method of the AOAC. Good agreement was obtained except with
natural products such as cottonseed meal, wheat bran, rice feed, linseed oil meal, and also magnesium ammonium phosphate solutions.
These authors believe that the relatively large amounts of magnesium
and phosphorus present in natural products tend to give low results
with the method. If the flask is warmed during aeration, the results
more nearly approach true values. Dillingham (35), also, used the
aeration method on ammonium sulfate and reported no quantitative
recovery of nitrogen. In all cases the variation was from 3 to 15%
low. This residual nitrogen could be recovered either by steam distillation or by heating the flask over a small flame and continuing
aeration. When the latter procedure was followed and with an aeration
rate of 360 liters per hour maintained for 90 minutes, 99.8% recovery
was possible. Falk and Lugiura (36) conducted an extensive study of
the aeration method. A comparison with the heat distillation method
was made using 20 ml of concentrated sulfuric acid, 10 gm of potassium sulfate and 0.2 gm of anhydrous copper sulfate as the digestion

mixture. All digests were boiled for 1 hour after clearing. A period of 2 hours for aeration was established at a rate of 330–340 liters per hour. After aeration, each sample was subjected to heat distillation. The results in Table XXVIII are taken in part from Falk and Lugiura.

The over-all results showed a variation of 0.40 to 1.50%, and due to their uncertainty, the method was considered unreliable. More recently, Meldrum, Melampy, and Meyers (37) used aeration for the recovery of nitrogen in N-butyramide. The volume at the start of the distillation, after dilution and addition of caustic, was 250 ml. From the data obtained by varying both the aeration rate (0.2–0.8 liter per minute) and temperature (25°–100°C), and holding the distillation time at 20 minutes, 99.8% recovery was obtained at 100°C and an air flow rate of 0.8 liter per minute. At 90°C and 250 ml volume, recovery is complete in 60 minutes. When the ratio of aeration is doubled (i.e. 1.6 liters per minute), distillation is complete in 13 minutes. In a study of the application of the Kjeldahl method to various types of nitrogen linkage, Phelps and Daudt (38) compared the aeration procedure with the usual distillation. The apparatus for aeration is constructed with a divided air line so that the diluted digest is kept agitated while the caustic is admitted to the flask by air pressure at any predetermined rate. When as much as 0.24 gm of ammonium sulfate are present in 15–20 ml of sulfuric acid diluted with 75 ml of water and alkalinized with 125 ml of saturated sodium hydroxide, complete recovery of ammonia is effected in 25 minutes at room temperature and at an aeration

TABLE XXVIII

COMPARISON OF AERATION AND
HEAT DISTILLATION METHODS FOR THE RECOVERY OF NITROGEN

Sample	% N Calc.	% Nitrogen found with		
		Aeration	Aeration plus heat distillation	Heat distillation
Casein	—	14.65	15.16	15.12
		14.62	15.10	
Castor bean preparation	—	16.46	17.05	17.04
		16.75	17.11	
Tyrosine	7.74	7.44	7.71	7.66
		7.54	7.64	
Alanine	15.73	15.17	15.68	15.73
		15.48	15.76	
Urea	46.66	44.69	46.60	46.58
		44.99	46.54	
Uric acid	33.33	32.86	33.27	33.39
		32.78	33.34	

rate of 850 liters per minute. When a lesser amount of acid is present (10 ml), the diluted digest must be heated almost to boiling before addition of caustic and subsequent aeration. Aside from the possible physical advantages of aeration over the usual distillation procedure, there is no difference in nitrogen recovery.

When an ammonium salt and formaldehyde are reacted in neutral solution, hexamethylenetetramime and free acid are formed. This reaction is the basis of a method for determination of formaldehyde, and, conversely, for the determination of ammonia.

$$2(NH_4)_2SO_4 + 6HCHO \rightarrow (CH_2)_6N_4 + 2H_2SO_4 + 6H_2O$$

The advantage of this procedure is that no distillation is required. The digest is sufficiently diluted, carefully neutralized, formaldehyde added, and the acid formed is titrated with standard alkali. Rona and Ottenberg (39) used this method for the determination of nitrogen in urine. Digestion was carried out on a 5 ml sample with 10 ml of sulfuric acid and 5 drops of chlorplatinic acid as a catalyst. The digest is neutralized with standard alkali after diluting with 100 ml of water, and adding 6–7 drops of litmus solution. After addition of 30 ml of neutral formaldehyde and 1 ml of 0.5% phenolphthalein solution, titration is continued to an end point which is indicated by the appearance of a violet color. A comparison of the usual Kjeldahl distillation method and the formaldehyde modification was made by Wright (40) on such materials as meat extracts, dried blood, fertilizers, and tankage. Wright used only phenolphthalein as the indicator for neutralization of the digest and titration of the acid formed. Simpson (41) makes reference to Hermann's reaction (42), which is a method for determining formaldehyde by addition of excess of an ammonium salt. The digest is neutralized with standard alkali using methyl orange as an indicator. Before adding neutral formaldehyde, the solution is boiled to expel carbon dioxide. Titration of the liberated acid was made with 0.1 N alkali, using phenolphthalein as the indicator. Simpson used this procedure successfully on mixtures of ammonium salts with alkali hydroxides, carbonates, and bicarbonates, organic compounds, and sodium ammonium hydrogen phosphate. Shaw (43) applied the formol titration to both macro and semi-micro procedures. Copper sulfate was used as a catalyst in the macro digestion. For the semi-micro digestion, 1 gm of potassium sulfate, 0.02 gm of copper sulfate, 2 drops of 2.5% platinum chloride, and 5 ml of sulfuric acid were used. After digestion, 40% sodium hydroxide is cautiously added, cooling meanwhile, until the solution is only slightly acid. It is then diluted to 250 ml. A 25 ml aliquot is taken for titration. An excess of 0.1 N alkali is added, and the sample titrated with 0.1 N acid until just acid, using phenolphthalein as an indicator. Carbon dioxide is expelled by boiling. The solution is cooled rapidly and 0.1 N alkali added until an end point is reached. After addition of 55 ml of formaldehyde, the solution is allowed to stand for several minutes, and then titrated to the original phenolphthalein end point. A correction is made for the acidity of the formaldehyde. For the semi-micro procedure, the quantities and normalities are modified to conform with the smaller amounts of samples and solutions. In stead of the usual Kjeldahl flask, Marcali and Rieman (44) use a 500 ml round bottom flask with a 24/40 standard taper neck into which is fitted a 20 cm tube, for digestion. This allows removal of the tube, and subsequent titration of the sample in the flask. Digestion is carried out with 10 gm potassium sulfate, 15 ml sulfuric acid, and 0.6–0.7 gm mercuric oxide. A 20 minute boil period after clearing was used. After digestion the flask is cooled and 50 ml of water added. When the digest is completely dissolved, 10 ml of 60% sodium bromide are added. This serves to complex the mercury used as a catalyst and prevent precipitation. The sulfuric acid is neutralized with 10 N sodium hydroxide until the solution is just basic to methyl red. Normal sulfuric acid is added until the indicator turns pink and the solution is boiled to remove carbon dioxide, after which it is titrated with 0.1 N alkali to the methyl red end point. Formaldehyde, 30 ml of 18% solution, and 8 drops of phenolphthalein are added and the titration continued to an end point. The difference between the methyl red and phenolphthalein end points is the amount of standard alkali equivalent to the nitrogen present. It is stated that when more than 17 ml of acid remain in the digest that sufficient silica is introduced as an impurity of the sodium hydroxide to act as a buffer and prevent a sharp color change in the indicator. The presence of calcium, barium, iron, copper, or other elements that form insoluble hydroxides also tend to obscure the end point. Phosphorus (e.g. in fertilizers) interferes since between the methyl red and phenolphthalein end points the primary phosphate is titrated to the secondary phosphate. In a later paper (45), these authors give a procedure for elimination of phosphate interference. After the digestion and dilution with the water, the solution is transferred to a 250 ml volumetric flask, 15 ml of 60% sodium bromide, and 5 ml of 1 M zirconyl chloride (322 gm zirconyl chloride octahydrate dissolved in 600 ml of 1 N hydrochloric acid, further diluted to a liter with 1 N hydrochloric acid). Zirconyl chloride will also react with any carbonate present so that boiling to expel carbon dioxide is unnecessary. Ten normal sodium hydroxide is added dropwise until the solution is basic to methyl red, and normal sulfuric acid is then added until the indicator becomes pink. The solution is cooled and made up to volume at room temperature. After filtering, an aliquot of 100 ml is taken for titration using the same procedure as noted above. Adams and Spaulding (46) modified the Marcali and Rieman method so that selenium could be used as a catalyst. Digestion was carried out in 100 ml Kjeldahl flasks with 7.5 gm of potassium sulfate, 12.5 ml of sulfuric acid, one selenized granule, and 0.5 gm of sample. After digestion, 50 ml of water and 1 ml of sulfurous acid are added, and the solution is boiled for 30 minutes to precipitate the selenium. After cooling, it is transferred to a 25 ml volumetric flask and made up to volume. A 50 ml aliquot is taken for the titration. This is adjusted to pH 5 with 8 N sodium hydroxide and to pH 6.8 with 0.2 N alkali. Neutral formaldehyde, 12 ml of an 18% solution, is added. The pH will drop, after 10 minutes, to about 4.4. The solution is then titrated with 0.2 N sodium hydroxide using phenolphthalein as an indicator. Addition of formaldehyde at a pH of 6.8–6.9 was found most suitable. A lower pH gave lower values. A period of 10 minutes was necessary to allow the pH to reach the lowest value.

Another method of estimating nitrogen, and not involving distillation, is that of Chang (47). After the usual digestion in which selenium is used as a catalyst, the digest is diluted to 100 ml with distilled water. A 20 ml aliquot is taken and carefully neutralized to a phenolphthalein end point first with 30% caustic and finally with 0.1 N NaOH. An excess of 20 ml of 0.1 N caustic is added and the solution boiled for one hour. Excess caustic is then titrated with 0.1 N acid. Reported results indicate a deviation from distillation procedure between 0.94% and 2.13%.

The use of hypohalites for the determination of ammonia and as general oxidizing agents extends back for a considerable period. Solutions of hypochlorite and hypobromite should be prepared and stored under controlled conditions. Since both solutions deteriorate with time, they should be kept in brown bottles in a cool place and should always be restandardized just before use. Of the two, the hypochlorite is more stable. The determination of ammonia takes place in the following manner:

$$2\ NH_3\ +\ 3\ NaOBr\ \longrightarrow\ 3\ NaBr\ +\ N_2\ +\ 3\ H_2O$$

$$NaOBr\ (excess)\ +\ 2\ KI\ +\ 2\ HCl\ \longrightarrow\ 2\ KCl\ +\ NaBr\ +\ I_2\ +\ H_2O$$

$$I_2\ +\ 2\ Na_2S_2O_3\ \longrightarrow\ Na_2S_4O_6\ +\ 2\ NaI$$

Willard and Cake (48) appear to be the first to apply the above reaction to the Kjeldahl process. A standard 0.6 N hypobromite solution was prepared as follows: 50 gm of bromine were added slowly with stirring to a solution of 30 gm of sodium hydroxide in 800 ml of water, which must be kept well cooled during the addition. The solution is kept in the dark at as low a temperature as possible. It is standardized before use with standard sodium thiosulfate which in turn has been standardized with potassium dichromate. Over a period of a week at 0°–5°C, the change in normality was negligible. After digestion of the sample with 15 ml of sulfuric acid and oxidation with potassium persulfate, the digest is diluted with 70 ml of water and boiled to remove sulfur dioxide. After cooling, the solution is neutralized with 10 N alkali using methyl orange or methyl red as indicator. The solution should be cooled during addition of alkali to avoid any possible loss of ammonia. Enough hypobromite is added so that not over two thirds are reduced by the ammonia. Evolution of nitrogen takes place and after standing 5 minutes, 5 gm of potassium iodide and 6 ml of hydrochloric acid are added. The titration is completed with thiosulfate, using starch as an indicator. If iron is present, 1 ml of phosphoric acid should be added with the iodide and hydrochloric acid. Haanappl (49) states that the reaction of ammonia with hypobromite is not affected by the large amounts of sodium sulfate formed by the neutralization of the digest. After making up to a specified volume a 50 ml aliquot is buffered with 20 ml of a 4% borax solution. Standard 0.1 N hypobromite, 25 ml, is added, and after evolution of nitrogen, 10 ml of normal potassium iodide and 5 ml of 4 N hydrochloric acid are added. The liberated iodine is titrated with 0.1 N thiosulfate. For the micro-Kjeldahl determination of nitrogen in milk, Ling (50) used the following procedure: after digestion, in which copper sulfate was used as a catalyst, 1 ml of water is added and the digest boiled to remove sulfur dioxide. When cool, 10 ml of water are added and the solution again cooled to room temperature. It is neutralized with 4 N sodium hydroxide containing 30.9 gm of boric acid per liter, until a blue precipitate of copper hydroxide forms, then 1 ml in excess is added. When cool, 5 ml of hypobromite are added. This is freshly prepared by adding 8 gm of potassium bromide dissolved in water to 400 ml of 4 N sodium hydroxide containing 1 ml of bromine, and making up to a volume of one liter. After standing 2 minutes, the nitrogen is determined iodometrically. Ashraf, Bhatty, and Shah (51), after digestion in which mercury was used as a catalyst, neutralize dropwise with 60% alkali until a yellow precipitate of mercuric oxide is formed, and complete neutralization with sodium bicarbonate. Potassium bromide, 4 gm, is added and the solution shaken until clear. Enough 0.2 N sodium hypochlorite is added to produce a yellow color, and the solution allowed to stand for 5 minutes. An excess of 0.01 N arsenious oxide is added and back titrated with hypochlorite using Bordeaux indicator. Results obtained with this procedure are stated to be within ±0.2% of theory. A comparison of this method with the AOAC procedure (52) gave results within experimental error. In further work on the micro and semimicro determination of nitrogen (53), the same procedure was used with the exceptions that the amount of potassium bromide added was 2 gm and the normality of hypochlorite was 0.02 or 0.05 N. A 0.05% aqueous solution of tartrazine is used as an indicator. Both Bordeaux and tartrazine are excellent indicators for the hypohalite titration. The former is irreversible, the color changing from pink to a yellowish-green while the latter is reversible with the color changing from yellow to colorless. The addition of bromide serves several purposes. It is necessary when either mercury or copper is used as a catalyst, and apparently when hypochlorite is used as a titrant, since possible oxidation to nitrogen and nitrogen oxides can occur (54). Hypochlorite solutions are more stable than those of hypobromite. However, in the presence of bromide ions, a hypochlorite solution will produce the same effect as that of hypobromite. Kolthoff and Stenger (55) recommend the use of calcium hypochlorite because of its greater stability, and titrate the ammonia in a solution faintly alkaline with sodium bicarbonate. To 25 ml of solution having a nitrogen content of 5–25 mg is added 10 ml of a 10% potassium bromide solution containing 5% sodium bicarbonate. Calcium hypochlorite (0.1 N) is added until the solution appears yellow. After standing for 3–5 minutes, 10 ml of 0.01 N sodium arsenite are added and the solution shaken well. Bordeaux indicator (0.2% in water), 0.05 ml, is added and should give a pink color. If not, more arsenite and indicator must be added. The titration is completed with hypochlorite solution. For a total volume of 50 ml, the indicator correction for 0.0 ml is equivalent to 0.02 ml of 0.1 N hypochlorite plus a constant increase of 0.01 ml for each 50 ml.

The detection and estimation of extremely small quantities of nitrogen, as ammonia, can be made by the use of Nessler's reagent. This is potassium mercuric iodide in alkaline solution, and its reaction with ammonia produces a yellow color with small amounts, orange with large amounts, and a brown precipitate when very large amounts are present. The following reactions are involved in preparation and formation of the ammonia complex:

$$HgCl_2 + 2\ KI \longrightarrow 2\ KCl + HgI_2$$

$$HgI_2 + 2\ KI \longrightarrow K_2(HgI_4)$$

$$2\ K_2(HgI_4) + 3\ KOH + NH_3 \longrightarrow O\underset{Hg}{\overset{Hg}{\diagdown\diagup}}NH_2\!-\!I + 2\ H_2O + 7\ KI$$

This reagent, first reported in 1856, is widely used in water analysis, or where small amounts of ammonia are to be determined. It is relatively stable, but should be checked at intervals. Generally, in the Kjeldahl method, it is used to estimate ammonia in the distillate although there are examples of direct determination on the diluted digest. Since iron, magnesium, and manganese interfere by causing a cloudy solution, this procedure is not useful unless the composition of the sample is known. There are various ways of preparing Nessler's reagent, although probably most common is addition of mercuric chloride to a fairly concentrated solution of potassium iodide until a permanent red color is obtained. Potassium hydroxide solution is added, and the mixture made up to specified volume with ammonia-free water. Koch and McMeekin (56) using a micro-Kjeldahl procedure, prepared a modified Nessler reagent by adding 22.5 gm of iodine to a solution of 30 gm of potassium iodide in 20 ml of water. Thirty grams of mercury are added and the mixture shaken and cooled under the tap until the yellow color has disappeared. This is diluted to 200 ml and poured into 975 ml of 10% sodium hydroxide. For the determination of ammonia in water, by distillation (57), the reagent can be prepared using mercuric iodide: 100 gm of mercuric iodide and 70 gm of potassium iodide are dissolved in a small quantity of ammonia-free water. One hundred grams of sodium hydroxide in 500 ml of water are added slowly, with stirring. After mixing, the solution is diluted to one liter. Stored in Pyrex, and kept in the dark, the reagent is stable for about a year, and should give the characteristic color with ammonia within 10 minutes after addition, and no precipitate with small amounts within 2 hours. Numerous slight variations in the preparation of Nessler's reagent appear in the literature, which, however, do not change the basic structure of the reagent. The relative instability of the color complex is stated to be partially overcome by the addition of a protective colloid such as gum arabic (58, 59). The actual determination of ammonia can be made visually, colorimetrically, or spectrophotometrically. Visual determination is made in 50 ml Nessler tubes. The color is developed by adding the reagent to 50 ml of either distillate or neutralized digest, representing the whole or an aliquot. The developed colors are compared with freshly prepared standards. Comparisons are made after the same time of standing. A photoelectric colorimeter having a blue filter with a wavelength of 400–425 mμ can be used, and, in this case, a standard curve must be prepared. The conditions under which the color of the samples is developed must be the same as those of the standards. Spectrophotometrically, either absorbance or transmittance is read at the selected wavelength, and the representative amount of nitrogen taken from a standard curve. Hale, Hale, and Jones (60) use this procedure for the semi-micro determination of very small amounts of nitrogen present in petroleum feed stocks and other petroleum products. Ammonia is steam distilled until exactly 50 ml of distillate are obtained. The entire distillate, or an aliquot, is treated with 1 ml of Nessler's reagent, mixed well and allowed to stand from 5 minutes to one hour. The absorbances at three wavelengths, 450, 475, and 500 mμ, are read and the results, taken from the three standard curves, are averaged. It was observed by these authors that in using a Coleman Model 11 Universal spectrophotometer the straight line relationship of absorbance to concentration tended to curve slightly at the higher concentrations, hence by taking the readings at three different wavelengths and averaging, the errors of measurement were reduced. Burck (61) reads absorbance at the single wavelength of 450 mμ. After digestion with sulfuric acid and oxidation with hydrogen peroxide in a micro-Kjeldahl flask calibrated to 50 ml, the mixture is diluted to the mark with distilled water. An aliquot is taken, 2 ml of Nessler's solution added, and diluted to volume. After mixing and standing for exactly 15 minutes, the absorbance is read. West and Brandon (62) digest with acid using selenium oxychloride as a catalyst. The resulting digest is diluted to volume and nesslerized. The results from this procedure compare favorably with those obtained when peroxide is used.

A micro-Kjeldahl method described by Van Slyke (63) determines the nitrogen gasometrically. The sample is digested with a 3:1 mixture of sulfuric acid-phosphoric acid and potassium persulfate. After digestion, 3 ml of water and one drop of 1% alizarin sulfonate are added. Forty percent sodium hydroxide is added dropwise until the indicator changes, and the digest again made just acid with 10% sulfuric acid. The solution is transferred to the Van Slyke-Neill (64) blood gas apparatus, and the digestion tube washed with water so that the total volume is 10 ml. The gas chamber is evacuated and shaken 2 minutes to remove air from the solution; this is repeated if necessary.

A 1.5 ml volume of hypobromite solution is pipetted into the cup and 1 ml is allowed to run into the chamber. The chamber is removed and the stop cock sealed with mercury. The apparatus is evacuated and shaken for 2–3 minutes. The gas volume is then adjusted to 2 ml, and the pressure (p_1) and temperature are read. The gas is expelled from the chamber and the pressure (p_2) again read at 2 ml. Milligrams of nitrogen are calculated from the following equation:

$$\text{mg N} = (p_1 - p_2 - C) \times f$$

p_1 = total pressure in millimeters at 2 ml volume
p_2 = pressure after expelling gas and adjusting volume to 2 ml
$C = (p_1 - p_2)$ obtained from a blank determination
f = factor for conversion of 1 mm pressure to milligrams of nitrogen

A partial table of the conversion factor f taken from Van Slyke's article appears in Table XXIX.

TABLE XXIX
CONVERSION FACTORS FOR NITROGEN

T°C	Factor
20	0.003192
21	80
22	68
23	56
24	45
25	36
26	24
27	16
28	04
29	0.003092
30	80

Solutions of hypobromite tend to decompose on standing. Van Slyke found that the most satisfactory was one containing 1 ml of bromine in 50 ml of 40% sodium hydroxide.

For the determination of nonprotein nitrogen in blood, Stehle (65) used the gasometric method, first digesting with acid, sulfate, and copper sulfate as a catalyst. During the gasometric determination, oxygen was evolved necessitating removal by alkaline pyrogallol before the nitrogen could be estimated. In a later paper (66), Stehle found that copper reacted with the hypobromite solution to produce appreciable amounts of oxygen. To overcome the difficulty of spontaneous generation of oxygen in the alkaline hypobromite, separate solutions of caustic and bromine in potassium bromide were used. Van Slyke found, however, that after mixing, the solution generated more oxygen than the single Br-NaOH solution. It was found (67) that a stable reagent could be prepared by dissolving 60 gm of potassium bromide in 100 ml of water, and adding 2.5 ml of bromine. For use, 1.25 ml of 40% sodium hydroxide are placed in the cup, and 0.75 ml of the bromine solution placed in the cup.

Several other means are available for the determination of nitrogen. Taylor and Smith (68) absorb the ammonia from distillation in 4% boric acid and determine the nitrogen (or ammonia) by the change in pH. The volume of boric acid must be measured exactly. A dilution of 10 ml of boric acid to 150 ml was considered suitable, since at this point, addition of 10 ml of water changed the pH by only ±0.01, which can be considered to be within the precision of the usual laboratory pH meter. A calibration curve must be prepared from standard ammonium hydroxide by addition to the 10 ml of boric acid and further dilution to 150 ml; the pH of the solutions is taken. The amount of ammonia or nitrogen can then be plotted against the pH. After distillation into the boric acid, the volume is made up to 150 ml and a pH taken. The amount of ammonia or nitrogen is determined from the standard curve. The curve should be checked whenever a fresh solution of boric acid is used.

The phenol-hypochlorite reaction for the detection of ammonia is more sensitive than Nessler's solution. Thomas (69) reported it as one part in two million. One milliliter of a 4% phenol solution in water is mixed with 5 ml of the test solution, and 1–2 drops of Javelle water are added. Ammonia is present if a blue color is developed in 15–30 minutes. Orr (70) used this reaction for the direct estimation of ammonia in urine. In this case, 4.5 gm of phenol were added directly to 5 ml of diluted urine (20 ml diluted to 100 ml with water). To this were added 20 ml of sodium hypochlorite solution (one volume of freshly prepared commercial hypochlorite and one volume of water). After standing 5 minutes the solution is poured into a 250 ml volumetric flask containing 100 ml of water, made up to volume, and compared with a standard. Murray (71) also used this procedure for blood urea, and Van Slyke and Hiller (72) for ammonia in blood. The latter authors use a 5 ml sample (which has been suitably processed), to which is added 1 ml of sodium phenate solution made by dissolving 25 gm of phenol in a small amount of water, adding 50 ml of 40% sodium hydroxide, and diluting to 100 ml with water. The hypochlorite solution is prepared by dissolving 50 gm of calcium hypochlorite in 500 ml of water; this is then added to a solution of 50 gm of anhydrous potassium carbonate in 200 ml of cold water, and made up to one liter. After the addition of sodium phenate, 0.5 ml of the hypochlorite solution is added, mixed, and placed in a boiling water bath for 3 minutes, cooled to room temperature with cold water. The color intensity is compared with standards.

The determination of trace nitrogen in petroleum in the range of parts per million has been made by Noble (73). After digestion of the sample with sulfuric acid, it is distilled into 20 ml of water and 2 drops of 0.5 N sulfuric acid. Distillation is continued until bumping occurs. This volume of distillate is evaporated to 20 ml and washed into a 50 ml glass-stoppered graduate, the total volume being 40 ml. Five milliliters of an 8% phenol in water solution are added and mixed well; then 5 ml of sodium hypochlorite solution (Clorox, 5.25% by weight of hypochlorite) are added and mixed well. The cylinders are placed in a boiling water bath for 6–8 minutes (optimum time is reported to be 7 minutes), removed, and cooled quickly under the tap. Absorbance is read at 610 mμ using 1 cm cells, and the amount of nitrogen taken from a standard curve. The specified volumes and order of reagent addition are critical. If the reagents are added to less than 40 ml of transferred distillate and the volume made up to 50 ml and heated, a more intense color is developed. This is also true if the color is first developed and subsequently diluted to 50 ml. It is stated that neither the phenol nor the hypochlorite concentration is too critical—relative to the amounts specified. Milner *et al.* (74) used this procedure for the estimation of trace quantities of nitrogen in petroleum fractions. These authors found that the volume of hypochlorite necessary was less than that recommended by Noble (5 ml). Since the concentration of hypochlorite affects the intensity of the color, the optimum concentration or volume which will give maximum color intensity should be determined. Since this method requires strict attention to details, Milner and Zahner (75) modified the procedure by distilling 100 ml directly into 25 ml of 0.15% boric acid and titrating with 0.01 N sulfamic acid using methyl red-Alphazurine as an indicator (76). The color change is from green-gray to gray to purple-gray, and both the color change and the end point are sharp. The indicator solution is prepared by dissolving 0.45 gm of methyl red and 0.55 gm of Alphazurine in distilled water and diluting to one liter.

A coulometric method based on the determination of ammonia by hypobromite is described by Arcand and Swift (77). Bromine is generated electrolytically, at an indicator potential of 120 mv and a pH of 8.5. When the current is stabilized, at 10 μamp, 2 ml of concentrated perchloric acid are added, causing the indicator current to rise to about 25 μamp in 5 seconds; the determination is stopped. The apparatus used is that of Meier, Myers, and Swift (78), with modifications by Ramsey, Farrington, and Swift (79).

In 1910, Erdmann (80) investigated the possibility of the presence of amines in the Kjeldahl distillate and also their formation during the digestion. To prove the presence of amines in the distillate, it was first titrated to obtain total nitrogen, 5–10 ml of a mixture of 20% sodium hydroxide and 30% sodium carbonate were added and the whole made up to volume with distilled water. For the equivalent amount of ammonia (in terms of milliliters of 0.1 N ammonia), 0.1 gm of yellow oxide of mercury was added for each milliliter. After shaking for 1 hour, excluding light, and allowing the precipitate to settle, the solution is filtered, and an aliquot taken for distillation. Since mercuric oxide removes ammonia, the nitrogen found after treatment is presumed to be due to amine. Erdmann's experiments were made on methyl-, dimethyl-, and trimethylamine, creatine, creatinine, peptone, lecithin, glycocoll, uric acid, hippuric acid, and urea. These were digested with sulfuric acid, with and without a catalyst, in a lead bath to maintain a constant temperature. After digestion at various temperatures and time periods, the amine content was determined in the distillates. With the exception of urea, glycocoll, hippuric and uric acids, amines were found in the distillates. However, with increasing time and temperature, lesser amounts of amines were recovered. This would indicate that neither the temperature nor the digestion time were sufficient to decompose the samples with sulfuric acid alone. Further work on the presence of amines in the distillate was made by Gortner and Hoffman (81) who digested samples of casein, using the Kjeldahl-Gunning procedure, and copper wire as a catalyst. The boil period was 20 minutes. From these so-called normal digests, the amount of amines found in the distillates was approximately 7%. When wheat flour was digested without potassium sulfate, the amine content of the distillates rose as high as 14.7%. These authors also report that addition of calcium, strontium, or barium chloride to the Kjeldahl-Gunning digest, influences the formation of amines.

REFERENCES

1. J. Kjeldahl, *Medd. Carlsberg Lab.* **2**, 1 (1883); *Z. anal. Chem.* **22**, 366 (1883).
2. H. F. Wilson and F. Mattingley, *Analyst* **51**, 569 (1926).
3. L. Michaelis and M. Maeda, *Aichi J. Exptl. Med. (Tokyo)* **1**, 51–59 (1923).
4. H. Wilfarth, *Chem. Zentr.* [3] **16**, 113 (1885).
5. *U.S. Dept. Agr. Bull.* **107**, 6.
6. Assoc. Offic. Agr. Chem. "Methods of Analysis," p. 12, Sec. 2.036 (1960).
7. C. F. Davis and M. Wise, *Cereal Chem.* **8**, 349–360 (1931).
8. E. Salm and S. Prager, *Chem. Ztg.* **42**, 104–105 (1918).
9. A. Hiller, J. Plazin, and D. D. Van Slyke, *J. Biol. Chem.* **176**, 1401–1420 (1948).
10. L. W. Winkler, *Z. angew. Chem.* **26**, 231–232 (1913).
11. F. M. Scales and A. P. Harrison, *J. Ind. Eng. Chem.* **12**, 350–352 (1920).
12. K. S. Markley and R. M. Hann, *J. Assoc. Offic. Agr. Chem.* **8**, 455–467 (1925).
13. H. D. Spears, *J. Assoc. Offic. Agr. Chem.* **5**, 105–108 (1921).
14. N. M. Staver and R. B. Sandin, *Ind. Eng. Chem., Anal. Ed.* **3**, 240–242 (1931).
15. J. F. Reith and W. M. Klazinga, *Chem. Weekblad* **38**, 122–125 (1941).
16. C. O. Willits, H. J. John, and L. R. Ross, *J. Assoc. Offic. Agr. Chem.* **31**, 432–438 (1948).
17. J. T. Scanlan and J. D. Reid, *Ind. Eng. Chem., Anal. Ed.* **7**, 125–126 (1935).
18. S. H. Green and A. G. Pellard, *J. Sci. Food Agr.* **4**, 490–496 (1953).
19. E. C. Wagner, *Ind. Eng. Chem., Anal. Ed.* **12**, 771–772 (1940).
20. E. W. Meeker and E. C. Wagner, *Ind. Eng. Chem., Anal. Ed.* **5**, 396–398 (1933).
21. S. H. Yuen and A. G. Pollard, *J. Sci. Food Agr.* **4**, 490–496 (1953).
22. A. Eisner and E. C. Wagner, *Ind. Eng. Chem., Anal. Ed.* **6**, 473 (1934).
23. H. S. Miller, *Ind. Eng. Chem., Anal. Ed.* **8**, 50–51 (1936).
24. J. Speirs and W. J. Mitchell, *J. Inst. Brewing* **42**, 247–250 (1936).
25. A. A. Fridman and K. L. F. Komissarova, *Kozhevenno Obuvnaya Prom. S.S.S.R.* **19**, No. 9–10, 27–30 (1940).
26. E. Schulek, K. Burger, and M. Feher, *Z. anal. Chem.* **167**, 28–31 (1959); cf. *Ann. Univ. Sci. Budapest. Rolando Eotvos Nominatae, Sect. Chim.* **2**, 543–545 (1960).
27. J. A. Bradley, Jr., *Ind. Eng. Chem., Anal. Ed.* **14**, 705–706 (1942).
28. R. Chand, *J. Indian Chem. Soc.* **24**, 167–168 (1947).
29. R. C. Howes and E. R. Skavinski, *Ind. Eng. Chem., Anal. Ed.* **14**, 917–921 (1942).
30. J. A. Kuck, A. Kingsley, F. Sheehan, and G. F. Swigert, *Anal. Chem.* **22**, 604–611 (1950).
31. P. A. Kober, *J. Am. Chem. Soc.* **30**, 1131 (1908); **32**, 689–691 (1910); P. A. Kober and S. S. Graves, *Ibid.* **35**, 1594–1604 (1913).
32. J. Sebelien, A. Brynildsen, and C. Haavardsholm, *Chem. Ztg.* **33**, 795 (1909).
33. R. O. E. Davis, *J. Am. Chem. Soc.* **31**, 556–558 (1909).
34. F. W. Gill and H. S. Grindley, *J. Am. Chem. Soc.* **31**, 1249–1252 (1909).
35. F. L. Dillingham, *J. Am. Chem. Soc.* **36**, 1310–1312 (1914).
36. K. G. Falk and K. Sugiura, *J. Am. Chem. Soc.* **38**, 916–921 (1916).
37. W. B. Meldrum, R. Melampy, and W. D. Meyers, *Ind. Eng. Chem., Anal. Ed.* **6**, 63–64 (1934).
38. I. K. Phelps and H. W. Daudt, *J. Assoc. Offic. Agr. Chemists* **3**, 306–315 (1920).
39. P. Rona and R. Ottenberg, *Biochem. Z.* **24**, 354–356 (1910).

40. A. M. Wright, *Trans. Proc. New Zeal. Inst.* **42** 224–225 (1911).
41. G. Simpson, *Pharm. J.* **92**, 546–547 (1914).
42. F. Herrmann, *Chem. Ztg.* **35**, 25 (1911).
43. W. S. Shaw, *Analyst* **49**, 558–565 (1924).
44. K. Marcali and W. Rieman III, *Ind. Eng. Chem., Anal. Ed.* **18**, 709–710 (1946).
45. K. Marcali and W. Rieman III, *Anal. Chem.* **20**, 381–382 (1948).
46. C. I. Adams and G. H. Spaulding, *Anal. Chem.* **27**, 1003–1004 (1955).
47. K. Chang, *Huo Hsuch Tung Pao No.* **2** ,3–5 (1960).
48. H. H. Willard and W. E. Cake, *J. Am. Chem. Soc.* **42**, 2646–2650 (1920).
49. Th. A. G. Haanappel, *Pharm. Weekblad* **75**, 570–574 (1938).
50. E. R. Ling, *J. Soc. Chem. Ind.* **61**, 194–196 (1942).
51. M. Ashraf, M. K. Bhatty, and R. A. Shah, *Pakistan J. Sci. Ind. Research* **3**, 1–3 (1960).
52. M. Ashraf, M. K. Bhatty, and R. A. Shah, *Pakistan J. Sci. Ind. Research* **12**, 103–105 (1960).
53. M. Ashraf, M. K. Bhatty, and R. A. Shah, *Anal. Chim. Acta* **25**, 448–452 (1961).
54. I. M. Kolthoff and Belcher, "Volumetric Analysis," Vol. III, p. 581, Wiley (Interscience), New York (1957).
55. I. M. Kolthoff and V. A. Stenger, *Ind. Eng. Chem., Anal. Ed.* **7**, 79–81 (1935).
56. F. C. Koch and T. L. McMeekin, *J. Am. Chem. Soc.* **46**, 2066–2067 (1924).
57. "Standard Methods for the Examination of Water, Sewage and Industrial Wastes," 10th ed., p. 144, American Public Health Association, Inc., New York (1959).
58. H. M. Chiles. *J. Am. Chem. Soc.* **50**, 217–221 (1928).
59. K. R. Middleton, *J. Appl. Chem. (London)* **10**, 281–286 (1960).
60. C. H. Hale, M. N. Hale, and W. H. Jones, *Anal. Chem.* **21**, 1549–1551 (1949).
61. H. C. Burck, *Mikrochim. Acta* pp. 200–203 (1960).
62. E. S. West and A. L. Brandon, *Ind. Eng. Chem., Anal. Ed.* **4**, 314–315 (1932).
63. D. D. Van Slyke, *J. Biol. Chem.* **71**, 235–248 (1927); cf. A. Hiller, J. Plazin, and D. D. Van Slyke, *J. Biol. Chem.* **176**, 1401–1420 (1948).
64. D. D. Van Slyke and J. M. Neill, *J. Biol. Chem.* **61**, 523 (1924).
65. R. L. Stehle, *J. Biol. Chem.* **45**, 223–228 (1920).
66. R. L. Stehle, *J. Biol. Chem.* **47**, 11 (1921).
67. D. D. Van Slyke and V. H. Kugel, *J. Biol. Chem.* **102**, 489–497 (1933).
68. W. H. Taylor and G. F. Smith, *Ind. Eng. Chem., Anal. Ed.* **14**, 437–439 (1942).
69. P. Thomas, *Bull. soc. chim.* **13**, 398–400 (1912).
70. A. E. Orr, *Biochem. J.* **18**, 806–808 (1934).
71. M. M. Murray, *Biochem. J.* **19**, 294 (1925).
72. D. D. Van Slyke and A. Hiller, *J. Biol. Chem.* **102**, 499–504 (1933).
73. E. D. Noble, *Anal. Chem.* **27**, 1413–1416 (1955); cf. J. P. Riley, *Anal. Chim. Acta* **9**, 575 (1953).
74. O. I. Milner, R. J. Zahner, L. S. Hepner, and W. H. Cowell, *Anal. Chem.* **30**, 1528–1530 (1958).
75. O. I. Milner and R. J. Zahner, *Anal. Chem.* **32**, 294 (1960).
76. H. Fleisher, *Ind. Eng. Chem., Anal. Ed.* **15**, 742 (1944).
77. G. M. Arcand and E. H. Swift, *Anal. Chem.* **28**, 440–443 (1956).
78. D. J. Meier, R. J. Meyers, and E. H. Swift, *J. Am. Chem. Soc.* **71**, 2340 (1949).
79. W. J. Ramsey, P. S. Farrington, and E. H. Swift, *Anal. Chem.* **22**, 332 (1950).
80. C. C. Erdmann, *J. Biol. Chem.* **8**, 41–55 (1911).
81. R. A. Gortner and W. F. Hoffman, *J. Biol. Chem.* **70**, 457–459 (1926).

General Bibliography

This section, in good part, represents the extensive work done on the Kjeldahl method. It has been divided into various classifications, and arranged in chronological order. In many cases—where it has seemed of sufficient importance—the same titles appear in more than one classification. In the following outline, no attempt has been made to classify the component parts of the Kjeldahl method in order of their importance.

1. Reviews
2. General
3. Oxidizing Agents
4. Reducing Agents
5. Catalysts
6. Natural Products
7. Nitro and Non-Aminoid Nitrogen
8. Distillation and Estimation of Nitrogen
9. Apparatus

Reviews

The Modification of the Kjeldahl Method for the Quantitative Determination of Nitrogen.
J. S. Hepburn, *J. Franklin Inst.* **166**, 81 (1908).

Kjeldahl and The Determination of Nitrogen.
R. E. Oesper, *J. Chem. Educ.* **11**, 457-462 (1934).

The Kjeldahl Determination of Organic Nitrogen.
R. B. Bradstreet, *Chem. Rev.* **27**, 331-350 (1940).

The Kjeldahl Method in the Past and Present.
A. Frankignoulle, *Z. ges. Brauw.* **65**, 33-39 (1942).

Sarudi's Rapid Method for Kjeldahl Nitrogen Determination.
I. Smith, *Tidsskr. Norske Landbruk* **49**, 197-198 (1942).

The Position of Arnold in Relationship to the Kjeldahl Method.
H. B. Vickery, *J. Assoc. Offic. Agr. Chemists* **29**, 358-370 (1946).

Determination of Kjeldahl Nitrogen in Foodstuffs and the Influence of Various Catalysts.
H. Hadorn, R. Jungkunz, and K. W. Biefer, *Mitt. Lebensm. u. Hyg.* **44**, 14-29 (1953).

Selenium Catalysis, A Review of the Literature on Its Use in the Kjeldahl Method for Nitrogen.
R. E. Seebold, *J. Am. Leather Chemists Assoc.* **42**, 2204 (1947).

Kjeldahl Method for Organic Nitrogen.
R. B. Bradstreet, *Anal. Chem.* **26**, 185-187 (1954).

The Use of Microchemical Methods in Food Research. I. Kjeldahl Micro and Semi-Micro Method.
C. Rzymowska, I. Bernsteinowna, and J. Grochowska, *Roczniki Panstwowego Zak adu Hig.* pp. 1-21 (1953) (English Summary).

Determination of Nitrogen by the Kjeldahl Method.
P. Fontana Jr., *Mem. inst. Oswaldo Cruz* **51**, 277-288(1953).

The Determination of Nitrogen by the Kjeldahl Method.
F. Abaffy, *Farm. G asnik* **12**, 283-288 (1956).

Kjeldahl Nitrogen Determination.
F. G. Seitz, *Chem. Ztg.* **84**, 362-364 (1960).

The Determination of the Protein Content of Milk by the Kjeldahl Method.
J. Eisses, *Neth. Milk Dairy J.* **14**, 334-351 (1960).

General

Comparative Work on Nitrogen Estimation by the Kjeldahl and Gunning Methods, and By a Combination of the Two Methods.
T. S. Gladding, Proc. Assoc. Offic. Agr. Chemists p. 85 (1906).

Physiological Chemical Notes. IV. Notes on Kjeldahl Determinat ons.
E. Salkowski, *Z. physiol. Chem.* **57**, 523-526 (1907).

Note on Kjeldahl Determinations of Nitrogen.
E. F. Harrison and P. A. W. Self, *Pharm. J.* **85**, 4 (1911).

Alkylamines as Products of the Kjeldahl Digestion.
C. C. Erdmann, *J. Biol. Chem.* **8**, 41-55 (1911).

The Estimation of Nitrogen by the Method of Kjeldahl.
A. C. Andersen, *Skand. Arch. Physiol.* **25**, 96-104 (1911).

Contribution to the Technique of Kjeldahl Nitrogen Estimations.
W. von Rijn, *Pharm. Weekblad* **48**, 27-28 (1911).

Source of Error in the Kjeldahl-Gunning Method for the Determination of Nitrogen.
E. Carpiaux, *Bull. soc. chim. Belges* **27**, 13-14 (1914).

An Important Source of Error in Kjeldahl Determinations of Urine.
G. von Spindles, *Schweiz. Wochschr.* **51**, 517-521 (1913).

Destruction of Large Amounts of Organic Material by the Kjeldahl Method.
E. Carpiaux, *Bull. soc. chim. Belges* **27**, 333-334 (1914).

A Note Upon the Kjeldahl Method for Nitrogen Determination.
P. L. Blumenthal and G. P. Plaisance, *J. Ind. Eng. Chem.* **7**, 1044-1045 (1915).

Determination of Nitrogen According to Kjeldahl.
O. Nolte, *Z. anal. Chem.* **54**, 259-262 (1915).

The Kjeldahl-Gunning-Arnold Method for Nitrogen.
J. M. Pickel, *J. Ind. Chem. Eng.* **7**, 357 (1915).

Estimation of Nitrogen by Kjeldahl's Method. II.
O. Nolte, *Z. anal. chem.* **55**, 185-189 (1916).

Micro-Kjeldahl Methods.
E. Abderhalden and A. Fodor, *Z. physiol. Chem.* **100**, 190-201 (1917).

Kjeldahl's Method.
O. Nolte, *Z. anal. Chem.* **56**, 391-393 (1917).

Some Limitations of the Kjeldahl Method.
H. C. Brill and F. Agcaoili, *Philippine J. Sci.* **12A**, 261-265 (1917).

The Estimation of Nitrogen by the Kjeldahl Process.
E. Salm and S. Prager, *Chem. Ztg.* **42**, 194-195 (1918).

The Determination of Nitrogen by the Kjeldahl Process.
A. Villiers and A. Moreau-Talon, *Ann. chim. anal. et chim. appl.* **1**, 183-185 (1919).

Simplification of the Kjeldahl Method in Clinical Medicine.
E. Pittarelli, *Riv. crit. clin. med.* **12**, (1919); *J. Pharm. Chim.* **20**, 32-34 (1919).

Investigation of the Kjeldahl Method for the Determination of Nitrogen.
I. K. Phelps and H. W. Daudt, *J. Assoc. Offic. Agr. Chemists* **3**, 218-220 (1919).

Report on Nitrogen.
R. N. Brackett and H. D. Haskins, *J. Assoc. Offic. Agr. Chemists* **3**, 207-217 (1919).

Modified Kjeldahl Method for the Estimation of Nitrogen – Test for Nitrates – Color Test for Tryptophan in Urine.
W. R. Fearon, *Dublin J. Med. Sci. March 1920, p. 28; J. Am. Med. Assoc.* **74**, 1128.

Investigations of the Kjeldahl Method for Determining Nitrogen.
I. K. Phelps and H. W. Daudt, *J. Assoc. Offic. Agr. Chemists* **3**, 306-315 (1920).

Investigation of the Kjeldahl Method for Determining Nitrogen.
I. K. Phelps, *J. Assoc. Offic. Agr. Chemists* **4**, 72-76 (1920).

Micro-estimation of Nitrogen in Agricultural Products.
W. Geilmann, *J. Landwirtsch* **68**, 235-254 (1920).

Report on Special Study of the Kjeldahl Method.
H. W. Daudt, *J. Assoc. Offic. Agr. Chemists* **4**, 366 (1921).

The Kjeldahl Nitrogen Method and Its Modifications.
A. E. Paul and E. H. Berry, *J. Assoc. Offic. Agr. Chemists* **5**, 108-132 (1921).

A Micro-Kjeldahl Method for Determining Nitrogen.
A. R. Ling and W. J. Price, *J. Soc. Chem. Ind.* **41**, 149-151T (1921).

Microchemical Determination of Nitrogen.
H. Luhrig, *Pharm. Zentralhalle* **62**, 437-444 (1921).

Comparative Determinations of Nitrogen by the Kjeldahl Method
and by the Folin Method.
L. Hannaelt and R. Wodon, *Bull. soc. med. nat. Bruxelles* pp. 30-31
(1921).

The Kleeman Modification of the Kjeldahl Process.
F. Skutil, *Chem. Listy* **16**, 173-177 (1922).

Determination of Nitrogen by the Kjeldahl Method and Modifications.
P. Fleury and H. Levaltier, *J. pharm. chim.* **29**, 137-147 (1924).

A Contribution to the Bang Micro-Kjeldahl Procedure.
S. Kasamori, *J. Biochem. Tokyo* **4**, 33-41 (1924).

Determination of Nitrogen by the Kjeldahl Method. An Attempt at
Generalization. A cause of Error; the Liberation of Nitrogen Gas.
P. Fleury and H. Levaltier, *J. pharm. chim.* **30**, 265-272 (1924); *Bull.
soc. chim. France* **37**, 330-335 (1925).

The Quickest Micromethod for Determining Nitrogen.
A. Kultjugin and E. Gubareff, *Biochem. Z.* **164**, 437-441 (1925).

Determination of Nitrogen by the Kjeldahl Method.
A. C. Andersen and B. N. Jensen, *Z. anal. Chem.* **67**, 427-448
(1926).

The Micromethod of Kjeldahl Simplified (Procedure without Distillation).
Mme. B. Pohorecka-Lelesz, *Bull. soc. chim. biol.* **7**, 1039-1043
(1925).

The Presence of Amines in the Distillate from Kjeldahl-Gunning
Nitrogen Determinations. Preliminary Paper.
R. A. Gortner and W. F. Hoffman, *J. Biol. Chem.* **70**, 457-459
(1926).

The Microchemical Determination of Nitrogen by Kjeldahl's
Method.

V. Sazavsky, *Z. Zuckerind. cechoslov. Rep.* **50**, 518-522 (1926); *Listy cukrovar.* **43**, 151 ff. (1924-1925).

Gasometric Micro-Kjeldahl Determination of Nitrogen.
D. D. Van Slyke, *J. Biol. Chem.* **71**, 235-248 (1927).

Rapid Boiling as an Aid to a Shortened Period of Digestion in the Determination of Nitrogen.
O. M. Shedd, *J. Assoc. Offic. Agr. Chemists* **10**, 507-520 (1927).

Reaction Accelerators in the Determination of Organic Nitrogen by Kjeldahl's Method.
F. Provvedi, *Atti accad. fisiocrit. Siena* [10] **3**, 423-425 (1928).

Relation of Quantity of Sodium Sulfate to Time of Digestion in Protein Determination.
C. G. Harrel and J. H. Lanning, *Cereal Chem.* **6**, 72-78 (1929).

Rapid Determination of Nitrogen by Kjeldahl's Method. II.
J. Ellborg, *Svenska Bryggareforen Manadsbl.* **46**, 333-334 (1931).

Notes on the Kjeldahl Determination.
V. A. Toscani, *Chemist Analyst* **20**, No. 5, 18-20 (1931).

Determination of Nitrogen by a Micro-Kjeldahl Method.
A. C. Andersen and B. N. Jensen, *Z. anal. Chem.* **83**, 114-120 (1931).

Suppression of Sulfuric Acid Mist in Kjeldahl Digestions.
A. Henwart and R. M. Garey, *Science* **76**, 524 (1932).

A New Micro-Kjeldahl Method.
S. Balarhovskii and K. Bruns, *Biochem. Z.* **256**, 292 (1932).

An Accurate Semi-Micro Kjeldahl Method.
D. I. Hitchcock and R. C. Belden, *Ind. Eng. Chem., Anal. Ed.* **5**, 402 (1933).

The Assumed and Actual Errors in the Macro-and Micro-Kjeldahl Distillation.
E. Schulek and G. Vastagh, *Z. anal. Chem.* **92**, 352-357 (1933).

Kjeldahl Determination of Nitrogen by the Suggested F.I.P. (Federation Internationale Pharmaceutique) Method.
H. J. van Giffen, *Pharm. Weekblad* **70**, 1005-1007 (1933).

Value of the Kjeldahl Method.
M. Lemoigne, R. Desveaux, and P. Monguillon, *Ann. fals. et fraudes*
27, 216-219 (1934).

Comparison of the Kjeldahl and Dumas Methods for Some Agricultural Products.
P. Anne, *Ann. fals. et fraudes* **27**, 220-222 (1934).

Dilution Method for Micro-Kjeldahl Determination.
O. Hartley, *Ind. Eng. Chem., Anal. Ed.* **6**, 249 (1934).

Quantitative Drop Analysis. III. Kjeldahl Nitrogen Determination and the Nonprotein Nitrogen of Blood.
P. L. Kirk, *Mikrochemie* **16**, 13-24 (1934).

Rapid Determination of Nitrogen by the Kjeldahl-Nessler Process.
W. H. Kitto, *Analyst* **59**, 733-735 (1934).

Fumeless Digestion of Nitrogen.
Y. V. Marayanayya and V. Subrahmanyan, *Current Sci.* **3**, 423 (1935).

A Chromic Acid Modification of the Kjeldahl Method for the Determination of Nitrogen in Organic Compounds.
J. M. Shewan, *J. Soc. Chem. Ind.* **54**, 172-4T (1935).

Rapid Determination of Nitrogen by the Kjeldahl Method.
H. Lundin, J. Ellburg, and H. Riehm, *Z. anal. Chem.* **102**, 161-172 (1935).

Estimation of Nitrogen by Fumeless Digestion. I.
Y. V. Marayanayya and V. Subrahmanyan, *Proc. Indian Acad. Sci.*
2B, 213-235 (1935).

Degradation of Simple Amines During Kjeldahlization.
E. Kahane and J. Gonzalez Carrero, *Anales soc. espan. fis. y quim.*
33, 864-876 (1935).

Modified Technique for the Kjeldahl Procedure.
A. Henwood and R. M. Garey, *J. Franklin Inst.* **221**, 531-538 (1936).

The Kjeldahl Method.
Le Tourneur-Hugon and Chambionnat, *Ann. fals. et fraudes* **29**, 227-229 (1936).

Mineralization in the Kjeldahl Procedure.
L. Palfrey, *Document. sci.* **6**, 305-308 (1937).

The Kjeldahl Method for Determining Nitrogen by the Method of Parnas and Wagner.
J. K. Parnas, *Z. anal. Chem.* **114**, 261-275 (1938).

A Micro-Kjeldahl Method Including Nitrates.
R. H. Moore, *Botan. Gaz.* **100**, 250-252 (1938).

Determination of Organic Nitrogen.
G. E. Mordovskii and A. E. Rukhman, Russian patent 54056 (1938).

The Rapid Determination of Nitrogen by a Modified Kjeldahl Method.
A. N. Temp and G. A. Aleksandrov, *Trudy Uzbeksk. Gos. Univ. Sbornik Rabot Khim.* **15**, 4-6 (1939).

A Rapid Method for Determining Nitrogen by the Kjeldahl Method.
L. G. Gorelik, *Nauch-Issled. Inst. Pishchevoi Prom. Belorusskoi S.S.R. Sbornik Rabot Molodykh Nauch. Rabotnikov (Minsk)* pp. 110-113 (1939); *Khim. Referat. Zhur. No.* **5**, 82-83 (1940).

The Analytical Error of the Kjeldahl Nitrogen Test.
W. F. Geddes and N. Milton, *Cereal Chem.* **16**, 392-404 (1939).

An Ultramicro-Kjeldahl Technique.
J. Needham and E. J. Boell, *Biochem. J.* **33**, 149-152 (1939).

A Rapid Micro-Kjeldahl Method.
A. Keys, *J. Biol. Chem.* **132**, 181-187 (1940).

Determination of Organic Nitrogen.
J. Cartiaux, *Ann. chim. anal. chim. appl.* **22**, 92 (1940).

The Effect of Halogen Compounds on Kjeldahl Nitrogen Digestions.
E. Modeer, *Wyoming Univ. Publ.* **7**, 13-26 (1940).

Report on Microchemical Methods. Kjeldahl Nitrogen Method.
E. P. Clark, *J. Assoc. Offic. Agr. Chemists* **24**, 641-647 (1941).

Semimicro Method for the Determination of Nitrogen.
R. Belcher and A. L. Godbert, *J. Soc. Chem. Ind.* **60**, 196-198 (1941).

Collaborative Report on the Micro and Semi-Micro Kjeldahl Nitrogen Method.
F. Acree Jr., *J. Assoc. Offic. Agr. Chemists* **24**, 648-651 (1941).

Various Methods for Digestion of Organic Substances in the Kjeldahl Nitrogen Determination.
E. Rauterberg and H. Benischke, *Bodenk. u. Pflanzenernahr.* **26**, 97-105 (1941).

Reactions in Sulphuric Acid. XXXII. A Universal Method for Nitrogen Determination by Mineralization with This Acid.
J. Milbauer, *Chem. obzor* **16**, 97-98 (1941); *Chem. Zentr.* Part I, p. 1592 (1942).

Micro-Kjeldahl Nitrogen Determination without the Use of Titration Procedure.
W. H. Taylor and G. F. Smith, *Ind. Eng. Chem., Anal. Ed.* **14**, 437-9 (1942).

Effect of Nitrates on the Determination of Protein Nitrogen by Kjeldahl Method.
E. I. Whitehead and O. E. Olson, *J. Assoc. Offic. Agr. Chemists* **25**, 769-772 (1942).

Diffusion Micro-Method for Nitrogen.
R. C. Hawes and E. R. Skavinski, *Ind. Eng. Chem., Anal. Ed.* **14**, 917-921 (1942).

Sarudi's Rapid Method for Kjeldahl Nitrogen Determination.
I. Smith, *Tidsskr. Norske Landbruk* **49**, 197-198 (1942).

Determination of Nitrogen by the Kjeldahl Method.
J. Soos, *Magyar Kém. Folyóirat* **49**, 81-100 (1943); *Chem. Zentr.* II, 344-345 (1944).

Notes on the Work of Imre Sarudi: On a Quick Method for Kjeldahl Nitrogen Determination.
H. Leopold, *Z. Lebensm. - Untersuch. u. Forsch.* **86**, 220-223 (1943).

A Micromethod for the Determination of Total Nitrogen.
D. Brüel, H. Holter, K. Linderstrøm-Lang, and K. Rozits, *Compt. rend. trav. Lab. Carlsberg, Ser. chim.* **25**, No. 13, 289-324 (1946) (separate English translation).

Micro-Kjeldahl Determination of Nitrogen.
R. Ballentine and J. R. Gregg, *Anal. Chem.* **19**, 281-283 (1947).

A Simplified Ultramicro Kjeldahl Method for the Estimation of Protein and Total Nitrogen in Fluid Samples of Less Than One Microliter.
J. Shaw and L. C. Beadle, *J. Exptl. Biol.* **26**, 15-24 (1949).

Determination of Traces of Nitrogen in Organic Substances by the Kjeldahl Method.
E. Schulek and Gyorgy Foti, *Magyar Kem. Lapja* **4**, 406-409 (1949).

Spectrophotometric Determination of Total Nitrogen in Oils.
C. H. Hale, M. N. Hale, and W. H. Jones, *Anal. Chem.* **21**, 1549-1551 (1949).

A New Micro-Kjeldahl Method.
M. T. S. Mogensen, *Proc. 12th Intern. Dairy Congr., Stockholm* **2**, 652-60 (1949).

Boiling Temperatures of Kjeldahl Digestion Mixtures.
C. L. Ogg and C. O. Willits, *J. Assoc. Offic. Agr. Chemists* **33**, 100-103 (1950).

Kjeldahl Ultramicro Determination of Nitrogen. Applications in the Industrial Laboratory.
J. A. Kuck, A. Kingsley, D. Kinsey, F. Sheehan, and G. F. Swigert, *Anal. Chem.* **22**, 604-611 (1950).

Kinetics of the Kjeldahl Reaction.
G. M. Schwab and E. Schwab-Agallidis, *J. Am. Chem. Soc.* **73**, 803-809 (1951).

Standardization of Digestion in Kjeldahl Nitrogen Determinations.
G. Middleton and R. E. Stuckey, *J. Pharm. and Pharmacol.* **3**, 829-841 (1951).

Effects of Digestion Temperature on Kjeldahl Analyses.
G. R. Lake, P. McCutchan, R. Van Meter, and J. C. Neal, *Anal. Chem.* **23**, 1634-1638 (1951).

Development of the Kjeldahl Method to a General Method for Nitrogen Determination.
F. Zinncke, *Angew. Chem.* **64**, 220-222 (1952).

Evaluation of Ronchese and Colobraro's Modification of the Kjeldahl Method.
V. Colobraro and J. C. Sanahuja, *Anales bromatol. (Madrid)* **4**, 51-56 (1952).

Kjeldahl Determination with Sealed Tube Digestion Microgram Analysis.
B. W. Grunbaum, F. L. Schaffer, and P. L. Kirk, *Anal. Chem.* **24**, 1487-1490 (1952).

The Kjeldahl Determination of Nitrogen.
S. V. Anantakrishman and K. V. Srinivasan, *Proc. Indian Acad. Sci.* **36A**, 299-305 (1952).

A Comparison of Semi-Micro and Macro Kjeldahl Determinations.
M. L. Belfort Bethlem, *Rev. brasil. farm.* **33**, 415-423 (1952).

Rapid Modified Procedure for Determination of Kjeldahl Nitrogen.
C. H. Perrin, *Anal. Chem.* **25**, 968-971 (1953).

A Comparative Study of Four Kjeldahl Methods.
K. Nuna, *Bull. Govt. Forest Expt. Sta. (Japan)* **53**, 127-134 (1952).

Digestion of Organic Compounds in the Kjeldahl Method.
I. Ribas and D. Vazquez-Gesto, *Inform quim. anal. (Madrid)* **7**, 29-42 (1953).

Kjeldahlization of Urea. II. Kinetics of the Kjeldahl Reaction.
G. M. Schwab and E. Schwab-Agallidis, *Angew. Chem.* **65**, 418-421 (1953).

Semi-Micro Kjeldahl Method for Nitrogen Determination.
Y. Mihashi and M. Tatsumi, *Ann. Rept. Tokyo Coll. Pharm.* **3**, 189-191 (1953).

Mineralization of Nitrogen in the Micro-Kjeldahl Method.
P. Fontana, *Eng. e quim. (Rio de Janeiro)* **5**, No. 6, 16-20 (1953).

The Kjeldahl Determination of Nitrogen: A Critical Study of Digestion Conditions—Temperature, Catalyst, and Oxidizing Agent.
H. A. McKenzie and H. S. Wallace, *Australian J. Chem.* **7**, 55 (1954).

Kjeldahl Determination of Nitrogen in Organic compounds. A Preliminary Report—Selection of Digesting Conditions.

A. Takeda and J. Senda, *Nogaku Kenkyu (Rept. Ohara Inst. Agr. Biol.)* **41**, 97-108 (1954).

An Improved Ultramicro-Kjeldahl Technique.
E. J. Boell and S. C. Shen, *Exptl. Cell Research* **7**, 147-152 (1954).

Ultramicro Determination of Ammonia or Organic Nitrogen.
Y. Okada and H. Hanafusa, *Bull. Chem. Soc. Japan* **27**, 478 (1954).

Kjeldahl Method with Sealed Tube Digestion.
B. W. Grunbaum, P. L. Kirk, and C. W. Koch, *Anal. Chem.* **27**, 384-388 (1955).

Determination of Organic Nitrogen by Kjeldahl Method without Distillation.
C. I. Adams and G. H. Spaulding, *Anal. Chem.* **27**, 1003-1004 (1955).

Rapid Mineralization of Ammonia in the Kjeldahl Determination.
S. Dittrich and J. X. de Vries, *pR (Montevideo)* **5**, No. 4, 78D-83D (1955).

The Kjeldahl Reaction.
G. M. Schwab and S. Caramanos, *Monatsh.* **86**, 341-374 (1955).

Causes of Error in the Microdetermination of Nitrogen by Kjeldahl Followed by Nesslerization.
J. Gonzalez Carrero, O. Carballido Ramallo, and F. Gomez Vigide, *Inform. quim. anal. (Madrid)* **10**, 199-208(1956).

Determination of 0.02 - 0.10 Gamma Quantities of Organic Nitrogen.
D. Exley, *Biochem. J.* **63**, 496-501 (1956).

Acid Requirements of the Kjeldahl Digestion.
R. B. Bradstreet, *Anal. Chem.* **29**, 944-947 (1957).

The Kjeldahl Reaction. IV.
G. M. Schwab and O. Neuwerth, *Monatsh.* **88**, 288-291 (1957).

Submicromethods for the Analysis of Organic Compounds.
I. Determination of Nitrogen.
R. Belcher, T. S. West, and M. Williams, *J. Chem. Soc.* pp. 4323-4328 (1957).

Modification of the Kjeldahl Method for the Determination of Total Nitrogen.
N. B. Myakina, *Pochvovedenie No.* **1**, 106-110 (1958).

Kjeldahl-Ronchese Method for Rapid Determination of Organic Nitrogen.
R. F. Gomez Vigide, *Inform. quim. anal. (Madrid)* **12**, 9-12 (1958).

The Determination of Nitrogen in Certain Fluorinated Nitrogen Compounds by the Kjeldahl Method.
T. R. F. W. Fennell and J. R. Webb, *Analyst* **83**, 694-695 (1958).

Effect of the Mode of Combustion on Nitrogen Determination by Kjeldahl's Method.
L. Rozental, *Roczniki Panstwowego Zaklada Hig.* **9**, 183-197 (1958).

Evaluation of Six Methods for Determination of Nitrogen in Nitroguanidime.
M. I. Fauth and H. Stalcup, *Anal. Chem.* **30**, 1670-1672 (1958).

Microdetermination of Nitrogen by the Kjeldahl Method.
P. Haack, *Lab. Sci. (Milan)* **7**, 1-8 (1959).

Determination of Nitrogen by the Micro-Kjeldahl Method.
C. L. Ogg, *J. Assoc. Offic. Agr. Chemists* **43**, 689-693 (1960).

Action of Perchloric Acid and Perchloric Acid Plus Periodic Acid on Ammonia and Amino Nitrogen.
F. B. Moore and H. Diehl, *Anal. Chem.* **34**, 1638-1642 (1962).

Simple Methods for the Determination of Very Small Amounts of Nitrogen in Organic Matter.
G. H. Sloane-Stanley and G. R. N. Jones, *Biochem. J.* **86**, 16 pp. (1963).

Submicromethods for the Analysis of Organic Compounds. XVI. The Determination of Nitrogen by a General Procedure.
R. Belcher, A. D. Campbell, and P. Gouverneur, *J. Chem. Soc.* pp. 531-533 (1963).

Oxidizing Agents

A Source of Error in the Determination of Total Nitrogen by the Persulfate Method.
P. Lemaire, *Bull. soc. pharm. Bordeaux* **50**, 306-311 (1909).

Kjeldahl Nitrogen Determination.
M. Siegfried and O. Weidenhaupt, *Z. physiol. Chem.* **76**, 238-240 (1911).

The Use of Potassium Persulfate in the Determination of Total Nitrogen in Urine.
L. C. Scott and R. G. Meyers, *J. Am. Chem. Soc.* **39**, 1044-1051 (1917).

Notes on the Use of Potassium Permanganate in the Determination of Nitrogen by the Kjeldahl Method.
W. Frear, W. Thomas, and H. D. Edmiston, *J. Assoc. Offic. Agr. Chem.* **3**, 220-224 (1919).

The Influence of Potassium Permanganate on Kjeldahl Nitrogen Determinations.
D. C. Cochrane, *J. Ind. Eng. Chem.* **12**, 1195-1196 (1920).

The Use of Permanganate in the Kjeldahl Method Modified for Nitrates.
I. K. Phelps, *J. Assoc. Offic. Agr. Chemists* **4**, 69-71 (1920).

Note on the Use of Potassium Permanganate in the Determination of Nitrogen by the Kjeldahl Method.
C. T. Dowell and W. G. Friedemann, *J. Ind. Eng. Chem.* **13**, 358 (1921).

The Use of Potassium Permanganate in the Determination of Nitrogen by the Kjeldahl Method.
D. C. Cochrane, *J. Ind. Eng. Chem.* **13**, 358 (1921).

The Use of Perchloric Acid as an Aid to Digestion in the Kjeldahl Nitrogen Determination.
B. Mears and R. E. Hussey, *J. Ind. Eng. Chem.* **13**, 1054-1056 (1921).

The Use of Perchloric Acid for Kjeldahl Digestions in the Determination of Nitrogen in Leather.
J. G. Parker and J. T. Terrell, *J. Soc. Leather Trades' Chemists* **5**, 380-384 (1921).

The Effect of Hydrogen Peroxide Upon the Decomposition of Plant and Animal Substances.
Kleeman, *Z. angew. Chem.* **34**, 625-627 (1921).

The Kleeman Modification of the Kjeldahl Process.
F. Skutil, *Chem. Listy* **16**, 173-177 (1922).

The Action of Hydrogen Peroxide on the Decomposition of Plant and Animal Substances.
R. Heuss, Z. ges. Brauw. **6**, 44-46 (1922).

Hydrogen Peroxide in Kjeldahl Digestion of Nitrogen.
S. Liljevall, *Svensk Kem. Tidskr.* **39**, 187-198 (1923).

The Use of Persulfate in the Estimation of Nitrogen by the Arnold-Gunning Modification of Kjeldahl's Method.
S. Y. Wong, *J. Biol. Chem.* **55**, 427-430 (1923).

The Use of Persulfate in the Estimation of Nitrogen by Folim's Nesslerization Method.
S. Y. Wong, *J. Biol. Chem.* **55**, 431-435 (1923).

Use of Hydrogen Peroxide in the Estimation of Nitrogen.
R. Heuss, *Wochschr. Brau.* **40**, 73-74 (1923).

The Quickest Micromethod for Determining Nitrogen.
A. Kultjugin and E. Gubareff, *Biochem. Z.* **164**, 437-441 (1925).

The Use of Perhydrol for the Determination of Nitrogen According to Kjeldahl.
P. Saccardi, *Biochem. e terap. sper.* **14**, 252-255 (1927).

Hydrogen Peroxide as an Oxidizing Agent in the Kjeldahl Method for Determining Nitrogen.
E. Gubarev, *Zhur. Eksp. Biol. i Med.* **6**, 261-265 (1927).

Hydrogen Peroxide and Persulfuric Acid in the Determination of Nitrogen According to Kjeldahl.
E. Pittarelli, *Biochim. e terap. sper.* **14**, 308-310 (1927).

Rapid Estimation of Nitrogen by Kjeldahl's Method.
H. Lundin and J. Ellburg, *Wochschr. Brau.* **46**, 133-137, 147-149 (1929).

The Use of Hydrogen Peroxide in the Micro-Kjeldahl Nitrogen Method.
V. C. Meyers, *J. Lab. Clin. Med.* **17**, 272-273 (1931).

A Chromic Acid Modification of the Kjeldahl Method for the Determination of Nitrogen in Organic Compounds.
J. M. Shewan, *J. Soc. Chem. Ind.* **54**, 172-174 (1935).

The Use of Persulfate in the Determination of Nitrogen without Distillation.
K. Steinitz, *Mikrochim. Acta* **3**, 110-112 (1938).

The Kjeldahl Method.
Le Tourneur-Hugon and Chambionnat, *Ann. fals. et fraudes* **29**, 227-229 (1936).

Determination of Organic Nitrogen.
J. Cartiaux, *Ann. chim. anal. chim. appl.* **22**, 92 (1940).

A Rapid Method for Determining Nitrogen by the Kjeldahl Method.
L. G. Gorelik, *Nauch-Issled. Inst. Pishchevoi Prom. Belorusskoi S.S.R., Sbornik Rabot Molodykh Nauch Rabotnikov (Minsk)* 110-113 (1939); *Khim. Referat. Zhur. No.* **5**, 82-83 (1940).

A Rapid Kjeldahl Nitrogen Determination.
I. Sarudi, *Z. Untersuch. Lebensm.* **82**, 451-454 (1941).

Perchloric Acid in Micro-Kjeldahl Digestions.
L. F. Wicks and H. I. Firminger, *Ind. Eng. Chem., Anal. Ed.* **14**, 760-762 (1942).

Rapid Kjeldahl Digestion Method Using Perchloric Acid.
L. P. Pepkowitz, A. L. Prince, and F. E. Bear, *Ind. Eng. Chem., Anal. Ed.* **14**, 856-857 (1942).

Kjeldahl Nitrogen Determination. A Rapid Wet-Digestion Micro-Method.
L. P. Pepkowitz and J. W. Shive, *Ind. Eng. Chem., Anal. Ed.* **14**, 914-916 (1942).

Notes on the Work of Imre Sarudi: On a Rapid Method for Kjeldahl Nitrogen Determination.
H. Leopold, *Z. Lebensm. Untersuch. u. Forsch.* **86**, 220-223 (1943).

Rapid Method of Kjeldahlization by the Combined Catalytic Action of Selenium and Perchloric Acid.
A. Mallol Garcia, *Rev. real acad. cienc. exact., fis. y nat. Madrid* **39**, 207-228 (1945).

Formation of Ammonia by the Action of Oxidizing Agents on Nitrogen-Containing Substances.
L. Rosenthaler, *Mitt. Lebensh. u. Hyg.* **37**, 215-217 (1946).

Oxidation of Glycerinated Solutions in the Micro-Kjeldahl Determination of Nitrogen.
P. E. Portner, *Anal. Chem.* **19**, 502-503 (1947).

Micro-Kjeldahl Determination of Nitrogen.
R. Ballentine and J. R. Gregg, *Anal. Chem.* **19**, 281-283 (1947).

The Action of the Oxidizing Compounds in the Kjeldahl Procedure.
A. Quartaroli, *Ann. fac. agrar. univ. pisa* **9**, 90-99 (1948).

Determination of Nitrogen.
M. Carranza Marquez and G. Alliotta, *Tec. y econ. No.* **2**, 55-58 (1949).

Kjeldahl Decomposition with Perchloric Acid.
F. J. Koch, *Z. anal. Chem.* **131**, 426-427 (1950).

The Kjeldahl-Mallol Method in Agricultural Analyses.
J. de La Rubia Pacheco, F. B. Lopez-Rubio, and J. Garrido Marquez, *Inform. quim. anal. (Madrid)* **4**, 166-167 (1950).

The Kjeldahl Method Catalyzed by Selenic-Perchloric Acids.
A. Mallol Garcia, Anales real soc. españ. fis y quím. (Madrid) **47B**, 659-664 (1951).

Potassium Permanganate in the Kjeldahl Method for Determining Nitrogen in Organic Substances.
A. E. Beet, *Nature* **175**, 513-514 (1955).

Rapid Determination of Nitrogen in Crude Anthracene and Its Transformation Products.
I. D. Gluzman, R. I. Melamid, and D. M. Khimkis, *Zavodskaya Lab.* **21**, 1433-1435 (1955).

Reducing Agents

Analysis of Compounds Containing -N-N- Bonds by the Kjeldahl Method.
A. Flamand and B. Prager, *Ber.* **38**, 559-560 (1905).

Bohn-Schmidt Reaction in the Benzene Series and the Estimation of Nitrogen in Nitro Compounds by the Kjeldahl Method.
Alfred Eckert, *Monatsh.* **34**, 1957-1964 (1913).

New Modification of the Kjeldahl Method for Determining Nitrogen in Organic Substances.
M. Wunder and O. Lascar, *Ann. chim. anal.* **19**, 329-332 (1914).

Kjeldahl Modification for Determination of Nitrogen in Nitro Substitution Compounds.
W. C. Cope, *J. Ind. Eng. Chem.* **8**, 592-593 (1916).

Kjeldahl Experiments.
S. J. Lawellin, *J. Am. Assoc. Cereal Chemists* **8**, 148-151 (1923).

Estimation of Nitrate Nitrogen by a Modification of Kjeldahl's Method.
S. K. Deb, *Ind. Chemists* **1**, 452-453 (1925).

The Use of Powdered Copper in Analytical Chemistry.
K. Kurchner and K. Scharrer, *Z. anal. Chem.* **68**, 1-14 (1926).

Kjeldahl-Pregl Method Applied to Nitro Compounds.
A. Elek and H. Sobotka, *J. Am. Chem. Soc.* **48**, 501-503 (1926).

The Determination of Nitrogen by the Kjeldahl Method as Applied to Dyestuffs and Intermediate Products.
P. Sisley and M. David, *Bull. soc. chim.* [4] **45**, 312-324 (1929).

The Determination of Nitrogen in Osazones by the Kjeldahl Method.
G. Dorfmüller, *Z. Ver. deut. Zuckerind.* **80**, 407-412 (1930).

A Kjeldahl Method for Determining Nitro Nitrogen in Aromatic Compounds.
M. Weizmann, J. Yopf, and B. Kirzors, *Z. physiol. Chem.* **192**, 70-72 (1930).

The Determination of Nitrogen in Nitro and Azo Compounds by the Kjeldahl Method.
B. G. Simek, *Chem. Listy* **25**, 322-325 (1931).

Report of the Government Chemist for the year 1932.
B. W. Whitfield, Sudan Government, Wellcome Trop. Research Lab., Chem. Sect. Publ. No. 66, 14 pp. (1933).

The General Application of the Micro-Kjeldahl Determination.
A. Friedrich, E. Kühaus, and R. Schnurch, *Z. physiol. Chem.* **216**, 68-76 (1933).

Semi-Micro Kjeldahl Determination of Nitro and Azo Nitrogen.
R. A. Harte, *Ind. Eng. Chem., Anal. Ed.* **7**, 432-433 (1935).

Determination of Nitrogen in Mixed Fertilizers Containing Nitrates and Chlorides.
B. Dyer and J. H. Hamence, *Analyst* **63**, 866-870 (1938).

Determination of Nitrogen in Azo Compounds by the Kjeldahl Method.
V. I. Kuznetsov, *Zavodskaya Lab.* **9**, 1039 (1940); *Khim. Referat. Zhur.* **4**, No. 3, 62-63 (1941).

Adaptation of the Micro-Kjeldahl Method to the Estimation of Nitrogen in Organic Compounds Containing Nitro and Azo Groups.
R. V. Bhat, *Proc. Indian Acad. Sci.* **13A**, 269-272 (1941).

Determination of Nitrogen in Azo Compounds by the Kjeldahl Method.
Z. Csuros, E. Fodor-Kenczler, and I. Gresits, *Magyar Chem. Folyoirat* **47**, 195-209 (1941); *Chem. Zentr.* I, p. 545 (1943).

Semimicro Method for the Determination of Nitrogen.
R. Belcher and A. L. Godbert, *J. Soc. Chem. Ind.* **60**, 196-198 (1941).

Kjeldahl Nitrogen Determination. A Rapid Wet Digestion Micro Method.
L. P. Pepkowitz and J. W. Shive, *Ind. Eng. Chem., Anal. Ed.* **14**, 914-916 (1942).

Determination of Nitrogen in Nitro and Nitroso Compounds by the Kjeldahl Method.
Z. Csuros and E. Fodor-Kenczler, *Magyar Kém. Folyóirat* **48**, 33-42 (1942); *Chem. Zentr.* I, pp. 545-546 (1943).

Determination of Nitrogen in Nitriles.
E. L. Rose and H. Zilliotto, *Ind. Eng. Chem., Anal. Ed.* **17**, 211-212 (1945).

Determination of Nonaminoid Nitrogen in Aliphatic and Aromatic Compounds.
P. D. Somers, *Proc. Indiana Acad. Sci.* **54**, 117-120 (1945).

The Use of Titanium Chloride for Determining Nitro Nitrogen by the Kjeldahl Method.
A. Soler, *Anales fis. y quim. (Madrid)* **41**, 789-797 (1945).

A New Micro-Estimation Method of the Amino Group.
T. Soda and H. Terayama, *Bull. Chem. Soc. Japan* **20**, 8-15 (1947) (in English).

Application of the Kjeldahl Method to the Analysis of Hydrazine and Nitramine Derivatives.
R. Perrot and A. Barghow, *Proc. 11th Intern. Congr. Pure and Appl. Chem.* **2**, 247-251 (1947) (in French).

Applications of the Kjeldahl Method to Determine Nitrogen in Certain Nitrated Aromatic Derivatives.
J. Tirouflet, *Bull. soc. sci. Bretagne* **23**, 129-131 (1948) (Publ. 1949).

Kjeldahl Micro Digestions in Sealed Tubes at 470°C.
L. M. White and M. C. Long, *Anal. Chem.* **23**, 363-365 (1951).

Micro-Kjeldahl Method for Biologicals.
M. B. Jacobs, *J. Am. Pharm. Assoc.* **40**, 151-153 (1951).

Behavior of Ring Nitrogen in the Micro-Kjeldahl Procedure.
M. Marzadro, *Mikrochemie ver Mikrochim. Acta* **36/37**, 671-678 (1951).

Determination of Nitrile Type Nitrogen with Ordinary Kjeldahl Digestion.
C. H. Vanetten and M. B. Wiele, *Anal. Chem.* **23**, 1338-1339 (1951).

Selective Determination of Different Forms of Nitrogen by the Micro-Kjeldahl Procedure.
M. Marzadro, *Mikrochemie ver. Mikrochim. Acta* **38**, 372-375; *Ann. chim. (Rome)* **41**, 669-672; *Rend. ist. super. sanita's* **14**, 668-672 (1951).

Report on Microanalytical Determination of Nitrogen for N-N, NO, and NO₂ Linkages.
C. L. Ogg and C. O. Willits, *J. Assoc. Offic. Agr. Chemists* **35**, 288-291 (1952).

Determination of Nitrogen Modified Kjeldahl Procedure Using Thiosalicylic Acid.
P. McCutchan and W. F. Roth, *Anal. Chem.* **24**, 369-373 (1952).

Strong Reduction Preliminary to Kjeldahl Digestion in the Analysis of Refractory Compounds.
S. Works, D. Scheirer, and E. C. Wagner, *Anal. Chem.* **25**, 837-838 (1953).

Selective Determination of Different Forms of Nitrogen with the Micro-Kjeldahl Procedure. III.
M. Marzadro, *Mikrochemie ver. Mikrochim. Acta* **40**, 359-366 (1953).

Determination of Nitro Nitrogen by the Kjeldahl Method.
R. B. Bradstreet *Anal. Chem.* **26**, 235-236 (1954).

Kjeldahl Method for Organic Nitrogen.
R. B. Bradstreet, *Anal. Chem.* **26**, 185-187 (1954).

Kjeldahl Determination of Nitrogen in Organic Compounds. A Preliminary Report-Selection of Digesting Conditions.
A. Takeda and J. Senda, *Nogaku Kenkyu (Rept. Ohara Inst. Agr. Biol.)* **41**, 97-108 (1954).

Microdetermination of Nitrogen in Petroleum and Its Products.
S. Baibaeva and M. Orlova, *Novosti Neftyanoi Tekh. Neftepererabotki No.* **4**, 29-34 (1955).

Determination of Nitrogen in Nitro Compounds and Oximes by Iodic Acid Decomposition.
S. Ohashi, *Bull. Chem. Soc. Japan* **28**, 537-541 (1955).

Reduction of Nitro Groups in Organic Compounds before Digestion by the Kjeldahl Method.
R. Belcher and M. K. Bhatty, *Analyst* **81**, 124-125 (1956).

Determination of Nonaminoid Nitrogen by the Micro-Kjeldahl Methods. I. Aromatic Nitro Compounds.
T. S. Ma, R. E. Lang, and J. D. McKinley Jr., *Mikrochim. Acta* pp. 368-377 (1957) (in English).

Kjeldahl Determination of Nitrogen, Extension to Nitro and Nitrogen Single Bond Compounds.
W. E. Dickinson, *Anal. Chem.* **30**, 992-994 (1958).

Micro-Kjeldahl Method for Nitrogen in Certain Organic Compounds Containing N-N and N-0 Linkages.
A. Steyermark, B. E. McGee, E. A. Bass, and Ruth R. Kamp, *Anal. Chem.* **30**, 1961-1963 (1958).

Micro-Kjeldahl Determination of Nitrogen in Aromatic Nitro and Polynitro Compounds.
N. N. Bezinga, T. I. Ovechkina, and G. D. Gal'pern, *Zhur. Anal. Khim.* **17**, 1027-1028 (1962).

Modified Micro-Kjeldahl Procedure for the Determination of Nitrogen in Organic Compounds Containing Nitrogen-Oxygen Bonds.
J. Albert, *Mikrochem. J. Symp. Ser.* **2**, 527-534 (1962).

The Rapid Alkaline Reduction of the Nitro Group and the Kjeldahl Determination of Nitrogen.
T. G. Lunt, *Analyst* **88**, 466-467 (1963).

Catalysts

Early Applications of Catalysts: H. Wilfarth, *Chem. Zentr.* **16**, 17 (1885), oxides of mercury, manganese, bismuth, zinc, lead, iron, and copper; H. Wilfarth, *Chem. Zentr.* **16**, 113 (1885), ferric oxide; K. Ulsch, *Chem. Zentr.* **17**, 375 (1886), platinic chloride; C. Arnold, *Z. anal. Chem.* **26**, 249 (1887), mercury and copper sulfate; C. Arnold and K. Wedemeyer, *Z. anal. Chem.* **31**, 525 (1892), mercuric oxide and copper sulfate.

Notes on the Determination of Nitrogen by the Kjeldahl Method.
P. L. Hibbard, *J. Ind. Eng. Chem.* **2**, 463-466 (1910).

The Estimation of Nitrogen by the Method of Kjeldahl.
A. C. Andersen, *Skand. Arch. Physiol.* **25**, 96-104 (1911).

Kjeldahl Determinations with Vanadium Pentoxide.
Oefele, *Pharm. Zentralhalle* **52**, 1121-1122 (1911).

A New Modification of Kjeldahl's Method.
L. Marino and F. Gonelli, *Atti accad. nazl. Lincei Mem., Classe sci. fis. mat. e nat.* **23**, Sez. I, 523-530 (1914).

Differences in the Acceleration of the Kjeldahl Digestion of Coal and Coke.
B. M. Margosches and A. Lang, *Chem. Ztg.* **39**, 673-675 (1915).

Estimation of Nitrogen by Kjeldahl's Method. II.
O. Nolte, *Z. anal. Chem.* **55**, 185-189 (1916).

Some Limitations of the Kjeldahl Method.
H. C. Brill and F. Agcaoili, *Philippine J. Sci.* **12A**, 261-265 (1917).

Investigation of the Kjeldahl Method for the Determination of Nitrogen.
I. K. Phelps and H. W. Daudt, *J. Assoc. Offic. Agr. Chemists* **3**, 218-220 (1919).

Report on Special Study of the Kjeldahl Method.
H. W. Daudt, *J. Assoc. Offic. Agr. Chemists* **4**, 366 (1921).

A New Catalyst for the Destruction of Organic Matter in the Kjeldahl Nitrogen Determination.
S. Sborowsky and L. Sborowsky, *Ann. chim. anal. Chim. appl.* **4**, 266-267 (1922).

Destruction of Organic Matter in the Kjeldahl Method with Vanadium Salts.
W. Parri, *Giorn. farm. chim.* **71**, 253-259 (1923).

Nitrogen Determinations by the Kjeldahl Method.
M. Hassig, *Mitt. Lebensm. Hyg.* **14**, 101-102 (1923).

The Use of Mercurous Iodide in the Determination of Nitrogen.
E. S. Richards, *Chem. Eng. Mining Rev.* **15**, 369 (1923).

Determination of Nitrogen by the Kjeldahl Method and Modifications.
P. Fleury and H. Levaltier, *J. pharm. chim.* **29**, 137-147 (1924).

Micro-Kjeldahl Experiments.
B. Saika-Pittner, *Pharm. Presse* **33**, 60-61 (1928).

Reaction Accelerators in the Determination of Organic Nitrogen by Kjeldahl's Method.
F. Provvedi, *Atti accad. fisiocrit. Siena* [10] **3**, 423-425 (1928).

The Use of Copper Sulfate Instead of Mercury in the Kjeldahl Digestion.
F. Mach and W. Lepper, *Landwirtsch. Vers.-Sta.* **109**, 363-366 (1929).

The Use of Copper Sulphate in Place of Mercury for the Kjeldahl Analysis.
W. Lepper, *Landwirtsch. Vers.-Sta.* **111**, 155-158 (1930).

Use of Selenium as a Catalyst in the Determination of Nitrogen by the Kjeldahl Method.
M. F. Lauro, *Ind. Eng. Chem., Anal. Ed.* **3**, 401-402 (1931).

Nitrogen Determination in Coals by the Kjeldahl Method.
E. Bornstein and A. J. Petrick, *Brennstoff-Chem.* **13**, 41-45 (1932).

A Note on the Use of Selenium Oxychloride as a Catalyst in the Determination of Nitrogen by the Kjeldahl Method.
C. E. Rich, *Cereal Chem.* **9**, 118-120 (1932).

A Note on the Use of Selenium as a Catalyst in Kjeldahl Digestion with Natural Gas Heat.
R. M. Sandstedt, *Cereal Chem.* **9**, 156-157 (1932).

Application of Selenium as a Catalyst to the Kjeldahl Method for the Determination of Nitrogen in Coal and Coke.
H. E. Crossley, *J. Soc. Chem. Ind.* **51**, 237-8T (1932).

Metallic Selenium as a Catalyst in Kjeldahl Digestions.
H. C. Messman, *Cereal Chem.* **9**, 357 (1932).

Selenium in Determination of Nitrogen by Kjeldahl Method.
J. Tennant, H. L. Harrell and A. Stull, *Ind. Eng. Chem., Anal. Ed.* **4**, 410 (1932).

A Study of the Kjeldahl Method. I. Mercuric Oxide as a Catalyst when Block Tin Condensers Are Used.
R. A. Osborn and A. Krasnitz, *J. Assoc. Offic. Agr. Chemists* **16**, 107-110 (1933).

A Study of the Kjeldahl Method. I. Mercuric Oxide as a Catalyst when Block Tin Condensers Are Used.
R. A. Osborn and A. Krasnitz, *J. Assoc. Offic. Agr. Chemists* **16**, 110-113 (1933).

Selenium in the Determination of Phosphorus and Nitrogen in Phospholipides.
F. E. Kurtz, *Ind. Eng. Chem., Anal. Ed.* **5**, 260 (1933).

Selenium: The New Catalyst in Kjeldahl Digestions.
M. F. Lauro, *Oil & Soap* **10**, 149-150 (1933).

Report of the Sub-committee on Selenium as a Kjeldahl Catalyst in the Cereal Laboratory.
C. F. Davis and M. Wise, *Cereal Chem.* **10**, 488-493 (1933).

A New Rapid Method of Nitrogen Determination.
F. M. Wieninger, *Wochschr. Brau.* **50**, 124 (1933).

Use of Selenium as a Catalyst in the Determination of Nitrogen by the Kjeldahl Method.
N. Belov and O. Pakhomova, *Kozhevenno-Obuvnaya Prom. U.S.S.R.* **12**, 371-372 (1933); *Chim. & ind. (Paris)* **31**, 300 (1934).

A Study of the Kjeldahl Method, III. Further Comparisons of Selenium with Mercury and with Copper Catalysts.
R. A. Osborn and A. Krasnitz, *J. Assoc. Offic. Agr. Chemists* **17**, 339-342 (1934).

Some Observations on the Use of Selenium and Its Compounds as a Catalyst in the Determination of Protein in Wheat by the Kjeldahl Method.
S. R. Snider and D. A. Coleman, *Cereal Chem.* **11**, 414-430 (1934).

An Improved Kjeldahl Process for the Determination of Nitrogen in Coal and Coke.
A. E. Beet, *Fuel* **13**, 343-345 (1934).

Determination of Nitrogen and Phosphorus in the Kjeldahl Reaction with Selenium as a Catalyst.
K. Taufel, H. Thaler, and K. Starke, *Angew. Chem.* **48**, 191-192 (1935).

Mechanism of the Catalytic Effects of Selenium and Tellurium in the Sulphuric Acid Digestion of Organic Material Prior to the Kjeldahl Determination of Nitrogen.
V. V. Illarionov and N. A. Soloveva, *Z. anal. Chem.* **100**, 328-343 (1935).

Rational Procedure for the Use of Selenium in the Kjeldahl Determination of Nitrogen.
V. V. Illarionov and N. A. Soloveva, *Z. anal. chem.* **101**, 254-257 (1935).

The Most Rapid Oxidation of Organic Substances with Sulphuric Acid.
J. Milbauer, *J. Elektrochem.* **41**, 594-595 (1935).

A Study of the Kjeldahl Method. IV. Metallic Catalysts and Metallic Interferences.
R. A. Osborn and J. B. Wilkie, *J. Assoc. Offic. Agr. Chemists* **18**, 604-609 (1935).

The Determination of Nitrogen in Coal by the Kjeldahl Method, Using Selenium as a catalyst.
H. E. Crossley, *J. Soc. Chem. Ind.* **54**, 367-9T (1935).

Selenium as the Catalyst in Kjeldahl Digestions.
K. Scharrer, *Z. Pflanzenernahr., Dungung Bodenk.* **41**, 203-207 (1935).

Effect of the Constitution of the Oxidized Substances on the Activity of the Catalysts for Concentrated Sulphuric Acid and the Effect of Temperature on the Catalysts.
J. Milbauer, *Bull. soc. chim.* [5] **3**, 218-221 (1936).

Addendum to the Rapid Method of Estimating Nitrogen with Selenium as a Catalyst.
F. M. Wieninger, *Wochschr. Brau.* **53**, 251-252 (1936).

Kjeldahl Method for the Determination of Nitrogen in Foods, Feeding Stuffs, Leather, etc.
A. E. Beet and D. G. Furzey, *J. Soc. Chem. Ind.* **55**, 108-9T (1936).

Copper Selenite as a Catalyst in the Kjeldahl Nitrogen Determination.
E. J. Schwoegler, B. J. Babler, and L. C. Hurd, *J. Biol. Chem.* **113**, 749-751 (1936).

The Kjeldahl Decomposition with the Aid of Selenium.
K. Taufel, H. Thaler, and K. Starke, *Angew. Chem.* **49**, 265-266 (1936).

Selenium as a Catalyst in the Kjeldahl Method as Applied to Soil and Grass Analysis.
F. L. Ashton, *J. Agr. Sci.* **26**, 239-248 (1936).

Reactions in Concentrated Sulphuric Acid. VI. The Relation of the Substance to Be Oxidized to the Effectiveness of the Catalyst.
J. Milbauer, *Chem. obzor* **11**, 208-211 (in English, p. 211) (1936).

A New Method for Ttirating Ammonia in the Micro-Kjeldahl Determination.
C. Brecker, *Wien. klin. Wochschr.* **49**, 128-131 (1936).

Reaction in a Medium of Concentrated Sulphuric Acid. VIII. Equilibrium States with Catalysts.
J. Milbauer, *Chem. obzor* **11**, 233-240 (in English, p. 240) (1936).

Rapid Determination of Nitrogen (in Beet Pulp) by the Kjeldahl Method.
L. E. Volochanenko, *Sovet. Sakhar, No.* **9**, 44-46 (1936).

Reactions in a Medium of Concentrated Sulphuric Acid. IX. The Kjeldahl Reaction in a Current of Gases.
J. Milbauer, *Chem. Obzor* **12**, 17-19 (1937).

Speed and Accuracy in the Determination of Total Nitrogen. Use of Selenium and Other Catalysts.
A. E. Murneek and P. H. Helnze, *Missouri Agr. Expt. Sta. Research Bull.* **261**, 2-8 (1937).

Determination of Nitrogen in Complex Nitrogenous Substances.
H. C. Goswami and M. R. Ray, *Sci. and Culture (Calcutta)* **3**, 180 (1937).

The Use of Selenium in the Determination of Nitrogen in Potato Tubers.
A. M. Smith and W. Y. Paterson, *Analyst* **62**, 786-788 (1937).

Some Catalysts in the Kjeldahl Digestion.
T. Nagosi and I. Nakagawa, *J. Sci. Soil Manure, Japan* **11**, 433-438 (1937).

Rapid Estimation of Nitrogen with the Use of Mercury-Free Selenium Catalyst.
M. Lindemann, *Wochschr. Brau.* **54**, 155-156 (1937).

Tellurium as a Catalyst.
Y. D. Gresin, *Farm. Zhur. No.* **2**, 104-109 (1937).

Modification of the Kjeldahl Procedure.
J. Milbauer, *Z. anal. Chem.* **111**, 397-407 (1938).

Selenium Catalyst in the Determination of Nitrogen by Kjeldahl's Method.
K. Nokajima and M. Ikeda, *J. Agr. Chem. Soc. Japan* **13**, 1208-1214 (1937).

Modification of the Kjeldahl Method in Which Selenium Is Used as a Catalyst in the Digestion.
M. Ohmasa, *J. Sci. Soil Manure, Japan* **11**, 133-138(1937).

A New Catalyst for the Destruction of Organic Matter in the Kjeldahl Nitrogen Determination.

C. Dumazert and Y. Marcelet, *Bull. soc. chim. biol* **20**, 201-211 (1938).

Improved Micro-Kjeldahl Method for the Determination of Nitrogen in Coal.
A. E. Beet and R. Belcher, *Mikrochemie* **24**, 145-148(1938).

Use of Selenium as Catalyst in the Kjeldahl Method of Estimating Nitrogen.
C. S. Piper, *Australian Chem. Inst. J. & Proc.* **5**, 312-316 (1938).

New Catalyst for the Determination of Nitrogen by the Kjeldahl Method.
R. B. Bradstreet, *Ind. Eng. Chem., Anal. Ed.* **10**, 696 (1938).

Use of Mercuric Selenite as a New Catalyst for the Destruction of Organic Matter in the Kjeldahl Determination.
C. Dumazert and Y. Marcelet, *Bull. biologistes pharmaciens* **44**, 546-552 (1938).

A Remarkable Catalyst in the Destruction of Organic Matter by the Kjeldahl Method.
J. Vene, *Bull. soc. sci. Bretagne* **15**, 49-51 (1938).

Selenium Catalyst in Kjeldahl Digestion of Leather.
D. J. Lloyd, *J. Intern. Soc. Leather Trades' Chemists* **23**, 275 (1939).

The Mechanism of the Catalytic Effect of Selenium in the Kjeldahl Method for Determining Nitrogen.
A. Sreenivasan and V. Sadasivan, *Z. anal. Chem.* **116**, 244-252 (1939); *Ind. Eng. Chem., Anal. Ed.* **11**, 314-315 (1939).

Use of Selenium in the Kjeldahl Digestion of Leather for Nitrogen.
D. Williams, *J. Am. Leather Chemists' Assoc.* **34**, 261-263 (1939).

Selenium Catalyst in the Kjeldahl Digestion of Leather.
D. J. Lloyd, *J. Intern. Soc. Leather Trades' Chemists* **23**, 275 (1939).

Effect of Selenium on the Kjeldahl Digestion.
R. B. Bradstreet, *Ind. Eng. Chem., Anal. Ed.* **12**, 657 (1940).

A New Catalyst for the Kjeldahl Combustion of Coals.
H. E. Crossley, *Fuel* **20**, 144-146 (1941).

Selenium as a Catalyst in the Determination of Nitrogen According to Kjeldahl.

G. R. Kaneck, *Trudy Leningrad. Inst. Sovet. Targovti No.* **2**, 22-29 (1939); *Khim. Referat. Zhur.* **4**, No. 1, 89 (1941).

Anhydrous $CuSO_4$ in the Kjeldahl Nitrogen Determination.
C. Beatty, *Ind. Eng. Chem., Anal. Ed.* **15**, 426 (1943).

Collection of Micro-Kjeldahl Ammonia in Boric Acid and Precise Titration.
W. R. Thompson, N. Y. State Dept. Health Ann. Rept. Div. Labs. and Research pp. 23-29 (1943).

Determination of Nitrogen by the Kjeldahl Method.
J. Sovo, *Magyar Kém. Folyóirat* **49**, 81-100 (1943); *Chem. Zentr. II*, pp. 344-345 (1944).

Catalytic Activity of Selenates in the Kjeldahl Method for the Determination of Nitrogen.
R. S. Dalrymple and G. B. King, *Ind. Eng. Chem., Anal. Ed.* **17**, 403-404 (1945).

Rapid Method of Kjeldahlization by the Combined Catalytic Action of Selenium and Perchloric Acid.
A. Mallol, *Farm. nueva (Madrid)* **11**, No. 108, 7-17 (1946).

Comparison of Copper Sulphate and Mercuric Oxide as Catalysts in the Determination of Protein in Fish Meal.
T. J. Potts, M. A. Parkam, and I. M. Schafer, *J. Assoc. Offic. Agr. Chemists* **30**, 648-651 (1947).

Selenium as a Catalyst in Kjeldahl Digestions.
S. M. Patel and A. Sreenivasan, *Anal. Chem.* **20**, 63-65 (1948).

Comparison of Tellurium and Selenium as Catalysts for Kjeldahl Digestion.
R. B. Bradstreet, *Anal. Chem.* **21**, 1012-1013 (1949).

Selenium Catalysis of the Kjeldahl Reaction.
G. M. Schwab and E. Schwab-Agallidis, *Naturwissenschaften* **36**, 254 (1949).

The Kjeldahl Method Catalyzed by Selenic-Perchloric Acids.
A. Mallol García, *Anales real soc. españ. fis. y. quím.* **47B**, 659-664 (1951).

The Kjeldahl Determination in the Presence of Selenium Oxychloride; Quinoline and Quinaldine.

C. Moreau, *Compt. rend.* **233**, 1616-1617 (1951).

Determination of Nitrogen by the Kjeldahl Method.
J. Almeida Alves and E. L. Neves Alves, *Melhoramento* **4**, 135-187 (1951).

Nitrogen Loss When Selenium Mixture Is Used in the Kjeldahl Digestion as Described by F. M. Wieninger.
W. Lepper, *Z. anal Chem.* **134**, 248-252 (1951).

Report of the A.L.C.A. Hide-Substance Subcommittee.
H. B. Merrill, S. Dahl, R. M. Lollar, H. L. Ellison, and A. N. Kay, *J. Am. Leather Chemists Assoc.* **47**, 15-40 (1952).

The Kjeldahl Determination of Nitrogen.
S. V. Anantakrishman and K. V. Srinivasan, *Proc. Indian Acad. Sci.* **36A**, 299-305 (1952).

Determination of Kjeldahl Nitrogen in Foodstuffs and the Influence of Various Catalysts.
H. Hadorn, R. Jungkunz, and K. W. Biefer, *Mitt. Lebensm. Hyg.* **44**, 14-29 (1953).

Decomposition of Ammonia in Sealed-Tube Micro Digestions with a Selenium Catalyst.
P. R. W. Baker, *Analyst* **78**, 500-501 (1953).

The Catalytic Effect of Wieninger's Selenium Reaction Mixture Compared with Copper Sulfate Plus Potassium Sulfate in the Kjeldahl Decomposition of Feeds.
P. von Polheim, K. Jungermann, and A. E. von Mettenheim, *Landwirtsch. Forsch.* **6**, 194-199 (1954).

Comparison of Some Catalysts Used in the Kjeldahl Nitrogen Determinations.
D. F. Louw, *J. S. African Chem. Inst.* **8**, 39-42 (1955).

Note on the Catalyst in the Kjeldahl Procedure for Nitrogen in Fertilizer.
H. B. Allan, *J. Assoc. Offic. Agr. Chemists* **38**, 185 (1955).

Semimicro Kjeldahl Determination of Nitro and Amido Nitrogen.
I. Selenium Catalysts.
A. Takeda and J. Senda, *Ber. Ohara Inst. landwirtsch. Biol. Okayama Univ.* **10**, 241-244 (1956) (in English).

Effect of the Mode of Combustion on Nitrogen Determination by Kjeldahl's Method.
L. Rozental, *Roczniki Państwowego Zaklada Hig.* **9**, 183-197 (1948).

Micro-Kjeldahl Determination of Nitrogen. The Effects of Added Salts and Catalysts.
P. R. W. Baker, *Talanta* **8**, 57-71 (1961).

Natural Products

Determination of Total Nitrogen of Urine.
Huguet, *Repert. pharm.* **21**, 481 (1909).

The Determination of Organic Nitrogen, in Sewage by the Kjeldahl Process.
L. Whipple, *Tech. Quart.* **20**, 162-169 (1907).

On the Method of Nitrogen Determination in Urine.
P. Rona and R. Ottenberg, *Biochem. Z.* **24**, 354-356 (1910).

Notes on the Determination of Nitrogen in the Kjeldahl Method.
P. L. Hibbard, *J. Ind. Eng. Chem.* **2**, 463-466 (1910).

Determination of Nitrogen in Cerebrospinal Fluid.
P. Thomas, *Bull. soc. chim.* **13**, 398-400 (1912).

Decomposition of Organic Substances by Kjeldahl's Method and Estimation of Nitrogen in Barley.
K. Bunge, *Pharm. Zentralhalle* **54**, 1127-1128 (1914).

Simplification of Bang's Micro-Kjeldahl Method and the Nitrogen Content of the Vitreous Humor in the Eye of Rabbit and Dog.
M. Kochmann, *Biochem. Z.* **63**, 479-482 (1914).

Determination of Nitrogen in Coal. A Comparison of the Kjeldahl Method with the Dumas Method.
A. C. Fieldner and C. A. Taylor, *U. S. Bur. Mines Tech. Paper* **64**, 25 pp. (1915).

Rapid Manipulation of Kjeldahl's Method.
A. T. Hough, *Collegium* (London Edition) pp. 126-127 (1915).

Differences in the Acceleration of the Kjeldahl Digestion of Coal and Coke.
B. M. Margosches and Alfred Lang, *Chem. Ztg.* **39**, 673-675 (1915).

Note on Kjeldahl's Method for the Determination of Nitrogen as Applied to Gelatine.
H. G. Bennett and N. L. Holmes *J. Soc. Leather Trades' Chemists* **3**, 24-27 (1919).

A Simplified Macro-Kjeldahl Method for Urine.
O. Folin and L. E. Wright, *J. Biol. Chem.* **38**, 461-464 (1919).

Micro-Estimation of Nitrogen in Agricultural Products.
W. Geilmann, *J. Landwirtsch.* **68**, 235-254 (1920).

Use of Trichloracetic Acid and Copper Sulfate as Aids in the Method of Kjeldahl Application to Urine.
A. Gregaut and J. Thiery, *Compt. rend. soc. biol.* **84**, 716-718 (1921).

Shortening the Process of Digestion in Protein Determinations of Wheat and Flour.
R. K. Durham, *Modern Miller* **49**, No. 24, 26 (1922).

Quick Method for Determining Protein in Wheat.
P. H. Bimmerman and W. L. Frank, *J. Am. Assoc. Cereal Chem.* **8**, 49-53 (1923).

The Micro-Kjeldahl Method for Technical Tanning and Similar Investigations in the Albumin Industry.
O. Gerngross and W. E. Schaefer, *Z. angew. Chem.* **36**, 391-394 (1923).

The Estimation of Nitrogen in Coal.
L. A. Baranov and R. A. Mott, *Fuel* **3**, 31-34 (1924).

The Estimation of Nitrogen in Coal.
L. A. Baranov and R. A. Mott, *Fuel* **3**, 49-52 (1924).

A Modification of the Salicylic-Thiosulfate Method Suitable for the Determination of Total Nitrogen in Plants, Plant Solutions, and Soil Solutions.
R. Ranker, *J. Assoc. Offic. Agr. Chemists* **10**, 230-251 (1927).

Comparing Protein Determinations in Grain by the Quick Method.
H. Kuehl and P. G. Gottschalk, *Cereal Chem.* **6**, 512-514 (1929).

Nitrogen Determination in Coals by the Kjeldahl Method.
E. Börnstein and A. J. Petrick, *Brennstoff-Chem.* **13**, 41-45 (1932).

Further Experiments with the Kjeldahl Process. A Comparison Between Coal and Other Nitrogenous Substances.
A. E. Beet, *Fuel* **11**, 406-408 (1932).

Microdetermination of Protein in Cereal Products.
R. J. Robinson and J. A. Shellenberger, *Ind. Eng. Chem., Anal. Ed.* **4**, 243 (1932).

Determination of Nitrogen in Soils.
A. Sreenivasan, *Indian J. Agr. Sci.* **2**, 525-530 (1932).

Methodics of the Micro-Nitrogen Determination with Special Reference to Foodstuffs and Condiments.
E. Iselin, *Mitt. Lebensm. Hyg.* **24**, 267-273 (1933).

Use of a Selenium-Mercuric Oxide Combination in Determination of Nitrogen in Feed Materials.
L. V. Taylor, *Ind. Eng. Chem., Anal. Ed.* **5**, 263 (1933).

An Improved Kjeldahl Process for the Determination of Nitrogen in Coal and Coke.
A. E. Beet, *Fuel* **13**, 343-346 (1934).

Some Observations on the Use of Selenium and Its Compounds as a Catalyst in the Determination of Protein in Wheat by the Kjeldahl Method.
S. R. Snider and D. A. Coleman, *Cereal Chem.* **11**, 414-430 (1934).

Comparison of the Kjeldahl and Dumas Methods for Some Agricultural Products.
P. Anne, *Ann. fals. et fraudes* **27**, 220-222 (1934).

Dilution Method for Micro-Kjeldahl Determinations.
O. Hartley, *Ind. Eng. Chem., Anal. Ed.* **6**, 249 (1934).

Quantitative Drop Analysis. III. Kjeldahl Nitrogen Determination and the Non-Protein Nitrogen of Blood.
P. L. Kirk, *Mikrochemie* **16**, 13-24 (1934).

Rapid Technique for the Determination of Nitrogen by the Kjeldahl Method, Suitable for Determining the Total Protein of Wheat, Flour, and Mill Products.
R. Guillemet and C. Schell, *Bull. soc. chim. biol.* **16**, 1631-1636 (1934).

Determination of Nitrogen in Soils. Protective Action of Silica as a Factor in the Estimation of Nitrogen by the Kjeldahl Method.
A. Sreenivasan and V. Subrahmanyan, *Indian J. Agr. Sci.* **3**, 646-657 (1933).

Determination of Nitrogen in Soils. III. Further Observations on the Protective Action of Silica and Their Bearing on the Estimation of Nitrogen in Substances Which Are Admixed with Soil or Are Otherwise Rich in Silica.
A. Sreenivasan, *Indian J. Agr. Sci.* **4**, 320-326 (1934).

Determination of Nitrogen in Soils. IV. Pretreatment with Oxidizing Agents and Its Influence on the Progress of Acid Digestion.
A. Sreenivasan, *Indian J. Agr. Sci.* **4**, 546-553 (1934).

Micro-Kjeldahl Method in the Analysis of Silk Thread and Textiles.
M. Bonicotti, *Boll. uffic. regia Staz. sper. seta* **4**, 35-37 (1934).

Change in the Kjeldahl-Pregl Method for Determining Nitrogen, and Its Application to the Analysis of Canned Foodstuffs.
I. K. Kotlyar, *Z. anal. Chem.* **100**, 104-112 (1935).

Micromethods for the Determination of Ammonia, Urea, Total Nitrogen, Uric Acid, Creatinine (and Creatine), and Allantoin.
H. Borsook, *J. Biol. Chem.* **110**, 481-493 (1935).

Determination of Nitrogen in Soils. V, Estimation of Total Nitrogen to Include Nitrates.
A. Sreenivasan, *J. Indian Inst. Sci.* **18A**, Pt. 6, 25-38 (1935).

Determination of Protein Nitrogen. Accelerating the Kjeldahl-Gunning Digestion by Addition of Phosphates.
H. W. Gerritz and J. L. St. John, *Ind. Eng. Chem., Anal. Ed.* **7**, 380-383 (1935).

A Study of the Kjeldahl Method. IV. Metallic Catalysts and Metallic Interferences.
R. A. Osborn and J. B. Wilkie, *J. Assoc. Offic. Agr. Chemists* **18**, 604-609 (1935).

The Determination of Nitrogen in Coal by the Kjeldahl Method, Using Selenium as a Catalyst.
H. E. Crossley *J. Soc. Chem. Ind.* **54**, 367-9T (1935).

The Apparent Nitrogen Assimilation of Germinating Peas. (The

Applicability of Kjeldahl Method in Biological Assimilation Experiments.)
E. M. Smyth and P. W. Wilson, *Biochem. Z.* **282**, 1-25 (1935).

The Rapid Determination of Nitrogen in Beets and in Sugar Products by the Kjeldahl Method.
H. Riehm, *Listy cukrovar,* **54**, 41-44 (1935); *Z. Zuckerind. cechoslov. Rep.* **60**, 156-159 (1935).

The Micro-Kjeldahl Method for Determining the Total Nitrogen in Yeast.
M. Sobotka, *Mikrochemie* **19**, 81-88 (1936).

Kjeldahl Method for the Determination of Nitrogen in Foods, Feeding Stuffs, Leather, etc.
A. E. Beet and D. G. Furzey, *J. Soc. Chem. Ind.* **55**, 108-9T (1936).

Selenium as a Catalyst in the Kjeldahl Method as Applied to Soil and Grass Analysis.
F. L. Ashton, *J. Agr. Sci.* **26**, 239-248 (1936).

Analysis of Plant Tissue. Application of a Semi-Micro Kjeldahl Method.
W. W. Umbreit and V. S. Bond, *Ind. Eng. Chem., Anal. Ed.* **8**, 276-278 (1936).

Semi-micro Analysis of Nitrogen in Oil Cakes by the Kjeldahl Method.
S. S. Mirskaya, *Vsesoyuz. Nauch.-Issledovatel Inst. Zhirov. Analysemethoden in der Oel-u. Fettind. 1936,* pp. 99-106 (In German, pp. 106-107).

The Betaine Content and Nitrogen Distribution of Beet Molasses and Other Beet By-Products.
W. L. Davies and H. C. Dowden, *J. Soc. Chem. Ind.* **55**, 175-9T (1936).

Rapid Determination of Nitrogen (in Beet Pulp) by the Kjeldahl Method.
L. E. Volochanenko, *Sovet. Sakhar No.* **9**, 44-46 (1936).

The Acceleration of Digestion in the Kjeldahl Method as Applied to Soil and Grass Analysis.
F. L. Ashton, *J. Soc. Chem. Ind.* **56**, 101-4T (1937).

The Use of Selenium in the Determination of Nitrogen in Potato Tubers.
A. M. Smith and W. Y. Paterson, *Analyst* **62**, 786-788(1937).

Determination of Nitrogen in Flour.
B. Jelinek, *Bull. anciens eleves ecole franc. meunerie* pp. 233-234 (1937).

Determination of Nitrogen in Complex Nitrogenous Substances.
H. C. Goswami and M. R. Ray, *Sci. and Culture* **3**, 180 (1937).

The Determination of Nitrogen Distribution in Milk.
S. J. Rowland, *J. Dairy Research* **9**, 42-46 (1938).

The Determination of Total Nitrogen in Small Quantities of Agricultural Products.
H. Roth, *Angew. Chem.* **51**, 120-121 (1938).

Improved Micro-Kjeldahl Method for the Determination of Nitrogen in Coal.
A. E. Beet and R. Belcher, *Mikrochemie* **24**, 145-148(1938).

Applicability of the Method of Kjeldahl in the Determination of Nitrogen in Biochemical Research.
G. Bertrand, *Compt. rend. trav. lab. Carlsberg, Ser. Chim.* **22**, 67-72 (1938).

The Nitrogen Problem in the Brewing Industry.
G. Chabot, *Ann. soc. brass. enseignement profess.* **47**, 150-161 (1938).

Improved Micro-Kjeldahl Method for the Determination of Nitrogen in Coal.
A. E. Beet and R. Belcher, *Mikrochemie* **24**, 145-148(1938).

The Kjeldahl Determination of Nitrogen.
J. Jany and A. Morvay, *Z. anal. Chem.* **114**, 120-125 (1938).

Micro-Kjeldahl Method Including Nitrates.
R. H. Moore, *Botan. Gaz.* **100**, 250-252 (1938).

Application of the Kjeldahl Method to the Study of the Binding of Nitrogen by Leguminous Seeds During Germination.
V. Sadasivan and A. Sreenivasan, *Biochem. Z.* **296**, 434-442 (1938).

Determination of Nitrogen in Mixed Fertilizers Containing Nitrates and Chlorides.
B. Dyer and J. H. Hamence, *Analyst* **63**, 866-870 (1938).

Nitrogen Determination in Milk and Butter by the Kjeldahl and the ter Meulen Methods.
H. A. Serks, *Verslag. Landbouwk. Onderzoek. Sect. C* **45**, (2), 47-54 (1939).

Determination of Nitrogen in Leather.
W. F. Baker and S. G. Shuttleworth, *J. Intern. Soc. Leather Trades' Chemists* **23**, 488-491 (1939).

The Determination of Nitrogen in Plant Materials Containing Nitrates.
E. Rauterberg and E. Knippenberg, *Bodenk. u. Pflanzenernahr.* **13**, 194-198 (1939).

Rapid Determination of Total Nitrogen in Plants.
V. M. Panifilov, *Chemisation Socialistic Agr. (U.S.S.R.)* **8**, No. 5, 60-62 (1939); *Chim. et ind.* **43**, 164 (1940).

Note on the Kjeldahl Digestion of Sugar-Cane Juice.
L. G. Davidson, *J. Assoc. Offic. Agr. Chem.* **23**, 171-172 (1940).

A Semi-micro Kjeldahl Method for the Determination of Total Nitrogen in Milk.
S. G. Menefee and O. R. Overman, *J. Dairy Sci.* **23**, 1177-1185 (1940).

Determination of Nitrogen, Potassium, and Soluble Sugars in Small Samples of Plant Substances.
V. I. Shtatnov, *Chemisation Socialistic Agr. (U.S.S.R.) No.* **9**, 44-47 (1940); *Khim. Referat. Zhur.* **4**, No. 3, 63 (1941).

Analytical Methods in Rubber Chemistry. I (2).
G. R. Tristram, *Trans. Inst. Rubber Ind.* **16**, 261-267 (1941).

Effect of Nitrates on the Determination of Protein Nitrogen by Kjeldahl Method.
E. I. Whitehead and O. E. Olson, *J. Assoc. Offic. Agr. Chemists* **25**, 769-772 (1942).

The Determination of Ammoniacal and Urea Nitrogen in Feeds.
W. B. Griem, *J. Assoc. Offic. Agr. Chemists* **25**, 874-877 (1942).

The Total Nitrogen Content of Egg Albumin and Other Proteins.
A. C. Chibnall, M. W. Rees, and E. F. Williams, *Biochem. J.* **37**, 354-359 (1943).

Determination of Total Nitrogen in Proteins and Their Hydrolyzates. Improved Method and Apparatus.
R. Jonnard, *Ind. Eng. Chem., Anal. Ed.* **17**, 246-249 (1945).

Methods in Chemical Analysis of Soils. Determination of Total Nitrogen, Ammonia, Nitrates, and Nitrites in Soils.
A. L. Prince, *Soil Sci.* **59**, 57-52 (1945).

Micro-Kjeldahl Determination of the Nitrogen Content of Amino Acids and Proteins.
L. Miller and J. A. Houghton, *J. Biol. Chem.* **159**, 373-383 (1945).

Determination of Nitrogen in Foodstuffs by the Kjeldahl Method: Digestion Conditions.
R. S. Alcock, *Analyst* **71**, 233-234 (1946).

Determination of Nitrogen, Phosphorus, Potassium, Calcium, and Magnesium in Plant Tissue. Semimicro Wet Digestion Method for Large Number of Samples.
O. J. Kelley, A. S. Hunter, and A. J. Sterges, *Ind. Eng. Chem., Anal. Ed.* **18**, 319-322 (1946).

Micro-Kjeldahl Determination of Nitrogen in Gramicidin and Tryptophan. Comparison of Gunning-Arnold-Dyer and Friedrich Methods.
L. M. White and G. E. Secor, *Ind. Eng. Chem., Anal. Ed.* **18**, 457-458 (1946).

A New Micro-Estimation Method for the Amino Group.
T. Sada and H. Terayama, *Bull. Chem. Soc. Japan* **20**, 8-15 (1947) (in English).

Semimicro Determination of Amino Acid Nitrogen.
G. Frey, *Helv. Chim. Acta* **31**, 709-715 (1948).

Oxidation of Glycerinated Solutions in the Micro-Kjeldahl Determination of Nitrogen.
P. E. Portner, *Anal. Chem.* **19**, 502-503 (1947).

Determinations of Nitrogen in Crude Rubber.
G. J. van der Bie, *Mededeel. Ned.-Indisch Inst. Rubberonderzoek, Buitenzorg* **64**, 8 pp. (1948).

Study of Conditions for the Kjeldahl of Nitrogen in Proteins. Description of Methods with Mercury as a Catalyst, and Titrimetric and Gasometric Measurements of the Ammonia Formed.
A. Hiller, J. Plazin and D. D. Van Slyke, *J. Biol. Chem.* **176**, 1401-1420 (1948).

Spectrophotometric Determination of Total Nitrogen in Oils.
C. H. Hale, M. N. Hale and W. H. Jones, *Anal. Chem.* **21**, 1949-1951 (1949).

The Kjeldahl Method in Agricultural Analyses.
J. de La Rubia Pacheco, F. B. Lopez-Rubio, and J. Garrido Marquez, *Inform. quim. anal. (Madrid)* **4**, 166-167 (1950).

A Modified Procedure for the Determination of Niacin in Cereal Products.
O. Pelletier and J. A. Campbell, *J. Assoc. Offic. Agr. Chem.* **42**, 625-630 (1950).

Determination of Nitrogen in Coal.
G. N. Badami and J. W. Whitaker, *Fuel* **30**, 8-9 (1951).

Micro-Kjeldahl Method for Biologicals.
M. B. Jacobs. *J. Am. Pharm. Assoc.* **40**, 151-153 (1951).

The Determination of Nitrogen in Leather by the Kjeldahl Method.
S. Dahl and R. Oehler, *J. Am. Leather Chemists' Assoc.* **46**, 317-335 (1951).

A Comparative Study of Four Kjeldahl Methods.
K. Nuna, *Bull. Govt. Forest Exptl. Sta. (Japan)* **53**, 127-134 (1952).

Report of the A.L.C.A. Hide-Substance Subcommittee.
H. B. Merrill, S. Dahl, R. M. Lollar, H. L. Ellison, and A. N. Kay, *J. Am. Leather Chemists' Assoc.* **47**, 15-40 (1952).

Determination of Kjeldahl Nitrogen in Foodstuffs, and the Influence of Various Catalysts.
H. Hadorn, R. Jungkunz, and K. W. Biefer, *Mitt. Lebensm. u. Hyg.* **44**, 14-29 (1953).

The Determination of Nitrogen Content of Solid Fuels with the Semimicro Kjeldahl Method.
W. Lange and W. Winzen, *Glückauf* **89**, 324-325 (1953).

The Use of Microchemical Methods in Food Research. I. Kjeldahl Micro and Semi-Micro Method.
C. Rzymowska, I. Bernsteinowna, and J. Grochowska, *Roczniki Panstwowego Zakladu Hig.* pp. 1-21 (1953). (English Summary).

The Estimation of Separated Milk Powder in Meat Products.
O. Jones and W. C. Avery, *Lab. Practice* **2**, 16 (1953).

Determination of Trace Kjeldahl Nitrogen in Petroleum Stocks.
H. J. Cahnmann, *Anal. Chem.* **27**, 1235-1240 (1955).

Microdetermination of Nitrogen in Petroleum and Its Products.
S. Baibaeva and N. Orlova, *Novosti Neftyanoi Tekh. Neftepererabotki No.* **4**, 29-34 (1955).

A New Semi-Micro Kjeldahl Method for the Determination of Nitrogen in Coals.
M. Dermelji and L. Strauch, *Bull. sci. Conseil. acad. RPF Yougoslavie,* **2**, 104-105 (1956) (in German).

Advancements in Bacteriology and Analytical Methods.
J. E. Kiker, Jr., *Public Works* **88**, No. 12, 89-90 (1957).

The Content of Amino Acids in Certain Foods and Their Biological Utilization. Contribution to the Analysis of Protein and to Problems Concerning the Biological Protein Values.
J. Wagner, *Kuhn-Arch.* **71**, No. 1, 1-74 (1957).

The Analysis of Nitrogen in the Smalley Oilseed Meal Series.
C. H. Perrin, *J. Am. Oil Chemists Soc.* **34**, 409-411 (1957).

Determination of Nitrogen in Polyacrylonitrile.
U. Bartels, *Faserforsch. u. Textiltech.* **8**, 194-195 (1957).

Determination of Total Protein in Cerebrospinal Fluid by an Ultramicro-Kjeldahl Nitrogen Procedure.
W. W. Tourtellotte, J. G. Parker, R. E. Alving, and R. N. De Jong, *Anal. Chem.* **30**, 1563 (1958).

The Determination of Trace Quantities of Nitrogen in Petroleum Fractions.

O. I. Milner, R. J. Zahner, L. S. Hepner, and W. H. Cowell, *Anal. Chem.* **30**, 1528-1530 (1958).

Simple Microdetermination of Kjeldahl Nitrogen in Biological Materials.
C. A. Long, *Anal. Chem.* **30**, 1692-1694 (1958).

Deproteinization Agents and the Kjeldahl Determination of Organic Nitrogen-Containing Compounds.
H. Slusanschi, M. Suteanu, and A. Lozinschi, *Acad. rep. populare Romine, Inst. biochim. Studii cercetari biochim.* **2**, 385-393 (1959).

The Determination of Protein Nitrogen in Wood.
S. Nickel, *Holzforschung* **14**, 150-152 (1960).

The Determination of the Protein Content of Milk by the Kjeldahl Method.
J. Eisses, *Neth. Milk Dairy J.* **14**, 334-351 (1960).

Some Methods for the Estimation of Protein in Milk.
C. W. Raadsveld, *Neth. Milk Dairy J.* **14**, 259-272 (1960).

Determination of Trace Amounts of Total Nitrogen in Petroleum Distillates.
M. Nakayama, Y. Sasaki, and H. Ito, *Shoseki Giho* **4**, 57-60 (1960).

An Accelerated Method for Protein Determination in Fatty Tissue.
T. K. Nikova, *Myasnaya Ind. S.S.S.R.* **31**, No. 6, 25-26 (1960).

Mineralization of Meat and Meat Products and Determination of Nitrogen in Protein by the Kjeldahl Method.
Z. Bozyk and Z. Godlewska, *Chem. Anal. (Warsaw)* **6**, 227-235 (1961).

Modified Method for Determining Protein in Cooked Foods.
N. M. Kaikov, *Gigiena i Sanit.* **26**, No. 3, 57-80 (1961).

Determination of Niacin in Cereals.
J. A. Campbell and O. Pelletier, *J. Assoc. Offic. Agr. Chemists* **44**, 431-436 (1961).

A Direct Determination of Nitrogen in Sulfuric Acid Digestion Mixture.
C. J. F. Boettcher, C. M. van Gent, and C. Pries, *Rec. trav. chim.* **80**, 1157-1168 (1961) (in English).

Nitro and Non-Aminoid Nitrogen

Bohn-Schmidt Reactio in the Benzene Series and the Estimation of Nitrogen in Nitro Compounds by the Kjeldahl Method.
A. Eckert, *Monatsh.* **34**, 1957-1964 (1913).

Some Limitations of the Kjeldahl Method.
H. D. Daken and H. W. Dudley, *J. Biol. Chem* **17**, 275-280 (1914).

Kjeldahl Modification for Determination of Nitrogen in Nitro Substitution Compounds.
W. C. Cope, *J. Ind. Eng. Chem.* **8**, 592-593 (1916).

Some Limitations of the Kjeldahl Method.
H. C. Brill and F. Agcaoili, *Philippine J. Sci.* **12A**, 261-265 (1917).

Application of the Kjeldahl Method to Compounds of Brucine with Reference to the Brucine Salt of a New Nucleotide.
W. Jones, *J. Pharmacol. Exptl. Therap.* **13**, 489-493 (1919).

Influence of the Position of Substituents in the Kjeldahl Estimation of Aromatic Nitro Compounds.
B. M. Margosches and E. Vogel, *Ber.* **52B**, 1992-1998(1919).

The Kjeldahlization of Mononitro Benzoic Acids and Mononitrocinnamic Acids.
B. M. Margosches and E. Vogel, *Ber.* **55B**, 1380-1389 (1922).

The Influence of the Nature and Position of Substitutents in Aromatic Nitro Compounds upon Kjeldahlization.
B. M. Margosches, W. Kristen, and E. Scheinost, *Ber.* **56B**, 1943-1950 (1923).

The Behavior of Aromatic Nitro Compounds in the Kjeldahl Process.
B. M. Margosches and W. Kristen, *Z. ges. Schiess-u. Sprengstoff w. Nitrocellulose* **18**, 73-76 (1923).

The Remarkable Behavior of Alkali Sulfates in the Kjeldahl Determination of Nitrogen in Nitroaniline.
B. M. Margosches, E. Scheinost, and M. Frissher, *Ber.* **58B**, 2233-2237 (1925).

Micro-Kjeldahl Experiments.
B. Saika-Pittner, *Pharm. Presse* **33**, 60-61 (1928).

The Determination of Nitrogen by the Kjeldahl Method as Applied to Dyestuffs and Intermediate Products.
P. Sisley and M. David, *Bull. soc. chim.* [4] **45**, 312-324 (1929).

The Determination of Nitrogen in Osazones by the Kjeldahl Method.
G. Dorfmüller, *Z. Ver. deut, Zuckerind.* **80**, 407-412 (1930).

A Kjeldahl Method for Determining Nitro Nitrogen in Aromatic Compounds.
M. Weizmann, J. Yopf, and B. Kirzors, *Z. physiol. Chem.* **192**, 70-72 (1930).

The Determination of Nitrogen in Nitro and Azo Compounds by the Kjeldahl Method.
B. G. Simek, *Chem. Listy* **25**, 322-325 (1931).

Adaptation of the Micro-Kjeldahl Method to the Estimation of Nitrogen in Organic Compounds Containing Nitro and Azo Groups.
R. V. Bhat, *Proc. Indian Acad. Sci.* **13A**, 269-272 (1941).

Determination of Nitrogen in Azo Compounds by the Kjeldahl Method.
V. I. Kuznetsov, *Zavodskaya Lab.* **9**, 1039 (1940); *Kim. Referat Zhur.* **4**, No. 33, 62-63 (1941).

Determination of Nitrogen in Nitro and Nitroso Compounds by the Kjeldahl Method.
Z. Csuros and E. Fodor-Kenczler, *Magyar Kém. Folyóirat* **48**, 33-42 (1942); *Chem. Zentr.* I, pp 545-546 (1943).

Determination of Nitrogen in Azo Compounds by the Kjeldahl Method.
Z. Csuros, E. Fodor-Kenczler, and I. Gresits, *Magyar Kém. Folyoirat* **47**, 195-209 (1941); *Chem. Zentr.* I, p. 545 (1943).

Determination of Nitrogen in Nitriles.
E. L. Rose and H. Zilliotto, *Ind. Eng. Chem., Anal. Ed.* **17**, 211-212 (1945).

Semi-micro Kjeldahl Determination.
I. A. Kaye and N. Weiner, *Ind. Eng. Chem., Anal. Ed.* **17**, 397-398 (1945).

Determination of Nitrogen in Pyridine Ring-type compounds by the Kjeldahl Method.

R. L. Shirley and W. W. Becker, *Ind. Eng. Chem., Anal. Ed.* **17**, 437-438 (1945).

Micro-Kjeldahl Determination of Nitrogen in Gramicidin and Tryptophan. Comparison of Gunning-Arnold-Dyer and Friedrich Methods.
L. M. White and G. E. Secor, *Ind. Eng. Chem., Anal. Ed.* **18**, 457-458 (1946).

Micro and Semimicro Determination of Nitrogen in Heterocyclic Nitrogen Ring Compounds by a Kjeldahl Method.
C. L. Ogg, R. W. Brand, and C. O. Willits, *J. Assoc. Offic. Agr. Chemists* **31**, 663-669 (1948).

Kjeldahl Determination of Nitrogen in Refractory Materials.
C. O. Willits, M. R. Coe, and C. L. Ogg, *J. Assoc. Offic. Agr. Chemists* **32**, 118-127 (1949).

Applications of the Kjeldahl Method to Determine Nitrogen in Certain Nitrated Aromatic Derivatives.
J. Tirouflet, *Bull. soc. sci. Bretagne* **23**, 129-131 (1948) (Publ. 1949).

The Friedrich Micro-Kjeldahl Method for Nitrogen; Effect of Potassium Sulfate Concentration.
G. E. Secor, M. C. Long, M. D. Kilpatrick, and L. M. White, *J. Assoc. Offic. Agr. Chemists* **33**, 872-880 (1950).

Kjeldahl Micro Digestions in Sealed Tubes at 470°C.
L. M. White and M. C. Long, *Anal. Chem.* **23**, 363-365 (1951).

Behavior of Ring Nitrogen in the Micro-Kjeldahl Procedure.
M. Marzadro, *Microchemie ver. Mikrochim. Acta* **36937**, 671-678 (1951).

The Study of the Determination of Pyridine by the Kjeldahl Method in the Presence of Selenium Oxychloride.
P. Dupuey, *Compt. rend.* **232**, 836-838 (1951).

Determination of Nitrite Type Nitrogen with Ordinary Kjeldahl Digestion.
C. H. Vanetten and M. B. Wiele, *Anal. Chem.* **23**, 1338-1339 (1951).

Selective Determination of Different Forms of Nitrogen by the Micro-Kjeldahl Procedure.

M. Marzadro, *Mikrochemie ver. Mikrochim. Acta* **38**, 372-375; *Ann. chim. (Rome)* **41**, 669-672; *Rend. ist. super. sanita* **14**, 668-672 (1951).

The Kjeldahl Determination in the Presence of Selenium Oxychloride: Quinoline and Quinaldine.
C. Moreau, *Compt. rend.* **233**, 1616-1617 (1951).

Determination of Nitrogen. Modified Kjeldahl Procedure Using Thiosalicylic Acid.
P. McCutchan and W. F. Roth, *Anal. Chem.* **24**, 369-370 (1952).

Hydrazones, Semicarbazones, and Other Nitrogenous Substances Requiring a Reductive Pretreatment.
V. B. Fish, *Anal. Chem.* **24**, 760-762 (1952).

Strong Reduction Preliminary to Kjeldahl Digestion in the Analysis of Refractory Compounds.
S. Works, D. Scheirer, and E. C. Wagner, *Anal. Chem.* **25**, 837-838 (1953).

Selective Determination of Different Forms of Nitrogen with the Micro-Kjeldahl Procedure. III.
M. Marzadro, *Mikrochemie ver. Mikrochim. Acta* **40**, 359-366 (1953).

Rapid Modified Procedure for Determination of Kjeldahl Nitrogen.
C. H. Perrin, *Anal. Chem.* **25**, 968-971 (1953).

Determination of Nitro Nitrogen by the Kjeldahl Method.
R. B. Bradstreet, *Anal. Chem.* **26**, 235-236 (1954).

Determination of Pyridinium Nitrogen.
F. E. Crane Jr. and R. M. Fuoss, *Anal. Chem.* **26**, 1651-1652 (1954).

Determination of Nitrogen in Organic Compounds by the Kjeldahl Method.
V. I. Esafov, *Zavodskaya Lab.* **21**, 1160-1163 (1955).

Determination of Nonaminoid Nitrogen by the Micro-Kjeldahl Method. I. Aromatic Nitro Compounds.
T. S. Ma, R. E. Lang, and J. D. McKinley Jr., *Mikrochim. Acta* pp. 368-377 (1957) (in English).

Micro-Kjeldahl Method for Nitrogen in Certain Organic Compounds Containing N-N and N-0 Linkages.

A. Steyermark, B. E. McGee, E. A. Bass, and R. R. Kamp, *Anal. Chem.* **30**, 1561-1563 (1958).

Determination of Nitrogen in Nitro Compounds and Oximes by Iodic Acid Decomposition.
S. Ohashi, *Bull. Chem. Soc. Japan* **28**, 537-541 (1955).

Evaluation of Six Methods for Determination of Nitrogen in Nitroguanidine.
M. I. Fauth and H. Stalcup, *Anal. Chem.* **30**, 1670-1672 (1958).

Semimicro-Kjeldahl Procedure for Pyridinium Halide and Oxyhalide Salts.
V. B. Fish and P. R. Collins, *Anal. Chem.* **30**, 151-152 (1958).

Submicromethods for the Analysis of Organic Compounds. VII. The Determination of Nitrogen in Heterocyclic Compounds and Azo, Hydrazo, and Nitro Compounds.
R. Belcher, R. L. Bhasin, and T. S. West, *J. Chem. Soc.* pp. 2585-2587 (1959).

Elemental Organic Analysis by the Wet Combustion Method. V. The Determination of Nitrogen in Pyridine Compounds.
A. P. Terent'ev and B. M. Luskina, *Zhur. Anal. Khim.* **17**, 227-230 (1962).

Distillation and Estimation of Nitrogen

An Ammonia Distillation with and without Cooling in Kjeldahl Determinations.
E. Preschek, *J. Landwirtsch.* **54**, 367-384 (1906).

Notes on Kjeldahl's Process.
V. Edwards and D. Chads, *Chem. News* **103**, 138 (1907).

Some Modifications in the Kjeldahl Method of Determining Nitrogen.
J. Sebelien, A. Brynildsen, and C. Haavardsholm, *Chem. Ztg.* **33**, 785-795 (1909).

Minor Communications on Various Subjects. The Kjeldahl Determination.
C. Neuberg, *Biochem. Z.* 423-442 (1909).

Determination of Nitrogen by Kjeldahl's Method, Especially in Milk.
G. Wiegner, *J. Landwirtsch.* **57**, 81-110 (1909).

On the Method of Nitrogen Determination in Urine.
P. Rona and R. Ottenberg, *Biochem. Z.* **24**, 354-356 (1910).

Color Reaction of Ammonia.
P. Thomas, *Bull. soc. chim.* **11**, 796-799 (1911).

The Formaldehyde Method for the Estimation of Nitrogen in Organic Substances.
A. M. Wright, *Trans. Proc. New Zealand Inst.* **42**, 224-225 (1911).

Simple Method for Determining Formaldehyde.
F. Herrmann, *Chem. Ztg.* **35**, 25 (1911).

Removal of Ammonia by Means of a Current of Air (Application to Analysis and to Industry).
G. A. Merlo, *Ind. chim. (Paris).* **12**, 17-20 (1912).

Quantitative Ammonia Distillation by Aeration, for Kjeldahl, Urea, and other Nitrogen Estimations.
P. A. Kober and S. S. Graves, *J. Am. Chem. Soc.* **35**, 1594-1604 (1913).

The Volumetric Determination of Ammonia.
L. W. Winkler, *Z. angew. Chem.* **26**, 231-232 (1913).

The Determination of Ammonia by the Boric Acid Method.
E. Bernard, *Z. angew. Chem.* **27**, 664 (1914).

Application of the Hexamethylenetetramine Titration Method to the Kjeldahl and Other Processes.
G. Simpson, *Pharm. J.* **92**, 546-547 (1914).

Comparative Study of Aeration and Heat Distillation in the Kjeldahl Method for the Estimation of Nitrogen.
K. G. Falk and K. Sugiura, *J. Am. Chem. Soc.* **38**, 916-921 (1916).

Total Nitrogen: Practical and Exact Method for the Volumetric Determination of Ammonia When the Organic Matter Is Destroyed in the Presence of Mercury.
E. Justin-Mueller, *Bull. sci. pharmacol.* **23**, 167-169 (1916).

Prevention of Loss of Ammonia in the Estimation of Nitrogen by Kjeldahl's Method.
A. Wolf-Joachimowitz, *Chem. Ztg.* **41**, 87 (1917).

The Distillation of Ammonia.
B. S. Davisson, *J. Ind. Eng. Chem.* **12**, 176-177 (1920).

Boric Acid Modification of the Kjeldahl Method for Crop and Soil Analysis.
F. M. Scales and A. P. Harrison, *J. Ind. Eng. Chem.* **12**, 350-352 (1920).

Gasometric Determination of Nitrogen and Its Application to the Estimation of the Non-Protein Nitrogen in Blood.
R. L. Stehle, *J. Biol. Chem.* **45**, 223-228 (1920).

Note on the Gasometric Determination of Nitrogen.
R. L. Stehle, *J. Biol. Chem.* **47**, 11 (1921).

Nitrogen Titratable by Kjeldahl' Method.
W. Mestrezat and M. P. Janet, *Bull. soc. chim. biol.* **3**, 105-130 (1921).

Boric Acid for Neutralizing Ammonia in Nitrogen Determinations.
H. D. Spears, *J. Assoc. Offic. Agr. Chemists* **5**, 105-108 (1921).

A Micro-Kjeldahl Method for Determining Nitrogen.
A. R. Ling and W. J. Price, *J. Soc. Chem. Ind.* **41**, 149-151 T (1921).

The Advantages of the Iodometric Method in Micro-Kjeldahl Determinations.
L. Michaelis and M. Maeda, *Aichi J. Exptl. Med.* **1**, 51-59 (1923).

New Direct Nesslerization Micro-Kjeldahl Method and Modification of the Nessler-Folin Reagent for Ammonia.
F. C. Koch and T. L. McMeekin, *J. Am. Chem. Soc.* **46**, 2006-2009 (1924).

The Micro-Estimation of Urea and of Ammoniacal Salts by Titration of Hypobromite.
Mme. B. Pohorecka-Lelesz, *Bull. soc. chim. biol.* **6**, 773-787 (1924).

A Contribution to the Bang Micro-Kjeldahl Procedure.
S. Kasamori, *J. Biochem. (Japan)* **4**, 33-41 (1924).

Application of "Formol Titration" to the Kjeldahl Method of Estimating Nitrogen.
W. S. Shaw, *Analyst* **49**, 558-565 (1924).

Colorimetric Method for the Direct Estimation of Ammonia in Urine.
A. E. Orr, *Biochem. J.* **18**, 806-808 (1924).

A Comparative Study of the Gunning-Arnold and Winkler Boric

Acid Modification of the Kjeldahl Method for the Determination of Nitrogen.
K. S. Markley and R. M. Hann, *J. Assoc. Offic. Agr. Chemists* **8**, 445-467 (1925).

The Presence of Amines in the Distillate from Kjeldahl-Gunning Nitrogen Determinations. Preliminary Paper.
R. A. Gortner and W. F. Hoffman, *J. Biol. Chem.* **70**, 457-459 (1926).

The Use of the Potassium Iodide and Iodate Method for the Titration of Kjeldahl Distillates.
H. F. Wilson and F. Mattingley, *Analyst* **51**, 569 (1926).

Gasometric Micro-Kjeldahl Determination of Nitrogen.
D. D. Van Slyke, *J. Biol. Chem.* **71**, 235-248 (1927).

Direct Nesslerization of Kjeldahl Digestions.
H. M. Chiles, *J. Am. Chem. Soc.* **50**, 217-221 (1928).

The Use of Steam in Kjeldahl Nitrogen Determinations.
F. T. Adriano, *Philippine J. Agr.* **17**, 509-510 (1929).

Use of Steam for Kjeldahl Distillation of Nitrogen.
J. Green, *Ind. Eng. Chem., Anal. Ed.* **3**, 160-161 (1931).

Colorimetric Estimation of Nitrogen by Direct Nesslerization with a Note on the Modified Nessler-Folin Reagent.
L. S. Walters, *Australian J. Exptl. Biol. Med. Sci.* **7**, 113-116 (1931).

Use of Boric Acid in Micro-Kjeldahl Determination of Nitrogen.
N. M. Staver and R. B. Sandin, *Ind. Eng. Chem., Anal. Ed.* **3**, 240-242 (1931).

Ammonia Distillation without Supervision.
K. F. Tromp, *Het Gas* **51**, 208-209 (1931).

Observations on the Precipitation of Mercury in the Kjeldahl Method.
C. F. Davis and M. Wise, *Cereal Chem.* **8**, 349-360 (1931).

Improved Direct Nesslerization Micro-Kjeldahl Method for Nitrogen.
E. S. West and A. L. Brandon, *Ind. Eng. Chem., Anal. Ed.* **4**, 314-315 (1932).

Determination of Ammonia in Blood.
D. D. Van Slyke and A. Hiller, *J. Biol. Chem.* **102**, 499-504 (1933).

The Determination of Nitrogen in Leather According to the Method of Kjeldahl by Distillation of the Ammonia into Boric Acid.
F. A. Sapegin and N. V. Ometov, *Izvest. Tsentr. Nauch-Issledovatel. Inst. Kozhevennoi Prom. No.* **697**, 54-58 (1932); *Chem. Zentr.* I, p. 3857 (1933).

Use of Aeration in Kjeldahl Distillations.
W. B. Meldrum, R. Melempy, and W. D. Meyers, *Ind. Eng. Chem., Anal. Ed.* **6**, 63-64 (1934).

Stability of Aqueous Solutions of Boric Acid Used in the Kjeldahl Method.
A. Eisner and E. C. Wagenr, *Ind. Eng. Chem., Anal. Ed.* **6**, 473 (1934).

Benzoyl Auramine G. A New Indicator for Kjeldahl Nitrogen Determinations.
J. T. Scanlan and J. D. Reid, *Ind. Eng. Chem., Anal. Ed.* **7**, 125-126 (1935).

A New Method for Titrating Ammonia in the Micro-Kjeldahl Determination.
C. Brecker, *Wien. Klin. Wochschr.* **49**, 1928-1931 (1936).

Source of Loss of Ammonia in Kjeldahl Distillations. Method of Eliminating this Loss.
H. S. Miller, *Ind. Eng. Chem., Anal. Ed.* **8**, 50-51 (1936).

Estimation of Nitrogen by Kjeldahl's Method. Note on the Ammonia Distillation.
J. Speirs and W. J. Mitchell, *J. Inst. Brewing* **42**, 247-259 (1936).

A New Method for Titrating Ammonia in the Micro-Kjeldahl Determination.
C. Brecker, *Wien. klin. Wochschr.* **49**, 1228-1231 (1936).

Quantitative Drop Analysis. VI. Total Nitrogen by Diffusion.
G. T. Bentley and P. L. Kirk, *Mikrochemie* **21**, 260-267 (1937).

A Method of Adding Alkali in the Kjeldahl Distillation.
L. A. Ynalvez, *Phillipine Agriculturist* **26**, 823-826 (1938).

Bromoiodometric Ammonia Determination and Its Application to Nitrogen Determination after Destructive Treatment According to Kjeldahl.
T. A. G. Haanappel, *Pharm. Weekblad* **75**, 570-574 (1938).

Final Titration of Ammonia in the Kjeldahl Microdetermination.
M. Nicloux, *Compt. rend. soc. biol.* **129**, 1171-1173 (1938).

Rapid Method of Determining Nitrogen for Estimation of the Protein Content of Grain and Feeding Stuffs.
H. Schroder and D. Seidel, *Muhlen-Ztg.* **42**, 215 (1939).

Titration of Ammonia in Presence of Boric Acid in the Macro, Semi-, Micro and Micro Procedures with Methyl Red Indicator and Color Matching End Point.
E. C. Wagner, *Ind. Eng. Chem., Anal. Ed.* **12**, 771-772 (1940).

New Method for Distilling Off Ammonia in the Determination of Nitrogen.
A. A. Fridman and K. L. F. Komissarova, *Kozhevenno-Obuvnaya Prom. S.S.S.R.* **19**, No. 9-10, 27-30 (1940).

Ammonia Distillation in the Kjeldahl Nitrogen Determination.
R. Lechner and M. Ross, *Z. Spiritusind.* **63**, 243 (1940).

Semi-Micro and Micro Kjeldahl Steam Distillation Unit.
J. H. Brant and D. C. Sievers, *Ind. Eng. Chem., Anal. Ed.* **13**, 133 (1941).

Absorption of Ammonia in Boric Acid Solution in the Determination of Nitrogen by the Kjeldahl Method.
J. F. Reith and W. M. Klazinga, *Chem. Weekblad* **38**, 122-125 (1941).

Quantitative Drop Analysis. XIII. The Formol Titration of Amino Nitrogen.
R. C. Sisco, B. Cunningham, and P. L. Kirk, *J. Biol. Chem.* **139**, 1-10 (1941).

Micro-Kjeldahl Determination for Nitrogen. A New Indicator and Improved Rapid Method.
T. S. Ma and G. Zuazaga, *Ind. Eng. Chem., Anal. Ed.* **14**, 280-282 (1942).

Micro-Kjeldahl Nitrogen Determination without the Use of Titration Procedure.
W. H. Taylor and G. F. Smith, *Ind. Eng. Chem., Anal. Ed.* **14**, 437-439 (1942).

Kjeldahl Distillation without Absorbing Acid.
J. A. Bradley Jr., *Ind. Eng. Chem., Anal. Ed.* **14**, 705-706 (1942).

Diffusion Micro-Method for Nitrogen.
R. C. Howes and E. R. Stavinski, *Ind. Eng. Chem., Anal. Ed.* **14**, 917-921 (1942).

Quantitative Drop Analysis. XVI. An Improved Diffusion Method for Total Nitrogen.
E. R. Tompkins and P. L. Kirk, *J. Biol. Chem.* **142**, 477-485 (1942).

Iodometric Determination of Nitrogen in Milk.
E. R. Ling, *J. Soc. Chem. Ind.* **61**, 194-196 (1942).

Collection of Micro-Kjeldahl Ammonia in Boric Acid and Precise Titration.
W. R. Thompson, N.Y. State Dept. Health Ann. Rept. Div. Labs and Research pp. 23-24 (1943).

Colorimetric Estimation of Small Amounts of Ammonia by the Phenol-Hypochlorite Reaction.
J. A. Russel, *J. Biol. Chem.* **156**, 457-461 (1944).

Titrimetric Ultramicromethod for the Estimation of Urea and Kjeldahl Nitrogen.
A. E. Sobel, A. M. Mayer, and S. Gottfried, *J. Biol. Chem.* **156**, 355-363 (1944).

Determination of Nitrogen by the Kjeldahl Method.
J. Soos, *Magyar Kém. Folyóirat* **49**, 81-100 (1943); *Chem. Zentr.* II, pp. 344-345 (1944).

Kjeldahl Determinations of Nitrogen. Elimination of the Distillation.
K. Marcali and W. Rieman III, *Ind. Eng. Chem., Anal. Ed.* **18**, 709-710 (1946).

Micro-Kjeldahl Determination of Nitrogen. Use of Potassium Biiodate in the Iodometric Titration of Ammonia.
R. Ballentine and J. R. Gregg, *Anal. Chem.* **19**, 281-283 (1947).

Determination of Nitrogen in Ammonium Sulphate.
H. A. Nicolas, *Chim. Anal.* **29**, 197 (1947).

Estimation of Ultramicro Quantities of Urea, and Kjeldahl and Amino Nitrogen. Improvements in Microaeration Technique.
A. E. Sobel, A. Hirschman, and L. Besman, *Anal. Chem.* **19**, 927-929 (1947).

Kjeldahl Distillation in a Closed Still.
R. Chand, *J. Indian Chem. Soc.* **24**, 167-168 (1947).

Kjeldahl Determinations of Nitrogen without Distillation. Application to Samples Containing Phosphorus.
K. Marcali and W. Rieman III, *Anal. Chem.* **20**, 381-382 (1948).

Determination of Nitrogen in Biological Materials.
G. L. Miller and E. E. Miller, *Anal. Chem.* **20**, 481-487 (1948).

Study of Conditions for the Kjeldahl Determination of Nitrogen in Proteins. Description of Methods with Mercury as a Catalyst, Titrimetric and Gasometric Measurements of the Ammonia Formed.
A. Hiller, J. Plazin and D. D. Van Slyke, *J. Biol. Chem.* **176**, 140-120 (1948).

Spectrophotometric Determination of Total Nitrogen in Oils.
C. H. Hale, M. N. Hale, and W. H. Jones, *Anal. Chem.* **21**, 154-151 (1949).

Improvements in Microaeration Technique for the Determination of Kjeldahl Nitrogen.
H. G. Day, E. Bernstoff, and R. T. Hill, *Anal. Chem.* **21**, 1290-1291 (1949).

Kjeldahl Ultramicrodetermination of Nitrogen. Applications in the Industrial Laboratory.
J. A. Kuck, A. Kingsley, D. Kinsey, F. Sheehan, and G. F. Swigert, *Anal. Chem.* **22**, 604-611 (1950).

Colorimetric Determination of Ammonia and Cyanate.
J. M. Kruse and M. G. Mellon, *Anal. Chem.* **25**, 1188-1192 (1953).

Spectro Determination of Ammonia in Natural Waters by the Phenol-Hypochlorite Method.
J. P. Riley, *Anal. Chim. Acta* **9**, 575-589 (1953).

Determination of Nitrogen in Soil and Plant Materials: Use of Boric Acid in the Micro-Kjeldahl Method.
S. H. Yuen and A. G. Pollard, *J. Sci. Food Agr.* **4**, 490-496 (1953).

Ultramicrodetermination of Ammonia or Organic Nitrogen.
Y. Okada and H. Hanafusa, *Bull. Chem. Soc. Japan* **27**, 478 (1954).

Two-Step Mixed Indicator for Kjeldahl Nitrogen Determination.
I. H. Sher. *Anal. Chem.* **27**, 8321-8323 (1955).

Alizarin as Alkalinity Indicator for Kjeldahl Digestions.
L. S. Malowan, *Chemist Analyst* **44**, 75 (1955).

Determination of Organic Nitrogen by the Kjeldahl Method Without Distillation.
C. I. Adams and G. H. Spaulding, *Anal. Chem.* **27**, 1003-1004 (1955).

The Micro-Distillation of Ammonia in the Kjeldahl Determination.
S. Dittrich and J. X. de Vries, *pH (Montevideo)* **5**, No. 4, 78-83D (1955).

Determination of 0.02-0.1 Gamma Quantities of Organic Nitrogen.
D. Exley, *Biochem. J.* **63**, 496-501 (1956).

Elimination of the Distillation Procedure in the Kjeldahl Method.
R. Belcher and M. K. Bhatty, *Mikrochim. Acta* pp. 1183-1186 (1956) (in English).

Coulometric Titration of Ammonia.
M. G. Arcand and E. H. Swift, *Anal. Chem.* **28**, 440-443 (1956).

The Hypobromite Method for the Determination of Nitrogen in Plants.
V. S. Iljin, *Agron. trop. (Maracay, Venezuela)* **4**, 191-205 (1958).

Determination of Trace Quantities of Nitrogen in Petroleum Fractions.
O. I. Milner, R. J. Zahner, L. S. Hepner, and W. H. Cowell, *Anal. Chem.* **30**, 1528-1530 (1958).

Can the Acid-Containing Adsorption Layer in the Kjeldahl Distillation Be Substituted by a Layer of Boiled Water?
E. Schulek, K. Burger, and M. Feher, *Z. anal. Chem.* **167**, 28-31 (1959).

Titration of Traces of Ammonia after Kjeldahl Distillation.
O. I. Milner and R. J. Zahner, *Anal. Chem.* **32**, 294 (1960).

New Nessler Reagent and Its Use in the Direct Nesslerization of Kjeldahl Digests.
K. R. Middleton, *J. Appl. Chem. (London)* **10**, 281-286 (1960).

The Direct Alkalimetric Determination of Ammonia in the Kjeldahl Method.
E. Schulek, K. Burger, and M. Fehér, *Magyar Kém. Folyóirat* **66**, 250-251 (1960).

Elimination of the Distillation Step in the Kjeldahl Method for the Determination of Nitrogen in Agricultural and Animal Products.
M. Ashraf, M. K. Bhatty, and R. A. Shah, *Pakistan J. Sci. Research* **12**, 103-105 (1960).

Photometric Determination of Organic Nitrogen by the Kjeldahl Method Without Distillation.
M. Kasagi and M. Ito, *Bunseki Kagaku* **9**, 105-109 (1960).

Determination of Nitrogen in Organic Compounds Without Distillation. II. Determination of Nitrogen in Nitro, Nitroso, and Azo Compounds.
M. Ashraf, M. K. Bhatty, and R. A. Shah, *Pakistan J. Sci. Ind. Research* **3**, 135-136 (1960).

Colorimetric Micro-Kjeldahl Method with Direct Nesslerization for Routine Determination of Nitrogen (Nitro and Nitroso Groups Excepted).
H. C. Burck, *Mikrochim. Acta* pp. 200-203 (1960).

Improved and Simplified Kjeldahl Nitrogen Determination.
K. Chang, *Hua Hsueh Tung Pao No.* **2**, 315 (1960).

Elimination of Distillation in the Kjeldahl Method for the Micro- and Semimicro Determination of Nitrogen in Nitro, Nitroso, and Azo Compounds.
M. Ashraf, M. K. Bhatty, and R. A. Shah, *Anal. Chim. Acta* **25**, 448-452 (1961) (in English).

Spectrophotometric Determination of Nitrogen in Organic Nitro Compounds.
M. Piazzi, *Ann. Chim. (Rome)* **51**, 886-890 (1961).

A Direct Determination of Nitrogen in Sulfuric Acid Digestion Mixtures.
C. J. F. Boettcher, C. M. van Gent, and C. Fries, *Rec. trav. chim.* **80**, 1157-1168 (1961) (in English).

Measurement of Total Nitrogen in Microgram Amounts.
C. A. Parker, *J. Exptl. Biol. Med. Sci.* **39**, 515-520 (1961).

Photometric Determination of Nitrogen in Organic Compounds by the Rubazonic Acid Method.
H. Kala, *Pharmazie* **18**, 29-34 (1963).

Apparatus

The Determination of Nitrogen.
F. Taurke, *Chem. Ztg.* **32**, 1176 (1909).

Modified Apparatus for Estimation of Nitrogen by the Kjeldahl Process.
F. E. Weston and H. R. Ellis, *Chem. News* **100**, 50 (1909).

A Modified Kjeldahl Connecting Bulb.
C. A. Jennings, *J. Ind. Eng. Chem.* **1**, 737 (1909).

A Modified Kjeldahl Connecting Bulb.
G. W. Gray, *J. Ind. Eng. Chem.* **1**, 813 (1909).

An Attachment to the Distillation Flask for Nitrogen Determination According to Kjeldahl.
F. Dudy, *Chem. Ztg* **33**, 1158 (1910).

A New Distillation Apparatus for the Determination of Nitrogen by the Kjeldahl Method.
W. Huehner and G. Wiegner, *J. Landwirtsch* **57**, 385-390 (1910).

A Digestion Flask for Kjeldahl Nitrogen Determinations.
R. A. Earp, *Collegium* p. 129 (1909).

Improvement of the Kjeldahl Apparatus for Determining Nitrogen.
L. von Lieberman, *Chem. Ztg.* **35**, 549 (1911).

Apparatus for Nitrogen Determination According to Kjeldahl.
Krieger, *Chem. Ztg.* **35**, 1083 (1911).

An Improvement in the Kjeldahl Distilling Apparatus.
W. L. Haddock, *J. Ind. Eng. Chem.* **4**, 22-23 (1912).

Apparatus for Nitrogen Determination According to Kjeldahl.
L. Dobzynski, *Chem. Ztg.* **35**, 1267 (1911).

Apparatus for Carrying Away Acid Fumes in Kjeldahl Determinations.
P. Wagner, *Chem. Ztg.* **35**, 1438.

An Apparatus for the Absorption of Fumes.
O. Folin and W. Denis, *J. Biol. Chem.* **11**, 503-560 (1912); *J. Chem. Soc.* **102**, II, 635 (1913).

Apparatus for Fumeless Kjeldahl Nitrogen Digestion.
A. P. Sy, *J. Ind. Eng. Chem.* **4**, 680-681 (1912).

One Piece Cooler for Kjeldahl Nitrogen Determinations.
E. Pescheck, *A. angew. Chem.* **26**, 176.

New Apparatus for the Distillation of Ammonia by the Kjeldahl Method.
M. G. Delattre, *Anal. Chem.* **18**, 223-226 (1913).

Receiver Specially Suited to Kjeldahl Distillations.
H. Lickfett, *Z. angew. Chem.* **26**, 688.

A New Flask for the Determination of Nitrogen.
D. G. Sjöquist, *Svensk Kem Tidskr.* **25**, 176-178 (1913).

A New and Improved Form of Kjeldahl Distillation Apparatus.
A. D. Holmes, *J. Ind. Eng. Chem.* **6**, 1010-1012 (1914); cf. **7**, 693-694 (1915).

A New Apparatus for the Ammonia Distillation in the Kjeldahl Method.
M. E. Pozzi-Escot, *Bull. assoc. chimistes sucr. dist.* **31**, 235-236 (1914).

A Compact Kjeldahl Apparatus.
H. G. Bennett, *Collegium* 482-484 (1914).

Several Changes in the Method of Nitrogen Estimation According to Kjeldahl.
R. Hottinger, *Biochem. Z.* **60**, 345-351 (1914).

Simplification of Bang's Micro-Kjeldahl Method and the Nitrogen Content of the Vitreous Humor in the Eye of Rabbit and Dog.
M. Kochmann, *Biochem. Z.* **63**, 479-482 (1915).

A Kjeldahl Distillation Apparatus.
J. M. Pickel, *J. Ind. Eng. Chem.* **7**, 787-789 (1915).

A New Tube for the Rapid Distillation of Ammonia.
M. E. Pozzi-Escot, *Ann. chim. anal.* **20**, 125-126 (1915).

A Micro-Kjeldahl Apparatus.
M. Morse, *Biochem. Bull.* **2**, 457-458 (1915).

A Kjeldahl Fume Remover.
F. G. Merkle, *J. Ind. Eng. Chem.* **8**, 521-522 (1916).

Weighing Boats for Kjeldahl Nitrogen Determination.
K. Bauman and J. Grossfeld, *Z. angew. Chem.* **29**, I, 364 (1916);
Chem. Ztg. **40**, 792 (1916).

Nitrogen Distillation Apparatus.
V. F. Murray, Can. Dept. Mines Summary Rept. No. 454 (1917);
Sess. Paper 26a, 75-78 (1917).

Some Laboratory Conveniences.
A. E. Perkins, *J. Ind. Eng. Chem.* **9**, 57-59 (1917).

A Simple and Entirely Adjustable Rack for Kjeldahl Digestion
Flasks.
F. E. Rice, *J. Ind. Eng. Chem.* **10**, 631-632 (1918).

A Scrubber for Ammonia Distillation.
B. S. Davisson, *J. Ind. Eng. Chem.* **11**, 465-466 (1919).

A Little Known Kjeldahl Distillation Attachment.
A. Prange, *Chem. Ztg.* **44**, 681 (1920).

A Modification and Simplification of Kjeldahl's Method for Determining Nitrogen.
H. Citron, *Deut. med. Wochschr.* **46**, 655-656 (1920).

Apparatus for Digestion in Micro-Chemical Kjeldahl Nitrogen Determinations.
H. Winkler, *Chem. Ztg.* **46**, 785 (1922).

Apparatus for Fume Conduction in the Kjeldahl Process.
W. H. Scott, U. S. Patent 1,542,843 (1925).

New Splash-Head for Kjeldahl Apparatus.
H. Lowe, *Analyst* **50**, 605 (1926).

Apparatus for Heating Kjeldahl Flasks.
P. A. Goldfisch, U.S. Patent 1,584,089 (1926).

A Simple and Inexpensive Kjeldahl Digestion Apparatus.
E. G. Hastings, E. B. Fred, and W. H. Peterson, *Ind. Eng. Chem.* **19**, 397 (1927).

Kjeldahl Digestion Apparatus.
H. W. Scott, *Ind. Eng. Chem.* **19**, 761 (1927).

Improved Micro-Kjeldahl Ammonia Distillation Apparatus.
G. Kemmerer and L. T. Hallett, *Ind. Eng. Chem.* **19**, 1295-1296 (1927).

Simplified Micro-Kjeldahl Apparatus.
J. G. Van der Sande, *Chem. Weekblad* **24**, 558 (1927).

Improved Ammonia Still.
L. G. Armstrong, *Chemist Analyst* **18**, No. 6, 17 (1929).

Micro-Kjeldahl Apparatus for the Proximate Determination of Assimilable Nitrogen in Molasses Solutions by Distillation with Caustic Soda.
F. Wagner, *Brennerei-Ztg.* **46**, 40 (1929).

Hot Bath for Decompositions in Kjeldahl Nitrogen Determinations.
E. Staudt, *Chem. Ztg.* **54**, 9 (1930).

Use of Steam for Kjeldahl Distillation of Nitrogen.
J. Green, *Ind. Eng. Chem., Anal. Ed.* **3**, 169-161 (1931).

Ammonia Distillation Without Supervision.
K. F. Tromp, *Het Gas* **51**, 208-209 (1931).

Fume Tube and Ejector Nozzle Suitable for Use with Kjeldahl Apparatus.
P. A. Goldfisch, U.S. Patent 1,842,378 (1932).

An Improved Device for Adding the Saturated Alkali Solution in the Kjeldahl Method for Nitrogen Determination.
F. T. Adriano, *Univ. Philippines Nat. and Appl. Sci. Bull.* **2**, 27-32 (1932).

Improved Distillation Trap.
E. S. West, *Ind. Eng. Chem., Anal. Ed.* **4**, 445 (1932).

A Modification of the Kjeldahl Apparatus for Nitrogen Determination.
M. Shoiri and A. Okuda, *Bull. Imp. Agr. Expt. Sta. (Japan)* **2**, 33-37 (1932); Abstr. Japan. Chem. Lit. **6**, 494 (1932).

New Form of Distillation Head Piece for the Nitrogen Determination.
W. Lepper, *Z. anal. Chem.* **91**, 15-16 (1932).

Distillation Apparatus for the Kjeldahl Method.
M. Shoiri and A. Okuda, *J. Imp. Agr. Expt. Sta., Nishigahara* **2**, 33-38 (1932).

A Micro-Kjeldahl Still.
T. P. Nash Jr., *J. Lab. Clin. Med.* **18**, 1285-1287 (1933).

Modified Ammonia Bulb.
L. J. Villanueva, *Univ. Philippines Nat. and Appl. Sci. Bull.* **3**, 451-452 (1933).

Modification of Kjeldahl Apparatus for Nitrogen Determination.
G. Colombo, *Boll. uffic. staz. sper. seta* **3**, 85-87 (1933).

An Absorption Apparatus for the Microdetermination of Certain Volatile Substances. I. The Microdetermination of Ammonia.
E. J. Conway and A. Byrne, *Biochem. J.* **27**, 419-420 (1933).

Improvement of the Micro-Kjeldahl Method.
B. Groak, *Biochem. Z.* **28**, 59-61 (1935).

A Simple Device to Be Used in Connection with the Kjeldahl Digestion Process.
H. Petersilie, *J. Lab. Clin. Med.* **19**, 672-673 (1934).

Apparatus for Use in Kjeldahl Digestions.
A. Henwood and R. M. Garey, U.S. Patent 2,004,868(1935).

Novelties in Micro-Chemical Apparatus. XVII. New Form of Micro-Kjeldahl Flask.
A. Solyts, *Microchemie* **19**, 304-305 (1936).

The Application of the Normal Ground Glass Connection to the Micro-Kjeldahl Apparatus.
J. Unterzaucher, *Mikrochemie* (Festschr. von Hans Molisch) pp. ^36-438 (1936).

A Simple Micro-and Macro-Kjeldahl Steam Distillation Apparatus.
J. M. Fife, *Ind. Eng. Chem., Anal. Ed.* **8**, 316 (1936).

An Auxiliary Apparatus of New Design for the Ammonia Distillation Apparatus for the Determination of Nitrogen According to the Method of Kjeldahl.
I. Esat, *Z. allgem. turk. Chem.-Ver.* **2**, 139-146 (1936); *Chem. Zentr.* p. 3525 (1937).

Simplified Micro-Kjeldahl Apparatus.
J. E. Scott and E. S. West, *Ind. Eng. Chem., Anal. Ed.* **9**, 50 (1937).

A One-Piece Glass Micro-Kjeldahl Distillation Apparatus.
P. L. Kirk, *Ind. Eng. Chem., Anal. Ed.* **8**, 223-224 (1936).

Studies on the Micro Nitrogen Determination According to Kjeldahl.
Z. Zakrzewski and H. J. Fuchs, *Biochem. Z.* **285**, 390-406 (1936).

A New Micro-Kjeldahl Apparatus.
A. R. Taborda, *Rev. brasil. chim.* **3**, 117-119 (1937).

A Kjeldahl Digestion Apparatus.
W. M. Clark, *Ind. Eng. Chem., Anal. Ed.* **9**, 338 (1937).

Electric Micro-Kjeldahl Heating Stand.
Lab. Staff Dartington Hall Trustees, *J. Soc. Chem. Ind.* **58**, 179-180 (1937).

Fume Tube for Micro-Kjeldahl Digestions.
J. S. Blair, *Ind. Eng. Chem., Anal. Ed.* **10**, 112 (1938).

A Method of Adding Alkalin in the Kjeldahl Distillation.
L. A. Ynalvez, *Philippine Agriculturist* **26**, 823-826 (1938).

A New Attachment for the Micro-Kjeldahl Distilling Apparatus.
H. Marzetowicz, *Mehl u. Brot.* **28**, No. 46, 3-4 (1938).

A Modified Fumeless Nitrogen Digestion Apparatus.
L. A. Ynalvez, *Phillipine Agriculturist* **27**, 510-511 (1938).

Attachment for Avoiding Sucking Over of Liquid in the Micro-Kjeldahl Apparatus of Parnas-Wagner.
P. E. Lindahl, *Mikrochemie* **27**, 195-196 (1939).

Semi-Micro Kjeldahl Distillation Apparatus.
C. E. Redemann, *Ind. Eng. Chem., Anal. Ed.* **11**, 635-636 (1939).

Apparatus for Carrying Out Chemical Digestions of the Kjeldahl Type.
May and Baker Ltd. and H. J. Barber, British Patent 522800 (1940).

New Apparatus for the Determination of Nitrogen after Kjeldahl Digestion.
H. Lecoq, *Bull. soc. chim. biol.* **22**, 112-113 (1940).

Convenient Method for Conducting the Kjeldahl Digestion.
B. O. Heston and S. R. Wood, *J. Chem. Educ.* **17**, 475 (1940).

Fume Tube Suitable for Kjeldahl Apparatus.
A. I. Newman, U.S. Patent 2210176 (1940).

Semi-Micro, and Micro-Kjeldahl Steam Distillation Unit.
J. H. Brant and D. C. Sievers, *Ind. Eng. Chem., Anal. Ed.* **13**, 133 (1941).

Apparatus for the Kjeldahl Determination of Nitrogen in Coal.
C. W. G. Ockelford, *Fuel* **20**, 139-143 (1941).

An Improved Micro-Kjeldahl Apparatus and Procedure for the Analysis of Milk.
M. C. Rhees, T. R. Freeman, and Charles T. Shipardson, *J. Dairy Sci.* **24**, 533-534 (1941).

A Steam Distilling Apparatus Suitable for Micro-Kjeldahl Analysis.
R. Markham, *Biochem. J.* **36**, 790-791 (1942).

A New Apparatus for the Determination of Nitrogen by the Kjeldahl Method.
B. Bencze, *Mezogazdasagi Kutatasok* 126-130 (1943); *Chem. Zentr.* II, p. 249 (1944).
A Semi-Micro Kjeldahl Apparatus.
B. T. Dewey and N. F. Witt, *J. Am. Pharm. Assoc.* **32**, 55-56 (1943).

Support for Kjeldahl Flasks.
J. S. Front. *Ind. Eng. Chem., Anal. Ed.* **16**, 324 (1944).

Kjeldahl Calculator.
O. A. Krober, *Trans. Am. Assoc. Cereal Chem.* **3**, 169-172 (1945).

An Improved Kjeldahl Trap and Ammonia Distillation Outfit.
A. Lovecy, *J. Soc. Chem. Ind.* **65**, 224-226 (1946).

Simple Apparatus for the Determination of Nitrogen.
M. Vignon, *Chim. anal.* **30**, 162-163 (1948).

Kjeldahl Distillation in a Closed Still.
R. Chand, *J. Indian Chem. Soc.* **24**, 167-168 (1947).

Manifold for Disposal of Fumes Given Off During Macro-Kjeldahl Digestive Process.
E. H. Tyner, *Anal. Chem.* **20**, 273 (1948).

Micro-Kjeldahl Distillation Apparatus.
R. Johanson, *Australian Chem. Inst. J. & Proc.* **15**, 183-184 (1948).

New Apparatus for Kjeldahl Determinations.
R. Dolique and M. T. Lacombe, *Trav. soc. pharm. Montpellier* **8**, 47-50 (1948).

New Apparatus for the Kjeldahl Determination of Nitrogen.
B. Bencze, *Z. anal. Chem.* **129**, 125-129 (1949).

Determination of Nitrogen by the Kjeldahl Method.
Y. O. Parnas, *Zhur. Anal. Khim.* **4**, 54-59 (1949).

A Rapid Distillation Apparatus for the Determination of Nitrogen by the Kjeldahl Method.
G. Nogrady, *Magyar Kem. Lapja* **4**, 350-352 (1949).

Modification of the Van Slyke and Cullen Aeration Apparatus and Its Application for Micro-Kjeldahl Procedure.
J. Lenquin and J. P. Delville, *Experientia* **6**, 273-275 (1950).

Simple Distillation Apparatus for Nitrogen Determinations According to the Micro-Kjeldahl Method.
E. Mohlan, *Pharm. Zentralhalle* **89**, 334-337 (1950).

Modified Micro-Kjeldahl Apparatus.
D. L. Shepard and M. B. Jacobs, *J. Am. Pharm. Assoc.* **40**, 154-155 (1951).

Apparatus for Use in Connection with the Sulfuric Acid Digestion of Protein-Containing Material.
A. J. G. Barnett and T. B. Miller, *Chem. & Ind. 246 (1951).*

Recommended Specifications for Micro-Chemical Apparatus. Micro-Kjeldahl Nitrogen.
A. Steyermark et al., *Anal. Chem.* **23**, 5231528 (1951).

Kjeldahl Flask Tray.
F. H. Smith, *Anal. Chem.* **23**, 687 (1951).

A Modified Kjeldahl Apparatus.
H. A. Hyde, *Chem. & Ind.* p. 1103 (1951).

Kjeldahl Nitrogen Determination with a U-shaped Tube as Distillation Apparatus.
A. P. De Groot and J. C. A. Mighorst, *Chem. Weekblad* **47**, 219-220 (1951).

Micro and Semi-Micro Kjeldahl Distillation Apparatus.
W. Kirsten, *Anal. Chem.* **24**, 1078 (1952).

Apparatus for the Rapid Determination of Nitrogen.
A. Budziszewski, *Roczniki Chem.* **28**, 145-147 (1952) (French Summary).

A New Apparatus for the Determination of Nitrogen.
E. Taucins, *Latvijas PSR Zinatnu akad. Vestis No.* **7** (Whole No. 60), 122 (in Russian pp. 122-124) (1952).

Nitrogen Determination Apparatus (Micro-Kjeldahl).
Brit. Standards Inst. London S. W. 7, *British Standards* 1428, Part Bl 15 pp. (1953).

Micro Kjeldahl Distillation Apparatus.
D. J. Jenden and D. B. Taylor, *Anal. Chem.* **25**, 685-686 (1953).

A Perfected Micro-Kjeldahl Apparatus.
L. Kehren, *Angis farm. e quím.* Saõ Paulo **6**, No. 5, 5-8 (1953) (in French).

Modification of Parnas-Wagner-Pregl Micro-Kjeldahl Apparatus.
E. H. Sheers and M. S. Cole, *Anal. Chem.* **25**, 1775 (1953).

Modified All Glass Apparatus for the Determination of Nitrogen by the Micro-Kjeldahl Method.
F. J. Scandrett, *Analyst* **78**, 734-737 (1953).

Adapter for Micro-Kjeldahl Distillation.
B. Berk, *Chemist-Analyst* **43**, 52 (1954).

Kjeldahl Distillation Apparatus.
D. W. Skidmore, *Ind. Chemist* **30**, 386 (1954).

Efficient Splash Trap.
C. O. Ingamells, *Chemist-Analyst* **45**, 53 (1956).

A Tested Distillation Apparatus for the microanalytical Determination of Nitrogen by the Kjeldahl Method.
W. Schoniger and P. Haack, *Mikrochim. Acta* pp. 1369-1372 (1956).

An Aid to the Micro-Kjeldahl Nitrogen Determination.
K. Eder, *Mikrochim. Acta* p. 227 (1957).

Mineralization Apparatus for Semimicro Determination of Nitrogen According to Kjeldahl and of Phosphorus According to Belcher and Godbert.
X. Bilger and G. Mnangeney, *Bull. soc. chim. France* pp. 1539-1540 (1958).

Improvements in the Kjeldahl Method.
N. F. Komishilov, *Invest. Karel'sk i Kol'sk. Filiala Akad. Nauk S.S.S.R. No.* 3, 137-138 (1958).

Microdetermination of Nitrogen by the Kjeldahl Method.
P. Haack, *Lab. Sci. (Milan)* 7, 1-8 (1959).

Improved Micro Steam Distillation Apparatus.
L. R. Fina and H. J. Sincher, *Chemist Analyst* 48, 83 (1959).

Micro-Kjeldahl Digestion Apparatus.
W. A. Evans, F. B. Johnston, and G. M. Ward, *Lab. Pract.* 8, 174-175 (1959).

Nitrogen Determination by a Continuous Digestion and Analysis System.
A. Ferrari, *Ann. N. Y. Acad. Sci.* 87, 792-800 (1960).

Combustion Apparatus for Semimicro and Micro-Kjeldahl Nitrogen Determination.
V. Fojtova, J. Purs, and J. Spidla, *Chem. Listy* 54, 1069-1071 (1960).

Modification of the Kjeldahl Flask for More Rapid Mineralization.
J. Herzmann and J. Janda, *Casopis Lékařå Ceskych* 99, 1493-1494 (1960).

New Type of Combustion Flask for the Micro-Kjeldahl Determination of Nitrogen.
V. Fojtova and J. Purs, *Chem. Listy* 55, 201-203 (1961).

Simple Micro-Kjeldahl Apparatus for Rapid Routine Analysis of Vegetable Materials.
L. Muller, *Turrialba* **11**, No. 1, 17-25 (1961).

"Direct Attachment" Kjeldahl Apparatus.
J. T. Stock and A. V. DeThomas, *J. Chem. Educ.* **40**, 87)1963).

Subject Index

A

Acetoxime, 126
Acid index, 13, 28
Acid requirements, 8–15
Aeration, 153–156
Alizarin red S, 111
Alkaline peroxide, 123
Amides, acid requirements, 17
Amines, acid requirements, 16
  in Kjeldahl distillate, 166
Amino Acids, digestion of, 46
  acid requirements, 17
Amino nitrogen, 113–115
Ammonia, absorption by boric acid, 150–152
  in water, 152
  determination of, 6
    with Nessler's reagent, 160–163
  distillation of, 147–166
  recovery by aeration, 153–156
Ammonium sulfate, recovery of, 12–14, 28, 32, 37, 38
Animal material, 40
Antipyrine, 131
Arsenic oxide, 81
Asbestos, platinized, 101
Azines, 130
Azo compounds, digestion of, 126, 139
  reduction of, 51, 52, 53, 55, 56, 119, 127
Azo dyes, 127
Azobenzene, 126, 127

B

Barley, 40
Beer, 31, 41
Beet juices, 41, 109
Beet products, 109
Benzidine transformation, 128
Benzoic acid, 3
Benzonitrile, 126
Benzophenone oxime, 126
Betaine, 109
Biological materials, 97–100
Bismuth oxide, 82
Blood, 44
  microdigestion of, 31, 100
Blood serum, deproteinized, 100
Boil period, 45–50
  time of, 48, 76
Borax, 28, 38
Boric acid, 150
  buffer action, 151, 152
  stability of, 152
Bromine, 41

C

Calcium hypobromite, 160
  preparation of, 159
Calcium hypochlorite, 160
  preparation of, 164
Casein, 30
Catalysts, 68–83
  copper, 72–73
  mercury, 71–72
  miscellaneous, 81–83
  mixed, 80–81, 82, 102, 105, 106
  selenium, 73–79
Catalyst activity, 69, 70, 81
Catalysts, effect of, 4
Cereals, 92–97
Chromic oxide, 82
Chromous chloride, 119